Premature Ejaculation

Premature Ejaculation presents a unique and innovative therapeutic programme for the successful treatment of premature ejaculation. This descriptive and well-structured programme is fundamentally different from traditional sex therapy and contemporary sexual medicine. Centred on the management of sexual excitement, it enables couples to prolong the length of intercourse without having to interrupt their lovemaking or resort to medication. The programme's sexological approach also empowers couples with the skills and knowledge to strengthen their sex life, leading to a healthier and happier relationship.

Combining theory and practical instruction, François de Carufel's book promotes a better understanding of premature ejaculation. It offers a new perspective on the causes of this dysfunction and provides practitioners and therapists with concrete ways to assist men and women in improving their sex life.

Premature Ejaculation will be of interest and value to health professionals and graduate students in all fields dealing with sexual difficulties, including psychology, social work, medicine, physical therapy, nursing and counselling.

François de Carufel, PhD, is the founder of Functional Sex Therapy. He has taught in the Department of Sexology at the Université du Québec à Montréal and now teaches in the École de Sexologie at the Université de Louvain, Belgium. He was editor-in-chief of the journal *Réalités en Gynécologie-Obstétrique/Sexologie* and is currently clinical director of the Functional Sex Therapy Unit at the Waterloo Hospital in Belgium.

‘The author is congratulated for successfully delivering his well-established sexual management program for men with ejaculatory problems. The integrated techniques are clearly described and should provide a valuable and accessible resource that can bring about meaningful change in this common and often challenging clinical situation for a man and his partner.’ – **Professor Kevan Wylie**, MD, FRCP, FRCPsych, FRCOG, FECSM, Honorary Professor, University of Sheffield, UK, President of the World Association for Sexual Health

‘At a time when we sometimes blindly turn to pharmacologic strategies for sexual problems, it is heartening to come across a thoughtful, evidence-based sexological approach to a common male sexual complaint. Dr. de Carufel’s concise yet comprehensive treatment guidance for men with premature ejaculation is a welcome addition to the clinical sexology toolbox.’ – **Marta Meana**, PhD, Professor, Department of Psychology, University of Nevada, Las Vegas, Past President of the Society for Sex Therapy and Research

‘This book provides a description of a unique approach to the treatment of premature ejaculation, which focuses on the management of sexual excitement rather than on the control of the ejaculatory process. The detailed description of this approach may be helpful to many clinicians.’ – **Robert Taylor Segraves**, MD, PhD, Professor of Psychiatry, Case Western Reserve University, Editor-in-chief of the *Journal of Sex and Marital Therapy*

‘This book is essential because it teaches men that their body is like a musical instrument on which they can play pleasurable melodies in harmony with their partner. To be read, meditated upon and applied!’ – **Mireille Bonierbale**, MD, Psychiatre-sexologue, Présidente de l’Association interdisciplinaire post universitaire de sexologie, Rédactrice en Chef de Sexologies: Revue Européenne de Santé sexuelle, Directrice de l’enseignement du DIU de Sexologie des CHU de Marseille et Montpellier.

Premature Ejaculation

Theory, evaluation and therapeutic treatment

François de Carufel

Routledge
Taylor & Francis Group
LONDON AND NEW YORK

First published in French 2009 as *L'éjaculation prématurée : Compréhension et traitement par la thérapie sexofonctionnelle* by Presses Universitaires de Louvain.

First published in English 2017
by Routledge
2 Park Square, Milton Park, Abingdon, Oxon OX14 4RN

and by Routledge
711 Third Avenue, New York, NY 10017

Routledge is an imprint of the Taylor & Francis Group, an informa business

British Library Cataloguing in Publication Data
A catalogue record for this book is available from the British Library

Library of Congress Cataloging in Publication Data
Names: Carufel, François de, author.
Title: Premature ejaculation : theory, evaluation and therapeutic treatment / François de Carufel, PhD.
Description: Milton Park, Abingdon, Oxon ; New York, NY : Routledge, 2016. | Includes bibliographical references.
Identifiers: LCCN 2015048766| ISBN 9781138122123 (hbk) | ISBN 9781138123113 (pbk) | ISBN 9781315641683 (ebk)
Subjects: LCSH: Premature ejaculation—Treatment. | Sex therapy.
Classification: LCC RC560.P73 C37 2016 | DDC 616.6/93—dc23
LC record available at http://lccn.loc.gov/2015048766

ISBN: 978-1-138-12212-3 (hbk)
ISBN: 978-1-138-12311-3 (pbk)
ISBN: 978-1-315-64168-3 (ebk)

Typeset in Times New Roman
by Swales & Willis Ltd, Exeter, Devon, UK

To my wife, Supatsa

Contents

Figures

Preface

Close to 30 percent of men ejaculate prematurely during lovemaking, and this condition is frequently the source of severe psychological and relationship problems. Fortunately, there are various therapeutic interventions available today to help couples extend the length of their sexual relations and enjoy better sex. Of all these interventions, the sexual excitement management programme for difficulty with prolonging intercourse proves the most versatile and comprehensive. Developed within functional sex therapy, this treatment is more effective than antidepressants or anaesthetic creams. Its techniques have been confirmed through experimental research conducted at the Université du Québec à Montreal in Canada and at the Université de Louvain-la-Neuve in Belgium. The findings of this research have been presented at several international medical, sexological and psychological congresses and published in diverse scientific journals in America, the United Kingdom and Europe.

The sexual excitement management programme for difficulty with prolonging intercourse is described in extensive detail in this book. General practitioners, urologists, psychologists, social workers and marriage counsellors will discover invaluable advice to provide to their patients. Sex therapists, for their part, will find a complete guide that will structure their therapeutic intervention step by step.

Managing sexual excitement has no side effects and does not impair erectile function or alter sexual desire as might antidepressants. In addition, unlike traditional sex therapy, the programme can be followed by the man alone without his spouse having to participate. The involvement of a supportive partner certainly facilitates the implementation of new ways of behaving, but is not absolutely necessary. Numerous men whose partners could not take part in this therapy process have been treated successfully and have achieved excellent results.

The sexual excitement management programme for difficulty with prolonging intercourse is also for single men. It is particularly practical for those who cannot or do not want to take medication, are beginning a new relationship and consider it quite inappropriate to ask their new partner to participate in sex therapy, or simply do not have a partner and do not want to get involved in a romantic relationship before finding a solution to their sexual problem. By following this programme, single men become able to extend the length of intercourse and enjoy more satisfying sexual relations with their new partner.

This book is divided into three parts. Chapter 1 is devoted to a review of the scientific literature on premature ejaculation. It provides an update on the current state of knowledge and dispels erroneous beliefs that still prevail today in the fields of sexology and medicine. Chapter 2 outlines the evaluation protocol for finding out the causes and establishing the diagnosis for this dysfunction. With this information, the clinician will be able to determine the best treatment to offer patients. Chapter 3 describes the treatment programme which fosters the acquisition of the fundamental skills and knowledge to efficiently manage sexual excitement. It will equip the therapist with all the necessary tools to help people who desire to extend the length of their sexual relations. This chapter includes information and very effective bodily exercises. There are also specific sections for unpartnered men, women and couples. Clinicians could, in many cases, apply this treatment to patients exactly as written in this book. When the need arises, they could equally modify or insert this treatment within a more global approach.

I hope the insights revealed in this book will contribute to a better understanding of the crucial role the management of sexual excitement plays in prolonging the duration of intercourse. I also trust the information will be highly useful for theorists, researchers and practitioners in their endeavour to help men and women overcome this difficulty and improve their overall sexual functioning.

Acknowledgements

I would like to express my utmost appreciation to the individuals who made this book possible.

First, I would like to thank Dr Jean-Yves Desjardins, co-founder of the Department of Sexology at the Université du Québec à Montréal. Both the originality of his thought and his clinical expertise proved to be priceless sources of inspiration and reflection.

I would like to equally convey my gratitude to Dr Pascal De Sutter, co-director of the Certificate of Clinical Sexology at the Université Catholique de Louvain. His observations and judicious recommendations allowed for the meticulous organization of the book's content.

To Dr Gilles Trudel, professor and researcher in the Department of Psychology at the Université du Québec à Montréal, I would like to say thank you. His support, open-mindedness and insightful advice were invaluable.

I would like to pay particular homage to Jean Asselin, artistic director of the corporeal mime company Omnibus; Mr Raymond Franchetti, director of dance at the Paris Opera; and Dr Jean Brunelle, professor in the Department of Physical Education at the Université Laval. Their science of movement and their exercise pedagogy significantly influenced the elaboration of the functional sex therapy treatment presented in this book.

I would like to thank Hélène de Carufel, linguistic editor, who revised the manuscript, and Flore Detilleux, graphic artist, who created the illustrations. Their work – which demonstrated exemplary professionalism – as well as their sagacious suggestions, elevated the quality of this book. In addition, I would like to acknowledge the excellent work of sexologists Hélène Dionne and Carol Cuppens who carried out the bibliographic research.

I am very grateful to Christina Wolaniuk who translated this book. Her commitment to the task, generosity, attention to detail, brilliant suggestions and intellectual elegance were extremely appreciated.

I would like to underscore the contribution of the men and women who, as patients, students or research subjects, participated in the development and enrichment of the functional sex therapy. Without their collaboration, this book could never have been written.

My appreciation also extends to the team at Routledge Mental Health: Joanne Forshaw, senior editor, Kirsten Buchanan, senior editorial assistant, Aiyana Curtis, editorial assistant, and Abigail M. Stanley, production editor. Their enthusiasm and commitment has made the realization of this work a more enjoyable experience. Special thanks goes also to Colin Morgan, project manager at Swales & Willis, for his dedicated and conscientious work, as well as his patience and understanding in the production of this book.

Finally, I would like to profess my deepest gratitude and offer my most heartfelt thanks to my wife, Supatsa Khamwongsa. Her understanding and love enabled me to realize this project under the most positive circumstances.

Introduction

Various terms have been used over the last three centuries to describe the fact of reaching ejaculation rapidly during sexual relations. These labels have in turn contributed to shaping and sometimes crystallizing the way scientists think about this phenomenon.

During the eighteenth, nineteenth and the first half of the twentieth centuries, numerous authors[1] labelled as 'sexual impotence' the ejaculatory reaction that occurs before, upon or shortly after penetration along with the ensuing loss of erection. This phrasing, by focusing on the man's incapacity to maintain an erection and satisfy his partner,[2] hence reinforced the way clinicians approached this dysfunction. Treatments like opiates (Marten, 1709), administration of electrical shocks (Roubaud, 1876), special diet (Gross, 1881), cold baths (Hammond, 1893) or psychoanalysis (Ferenczi, 1956) were then offered to patients to strengthen or restore their sexual potency.

In the twentieth century, in the wake of a better understanding of the physiology of sexual response, the emphasis shifted progressively away from potency to ejaculation. Expressions containing the word ejaculation, such as "premature ejaculation", "early ejaculation", "rapid ejaculation" or "ejaculatio praecox" were put forward to define the condition. With time, "premature ejaculation" became the term most used by therapists and researchers. This new perspective was followed by studies on the mechanism of ejaculation and the causes that facilitate its inception. Sexological and pharmaceutical treatments were developed to help couples enjoy longer sexual relations. However, this focus on ejaculation, combined with the medicalization of sexology, contributed over the years to many scientists overlooking sexual interaction as a whole (seduction, foreplay, intercourse) and the effects it has on the arrival of ejaculation, and instead targeting their research and treatments on a small part of this interaction (ejaculation and its physiology).

Today, a more global approach is emerging that takes into account the process leading up to ejaculation, namely sexual excitement. The term "premature ejaculation", despite being correct, is regarded as too narrow. Attention is shifting away from ejaculation to excitement which is, when not managed properly, the real cause of brief intercourse. New treatments dealing with the course taken by sexual excitement are being developed. Therapists teach patients sexological strategies and bodily techniques[3] to help them better manage their sexual excitement and, as a result, increase the length of intercourse. Sexology is getting "sexologized". The expressions "difficulty with extending the length of sexual activity prior to ejaculation" or "difficulty with managing sexual excitement in order to prolong intercourse" reflect this new trend. They open the door to a sexological understanding of the cognitive, emotional, physiological, behavioural and corporeal dimensions involved in human sexual functioning. They also contribute to broadening the conception of this dysfunction and moving away from the old erroneous dichotomy – characterized by the opposition between "psychological" and "organic" causal factors – in which clinicians were trapped when having to establish the aetiology of a sexual disorder. On the other hand, these expressions, being sexological in nature, limit the understanding of the problem presented by the patient to sexological factors. It should not be forgotten that organic, psychological and relational factors could often play a part in the creation of sexual symptoms by making it more arduous for the patient to function adequately sexually (for example, abandonment anxiety or hyperthyroidism could contribute to the difficulty of prolonging intercourse by making the management of sexual excitement more strenuous to accomplish).

The expressions "difficulty with extending the length of sexual activity prior to ejaculation" or "difficulty with managing sexual excitement in order to prolong intercourse", despite being the most accurate, are too long and, as such, not practical. The shorter expression "difficulty with prolonging intercourse" is more appropriate. As stated above, the term "premature ejaculation" is not wrong. However, it refers to a physiological activation in which a man cannot intervene voluntarily. I prefer the expression "difficulty with prolonging intercourse" as it relates to a condition that can be directly improved through behaviour. This expression places the emphasis on the acquisition of knowledge and skills and does not transform a cognitive-behavioural difficulty into a biological disorder like the expression "premature ejaculation" is liable to do. That being said, the expression "premature ejaculation" will still be used in this book when reporting on definitions, research and concepts by authors who employed it in order to accurately represent their point of view.

The first chapter of this book reviews the factors associated with premature ejaculation or the difficulty with prolonging intercourse. It provides answers to the following questions: What type of dysfunction is it? What are its causes? What solutions have been developed to deal with it?

To answer these questions, the scientific literature highlighting the ways in which this disorder has been tackled over the last eighty years will be examined. The definitions that have been given to it will be presented, the explanations that have been offered will be analysed and the treatments that have been proposed will be studied. Finally, the underlying principles of the sexual excitement management programme for the difficulty with prolonging intercourse will be explained and the findings from research on this treatment will be presented. This examination of the scientific literature will offer a global vision of premature ejaculation, also referred to as the difficulty with prolonging intercourse, and a greater understanding of the common clinical trends that prevail today. In addition, it will help practitioners determine, among a range of therapeutic modalities, those which are best suited to the needs of their patients.

The themes of this review of the scientific literature have been grouped into six sections. As already noted, the term used to describe the incapacity to delay the onset of ejaculation will be the one applied by the author(s) whose work is being examined in any given section. The first section presents the definitions of premature ejaculation that have been developed within the sexological, psychological and medical fields. The second section examines the epidemiological data collected in different eras and in various countries; this data will reveal the constancy and universality of this condition. The third section explores the continuum on which lies the capacity to prolong the length of sexual activity along with the sexual scripts which men suffering from this difficulty engage in to pursue their sexual encounters. The fourth section deals with the cognitive, emotional, behavioural and relational reactions of men and women confronted with this problem. The fifth section analyses the multiple hypotheses put forward as to the origins of this dysfunction; here, a distinction between the sexological causes on the one side and the psychological, relational and organic causes on the other side is established. Finally, the sixth section studies and evaluates the treatments most utilized at the present time.

Notes

1 Marten, 1709; Ryan, 1835; Gross, 1881; Shapiro, 1945.

2 For Marten (1709), an English surgeon, the ultimate proof of potency is conception. According to him, a woman needs to be pleasured in order to conceive, hence the sexual act must last long enough for her to be satisfied. Consequently, for one to be potent it is not sufficient to have a good erection and release a fruitful "seed" as the latter is "infertile when it is emitted in the act with too much precipitancy or haste, before the woman's parts are raised, or so fit to receive it, with that pleasure being necessary to occasion conception" (p. 33).

3 Crépault and Desjardins, 1978; de Carufel and De Sutter, 2001; De Sutter et al., 2002; de Carufel and Trudel, 2006; Desjardins, 2007; de Carufel, 2009: Kempeneers et al., 2012.

1 Factors associated with premature ejaculation

Definitions of premature ejaculation

Premature ejaculation has been defined in a great variety of ways by the many researchers who have studied the subject. For further clarity, these definitions have been grouped together into eight categories. Nevertheless, it is important to remember that the expression "premature ejaculation" embraces the same reality as the expression "difficulty with prolonging intercourse" but tends to convey a different understanding of this reality.

Definitions based on the number of pelvic thrusts

A few sex therapists use the number of in-and-out thrusts of the penis inside the vagina as the criterion for the definition of premature ejaculation. On that basis, some for example consider such an ejaculation to occur following fifteen thrusts or fewer after the beginning of intercourse (Colpi et al., 1986). The criticism that could be made of these definitions is that they are, to say the least, arbitrary. In fact, what rationale could explain that 5, 10 or 15 pelvic thrusts are symptomatic of premature ejaculation and that 20, 25 or 30 are not? As well, these thrusts could be carried out at different speeds, intensities or depths. Consequently, a man who, for example, executes ten movements of penetration slowly, deeply and in a relaxed manner will extend his lovemaking for a longer time than one who does twenty of these rapidly and vigorously. He will, nevertheless, be seen to suffer from premature ejaculation (whereas the other man will not), even though he prolongs further the length of intercourse and better manages his sexual excitement.

Definitions based on the length of intercourse

For many practitioners, the criterion for the definition of premature ejaculation rests on the length of time intercourse lasts. This problem is therefore considered to be present in an individual who ejaculates less than 15 seconds after the entry of the penis inside the vagina (World Health Organization, 1993), 1 minute (Cooper and Magnus, 1984), 1 minute and 30 seconds (Waldinger et al., 2005a), 1 minute and 48 seconds (Patrick et al., 2005), 2 minutes

(Spiess et al., 1984; Strassberg et al., 1990), 3 minutes (Rosen et al., 2007), 4 minutes (LoPiccolo, 1978), 5 minutes (Killmann and Auerbach, 1979; Zeiss et al., 1978) or 7 minutes (Schover et al., 1982). These definitions – regardless of whether they are founded on the opinion of their authors or on statistical data – possess the same flaw as the definitions based on the number of pelvic thrusts. They are not justified. In fact, the duration of intercourse stretches along a continuum. Consequently, any value of inclusion–exclusion, wherever it is situated, is open to the following two criticisms. The first is why do we choose this point of reference over another? For example, if the criterion of 1 minute 30 seconds is adopted, why do we choose one minute 30 seconds rather than 1 or 2 minutes? The second criticism hinges on what physiologically distinguishes a man who ejaculates 15 seconds below this benchmark from one who ejaculates 15 seconds above this benchmark? For example, how does the physiology of an individual who ejaculates in 1 minute differ from the physiology of another who ejaculates in 45 seconds or 1 minute 15 seconds? Up until now, no satisfactory answer has been given to this question.

Additionally, within a given time frame, a man could execute a different number of intravaginal movements and ultimately satisfy his partner. But because he has ejaculated within the fixed time frame, he would, nonetheless, be seen as suffering from a sexual dysfunction even if his partner reaches orgasm and expresses her satisfaction. Likewise, a man who ejaculates 15 or 30 seconds after the established time period would not be considered afflicted with a sexual difficulty despite his inability to effectively manage his sexual excitement and the fact that neither he nor his partner derive much pleasure from the experience.

Actually, Rowland et al. (2007) observed only a slight correlation between the length of intercourse and the following variables: lack of control, low sexual satisfaction, high personal distress and interpersonal difficulty. For their part, Barnes and Eardley (2007) did not find in the literature any specified duration time below which men develop de facto anxiety or any emotional distress. I tend to conclude from these observations that the problem of premature ejaculation does not rest in the length of intercourse as such. It is instead to be found in the attitude that people have towards it.

Definition based on the frequency of the woman's orgasm

Masters and Johnson (1970) state that a man suffers from premature ejaculation if he is unable to delay ejaculation long enough, during intercourse, to allow his partner to reach orgasm in at least 50 per cent of their sexual encounters. They add, however, that if the woman is anorgasmic for reasons other than the rapid ejaculation of her partner, their definition is no longer valid. This definition is interesting because it takes into account the partner's reaction. All the same, the designation of a percentage is just as arbitrary as setting a norm for the length of intercourse or the number of in-and-out thrusts. Without scientific data, we could always ask why Masters and Johnson opted for 50 per cent of encounters versus 25 per cent or 75 per cent.

Moreover, the criterion "to reach orgasm" is not judicious. In fact, many women may be very satisfied with their sexual experience even when they do not have an orgasm. In this case, sexual satisfaction becomes a better criterion than reaching orgasm in determining if the duration of intercourse was sufficient.

Finally, some women, in order to reach orgasm, require such prolonged stimulation that few men succeed in satisfying them irrespective of being able to fully extend the length of intercourse. Ejaculation clearly occurs prematurely for these women. But we could view things differently and juxtapose premature ejaculation of the male with delayed orgasm of the female. From a clinical perspective, it is more realistic to help these women accelerate the arrival of their orgasm than to get their partner to further prolong intercourse.

Definition based on control over the ejaculatory reflex

According to Kaplan (1974, 1989), premature ejaculation cannot be defined in quantitative terms. The cause of this sexual dysfunction is not related to the extent of intercourse or the number of coital thrusts. It is associated with the lack of control over the ejaculatory reflex, regardless of whether this occurs after "x" many pelvic thrusts or "y" minutes of intercourse. This notion is still endorsed today by a very large number of sex therapists, including Porst et al. (2007) and Rosen et al. (2007).

The major criticism we could direct at Kaplan is that she misses the fact that ejaculation is fundamentally a reflex process (Benson, 1988; Singer and Weiner, 1994) and that reflexes are outside voluntary control. Theoretically, no individual, whether he succeeds or not in extending the length of intercourse, has control over his ejaculation; he only has control over what leads to ejaculation, which is to say his sexual excitement (in the section *The third zone: The zone of ejaculatory imminence* we will examine in more detail the case of men who report having an orgasm without ejaculation). On the other hand, the advantage of Kaplan's approach to premature ejaculation is that she places the focus on the man's capacity to control himself and not on outside criteria. However, she positions the problem badly by defining the capacity of control as the ability to control the ejaculatory reflex and not as the aptitude to modulate sexual excitement.

Definition based on the capacity to ejaculate at the desired moment

For Hastings (1963) and Levine (1992), premature ejaculation is when a man ejaculates sooner than he wants. This definition pinpoints the real issues related to this problem by drawing out the subjective dimension. It falls short, however, because it focuses exclusively on the man's satisfaction. It ignores the wishes of the woman. For example, if a man is happy with intercourse that lasts 2 minutes but his partner is unsatisfied, in theory there would not be any sexual disharmony even though the dyadic adjustment leaves much to be desired.

Definition based on the subjective criteria of the couple

Some authors maintain that rapid ejaculation cannot be defined without considering the subjective satisfaction of the two partners involved (Jehu, 1979; Shilon and Paz, 1984; Rowland et al., 2001a.) This definition, based on the criteria of the couple, has considerable merit as it takes into account the views of both partners and situates sexuality within an interactive scope in which the personal and relational dimensions share an equal place. It also allows us to relativize the problem of premature ejaculation and to identify the existence of a sexual trouble from the perspective of dissatisfaction felt rather than the actual duration. For example, when one or both members of the couple like sexual relations that last more than 10 minutes and ejaculation occurs most of the time in under 5 minutes, the dissatisfaction that is felt becomes clinically legitimate and a sex therapist should help them. In contrast, some couples have a strong preference for sexual relations that take place quickly. As a result, it is not necessary for the sexual activity to last a long time in order for both partners to be satisfied. This approach to dealing with premature ejaculation avoids causing the couple the distress of a false diagnosis found within, for example, books or articles published in magazines.

Definitions of the American Psychiatric Association

The authors of the fourth revised *Diagnostic and Statistical Manual* (*DSM-IV TR*) of the American Psychiatric Association (2000) suggest that there is premature ejaculation when the individual ejaculates persistently or recurrently following minimal sexual stimulation before, on, or shortly after penetration, and this, before he wishes it. This definition is weighed by the clinician, who must take into account the factors that affect the duration of the excitement phase, such as the age of the person, the newness of the sexual partner, a change in the situation and the frequency of sexual activity. Finally, the sexual problem must lead to marked distress or interpersonal difficulties and cannot be caused exclusively by substance use.

The first criticism that could be taken into consideration with respect to this definition is the same one that was made against the definitions proposing an objective criterion for duration or for the number of movements of intercourse. "Minimal sexual stimulation" and "an ejaculation that occurs before, on, or shortly after intercourse" are unsubstantiated, arbitrary criteria. They delimit, on continua of stimulation and timing, particular points that indicate the presence or absence of premature ejaculation, and any selected point along a continuum is arbitrary because the reasons for which this point and not another was adopted may always be questioned.

The second criticism is that a physiological response (ejaculation) that occurs at a specific moment is classified a psychiatric disorder because an individual reacts badly to this condition or that his partner has difficulty adapting to it (marked distress or interpersonal difficulties). In reality, this is like affirming that not having a car becomes a psychiatric disorder when an individual is sad as a result of not having one or that his wife threatens to leave him because he does not have one. Conversely, not having a car is not seen as a psychiatric disorder if the people accept the fact and do not get upset about it. Confusion exists here between the phenomenon and the reaction people have towards it. The authors of the *DSM-IV TR* seem to have forgotten the old adage of the Greek philosopher Epictetus (which is at the root of modern psychotherapies such as cognitive behavioural therapy and rational-emotive therapy), which stipulates that it is not events that create human turmoil, but simply the ideas they have about these events. It follows from this analysis that an ejaculation occurring within 1, 3 or 5 minutes is not a problem in itself. It becomes a source of frustration only when the man or woman wishes otherwise.

This observation is supported by Patrick et al. (2005). These researchers have demonstrated that when experienced sex therapists tried to differentiate in accordance with the criteria of the *DSM-IV TR* men who ejaculate prematurely from those who do not, an overlap in the length of intercourse was observed. Of the 1,587 men they studied, 207 (13 per cent) were diagnosed as premature ejaculators and 1,380 as normal. The median length of intercourse of the men said to be premature ejaculators was 1.8 minutes, with variations ranging from 0 to 41 minutes. As to the length of the median length of intercourse of the so-called normal subjects, this clocked in at 7.3 minutes, with variations ranging from 0 to 53 minutes. Therefore, the diagnosis of premature ejaculation applied just as well to men who ejaculated within a minute as to those who ejaculated after more than 40 minutes of intercourse (because of the criteria "before the person wishes it" and "marked emotional distress or interpersonal difficulties"). Conversely, the diagnosis of normality was attributed to men ejaculating in less than a minute as well as those ejaculating after 52 minutes of intercourse. The same phenomenon was observed over the course of the study of Rowland et al. (2007). Of the 207 men who were diagnosed as premature ejaculators based on the criteria of the *DSM-IV TR*, 118 had a intercourse time equal to or greater than that of the men said to be normal, that which entails an overlap of 57 per cent. These research results are confirmed by those of the study by Giuliano and his colleagues (2007) that was conducted with 201 men and which demonstrates that the intravaginal ejaculatory latency time (length of intercourse) has no direct effect on satisfaction with sexual intercourse.

The third, and very important, criticism with regard to the definition of the American Psychiatric Association is that it fails by antinomy. By containing both an objective criterion ("ejaculation occurring before, on, or shortly after penetration") and a subjective criterion ("before the man wishes it"), it creates a dilemma impossible to solve. In fact, how could we reconcile these two criteria? The objective criterion is absolute and the time period it covers is very precise ("before, on, or shortly after penetration"). On the contrary, the subjective criterion is relative and the time interval it covers extends from zero to infinity ("before the man wishes it"). How, therefore, will the clinician decide between the proposed duration and his patient's request to determine if there is a sexual difficulty or not?

The fifth version of the Diagnostic and Statistical Manual of Mental Disorder (DSM-5) of the American Psychiatric Association (2013) provides a definition of premature ejaculation that differs from the one presented in the fourth edition. A man suffers from premature (early) ejaculation when there is "a persistent or recurrent pattern of ejaculation occurring during partnered sexual activities within approximately 1 minute following vaginal penetration and before the individual wishes it. The symptom must have been present for at least 6 months and must be experienced on almost all or all (approximately 75–100 per cent) occasions of sexual activity (in identified situational contexts or if generalized, in all contexts). The symptom causes clinically significant distress in the individual". We have already noted that the temporal criteria – 1 minute in this case – are completely arbitrary and the distress associated with a disorder can't be used to define its nature. As for the duration of the period during which the symptom had to have been present (six months) as well as the percentage of its occurrence (75–100 per cent of sexual activities), although equally arbitrary, these provide an acceptable reference point for clinicians to assess the severity of their patients' complaint.

Definition based on evolutionary criteria

Finally, one group of authors, far from viewing ejaculation occurring soon after the start of intercourse as a sexual dysfunction, consider it to be a biologically superior trait. According to Kinsey et al. (1948), a man who ejaculates early is completely normal among mammals and is an ordinary individual within his species. The authors add that it is curious that in the past we had qualified a reaction arising after so little stimulation as "impotence". A man who ejaculates rapidly is likely superior, even if this characteristic could prove disadvantageous for his partner.

Hong (1984) put forward the hypothesis that premature ejaculation is an adapted behaviour descended from the evolution of the species. An individual who ejaculates rapidly is less likely to be rejected by the female or attacked by other males. As a result, he increases his chances of reproducing and passing on his genetic traits to future generations. This adaptive capacity would have therefore led to an over-representation of males who ejaculate quickly in the human species. This assertion is supported by the research of Wainberg (1984), which ascertains that all large mammals, including primates, ejaculate immediately after penetration. Hong (1984) continues to develop his thesis by arguing that premature ejaculation has only recently become a dysfunctional trait in human beings, in fact since the loss of oestrus by the female, at the moment when sexual pleasure became dissociated from reproduction.

This concept of premature ejaculation leaves room for criticism. Indeed, Athanasiadis (1998) argues that this theory is contradicted by the observation that many species engage in seductive behaviour and lengthy foreplay. In addition the mere fact that it is possible to bring greater control to the majority of men who receive treatment based on the acquisition of knowledge and skills demonstrates that the behaviour that generates sexual excitement and promotes ejaculation is modifiable through learning (de Carufel and Trudel, 2006; Kempeners et al., 2012). It may be affirmed, as a result of these observations, that premature ejaculation is not revealing of a superior biological trait but rather of an uneducated response, just like eating quickly while making noise and not taking the time to taste food.

Theoretical and clinical considerations with regard to the definitions

This review of the sexological literature has made us aware of the vast number of definitions of premature ejaculation. Some authors maintain that this condition is a matter of personal pathology, others consider it to be a relational problem, and a last group thinks that it reflects a biological superiority. This diversity of opinions and these conceptual divergences make it currently very difficult, if not impossible, to formulate a definition that is universally acceptable to all. Actually, how can we reconcile definitions based on elements as diversified as the frequency of movements (from 8 to 15), the length of intercourse (from 15 seconds to 7 minutes), the attainment of the female orgasm, the moment of ejaculation (before, on, or shortly after penetration), the amount of stimulation received by the male (minimal), emotional distress, interpersonal difficulties, and the length of intercourse desired by the man or that wished by the woman?

One of the reasons why there exists such a great number of definitions is because premature ejaculation was determined by these researchers from different criteria. We know that the term "prematureness" describes a sequential relationship between two events. A phenomenon took place before another one occurred. Ejaculation appeared before . . . the man made "x" number of movements of penetration, the woman obtained "y" number of orgasms, the couple carried on intercourse for "z" minutes. "Prematurely" means before the accomplishment of a development, of a process or of a fact. But who defines the conditions of this accomplishment? The anthropologist who observes that 70 per cent of men have sexual relations that last more than 1 minute? The clinician who knows that a woman needs on average 8 minutes of intercourse to reach orgasm? The man who would like his lovemaking to last 45 minutes? The woman who desires to have an orgasm through intercourse? This would then make ejaculations premature that occur before a minute, or 8 minutes, or 45 minutes, or before the time required for a woman to be satiated. We therefore cannot give a universal definition of premature ejaculation. It is a relative condition and its definition is tributary of the norm – whether it is biological, statistical, social, clinical, personal or relational – on which we attach it. For example, premature ejaculation from an anthropological point of view could signal that a man ejaculates in less than a minute. From a conjugal perspective, this could indicate that he ejaculates before his wife is satisfied.

In observing nature, we recognize that it does not assign a duration to the excitement phase preceding ejaculation, whether the penis is outside or inside the vagina. It programmes many sexual physiological functions, but not the duration of sexual excitement (which is the cause of ejaculation). For example, it determines the pathway of spermatozoa during ejaculation. It ensures they travel from the epididymis to the far end of the urethra, passing through the vas deferens, the ejaculatory ducts and the ampulla, and receiving secretions from the seminal vesicles and the prostate to form semen. During this process, the sphincter of the bladder is shut to prevent semen from entering the bladder on its way out of the urethra. If the semen goes into the bladder, this means that nature's programming went wrong. This phenomenon is an organic condition called "retrograde ejaculation". But if nature plans or determines a set of physiological sexual processes, its programming does not include the length of time intercourse should last. It does not dictate whether intercourse should carry on "x" or "y" minutes in the same way it determines the path of sperm. There is not an organic condition labelled "premature ejaculation", which essentially would differ from the fixed length of intercourse determined by nature, as there is an organic condition called "retrograde ejaculation", which counters the path of sperm established by nature. It is human beings who express their own wishes as to the length of intercourse. And it is not because some find it difficult to manage their excitement during intercourse and, consequently, prolong its length, that we should assume there is a biological condition (even if a few organic factors could, to a certain extent, make this management more challenging). But unfortunately, as soon as we attach the term "premature" to the word "ejaculation", the resulting expression, namely "premature ejaculation", suggests that there is an organic condition that goes against biological programming when in fact it is but a normal physiological reaction whose activation occurs despite the contrary desires of individuals. It stems from these observations that therapists who assert that one cannot call any intercourse length "premature ejaculation" because there is a limit to prematurity, adhere to the belief that a pathological organic condition exists of a precise duration not conforming to the laws of nature and, as a matter of fact, these therapists deny the dissatisfaction of men or women who would like their lovemaking to last longer.

The expression "premature ejaculation" does not therefore describe a reality in itself. It does not refer to a phenomenon that is objective, observable and measurable (like diabetes, depression or a marital problem). It does not designate a particular physiological datum or a distinctive pathology. It only highlights a relationship between a physiological phenomenon (ejaculation) and its moment of arrival (which occurs earlier than a specified desire, criterion or norm).

As the term "premature" is relative, there is no absolute benchmark of premature ejaculation. In other words, we cannot qualify as "premature" an ejaculation that occurs in less than 1, 2, 5 or 7 minutes. We can only say that it takes place in less than 1, 2, 5 or 7 minutes. It becomes premature if it reveals itself before a specific desire, criterion or norm. Within a clinical context, this means before either member of the couple wishes. Only at this moment can we talk about it as a dysfunction or sexual difficulty. This observation is of critical importance because it depathologizes the reaction of people who ejaculate soon after the beginning of intercourse, but who do not wish otherwise. It is also crucial because it validates the desires and frustrations of individuals who seek treatment for an ejaculation occurring, for example, after 5, 8 or 10 minutes of intercourse, but who would like to prolong its duration even more. There are now very effective ways to help these people who experience a genuine dissatisfaction and it would be inappropriate not to do so under the pretext that their demand is beyond the limits of a certain standard. But these requests for a better sex life should not be confused with the delirious demands of some psychiatric patients or the solicitations of high-performing patients who lack points of reference on the subject of "normality".

The expression "premature ejaculation" does not therefore refer, in clinical practice, to an objective reality but to a condition relative to people's wishes. It denotes the inadequacy between the moment when people desire ejaculation to arrive and the actual moment it takes place. To say individuals suffer from premature ejaculation means in fact that they wish ejaculation to occur later than usual. And to say that they desire ejaculation to occur later means in fact that they wish to extend the length of their sexual activities long enough to, in general, experience all the pleasure they hope to get (there are obviously other reasons why people want to prolong their sexual activities). Accordingly, the problem does not lie with ejaculation but with the capacity to prolong the duration of sexual activities (in fact, with the capacity to prolong the length of intercourse for most people who encounter this difficulty). Ejaculation that occurs after the penis has been inside the vagina, regardless of the duration, is not an organic condition. It is the result of the way sexual excitement is managed during that period. The fact that this organicity does not exist explains why researchers were able to attribute, as we have seen earlier, a diverse range of values such as 15 seconds and 7 minutes to intercourse lengths deemed pathological.

From these considerations, I have come to the point, within a clinical context, to define premature ejaculation quite simply as "an ejaculation that occurs before the man or woman desires". We will see, however, in the section dealing with the causes of this dysfunction, that the use of the term "premature ejaculation" has led more than one to view it as a disorder related to the physiology of ejaculation rather than a dissatisfaction with sexual activities considered too brief. We will also see, within the larger approach developed inside this book, that the problem of ejaculation that happens earlier than expected is the equivalent of the difficulty with prolonging intercourse. This change of focus from an "ejaculation that happens earlier than expected" or "premature ejaculation" to a "difficulty with prolonging intercourse" allows a clinical shift away from an affliction to a behavioural cognitive limitation that can be handled with knowledge and skills.

Epidemiology

It is not easy to determine the prevalence of premature ejaculation (Costa, 2006). Many men experience difficulties managing the course of their sexual excitement at one time or another in their life, particularly when they are very sexually excited or with a new partner (Masters and Johnson, 1970). That being said, these difficulties will not prove to be problematic until they are considered unsatisfactory and become chronic (Jehu, 1979). Epidemiological studies on the prevalence of this condition demonstrate that between 4 per cent (Fugl-Meyer et al., 1999) and 66 per cent (Aschka et al., 2001) of men ejaculate shortly after the beginning of intercourse. Most studies, however, report a prevalence of 20 per cent to 30 per cent.

The National Health and Social Life Survey was the largest epidemiological research carried out in the United States on sexual disorders. Within this study, a representative sample of the American population whose age ranged between 18 and 59 years was interviewed. Among the men surveyed, about 28 per cent said their ejaculation occurred too quickly (Laumann et al., 1994). In Great Britain, a survey was conducted among a sample of individuals randomly chosen from a list of patients of general practitioners. Thirty-one per cent of these people stated that they suffered from this difficulty (Dunn et al., 1988). An extensive study (The Global Study of Sexual Attitudes and Behavior) was conducted with 27,500 subjects aged 40 to 80 years in 29 countries. Men from North America, Australia, New Zealand and South Africa complained in a proportion of 28 per cent that they ejaculated prematurely. This figure rose to more than 20 per cent among Europeans, Asians and South Americans and to 13 per cent among men in the Middle East (Laumann et al., 2005). A study on sexual behaviour carried out with a representative sample of 10,173 Australians aged 16 to 59 years indicated that 24 per cent among them ejaculated earlier than they desired (Richters et al., 2003). Finally, an Internet survey was conducted in the United States, Germany and Italy with 12,133 men aged 18 to 70 years. The prevalence of premature ejaculation reached 24 per cent among Americans, 20 per cent among Germans and 20 per cent among Italians (Porst et al., 2007).

Kinsey et al. (1948) mentioned in their report that 75 per cent of American men ejaculated in under 2 minutes and 90 per cent in under 3 minutes. A large multinational study conducted on the Internet with 11,543 subjects revealed that 25 per cent of men ejaculated in under 2 minutes (Rosen et al., 2004). Another survey was undertaken with 491 couples in five different countries in order to determine the length of intercourse in the general population (Waldinger et al., 2005b). The subjects measured, with the help of a stopwatch, the length of coitus from the time of insertion of the penis inside the vagina up until the moment when the man signalled to his partner the beginning of ejaculation. The median length of intercourse was 5.4 minutes, with a range of 0.55 to 44.1 minutes. There were, however, differences in duration from one country to the next: the United Kingdom led with (7.6 minutes) followed by the United States (7.0 minutes), Spain (5.8 minutes), Holland (5.1 minutes) and Turkey (3.7 minutes). It should be noted that these values decreased with age. If the median length of intercourse settled at 6.5 minutes among men aged 18 to 30 years, it was not more than 4.3 minutes among those older than 51 years.

As for women, they need intercourse to last on average around 8 minutes in order to reach orgasm; some climax in as little as 1 minute while others require up to 30 minutes of coital stimulation (Fisher, 1973). Weiss and Brody (2009), in contrast to the assumption of many sex therapists and educators, discovered that women's consistency of partnered orgasm is associated with a greater duration of penile–vaginal intercourse but not of foreplay. These researchers also found that orgasm obtained by penile–vaginal stimulation is associated with focusing attention to vaginal sensations during intercourse and with sex education which fosters that vaginal (and not clitoral) is an important region to be stimulated for female orgasm (Brody and Weiss, 2010). In a study published in 2004, Miller and Byers report that both sexes desire penile–vaginal intercourse to last 14–18.5 minutes in opposition to the 7–8 minutes they presently undergo. These figures clearly reveal the magnitude of the problem facing couples in search of mutual satisfaction. This is all the more alarming since the prevalence of this condition changes with age. There are proportionally more older men than younger men who are unable to prolong their sexual encounters (Laumann et al., 1999; Carson et al., 2003). In other words, with advancing age, a man will not increase his capacity to manage his sexual excitement if he does not receive outside help. Moreover, the increase in erectile disorders leads some to rush the act in order to be able to complete sexual relations before losing their erection. Finally, the changes taking place in modern societies contribute to altering women's expectations (Segraves, 2006). A study carried out in Sweden, Finland, Estonia and St Petersburg (Russia) demonstrates that women today are unsatisfied with the length of intercourse in greater numbers than their predecessors (Haavio-Manila and Kontula, 2003).

The importance for women of vaginal stimulation and sensations arising from penile–vaginal intercourse gives men a good reason to want to increase the length of intercourse. It also underscores the need for women to develop their own sexual competencies in order to achieve orgasm more often, more easily and more quickly.

The next step is to find out what activities are most conducive to producing orgasm in the woman during intercourse. Are they the movements of the woman's pelvis, the in-and-out movements by the man, the sentimental and emotional connection, the atmosphere of the encounter, the intimacy of the moment, the commitment? Should there be continuous pelvic movements? Do pauses during sex hinder or favour the rise of excitement and pleasure in the woman? Does the woman need to completely relax or move with some intensity? Is letting go essential for a woman to reach orgasm? What stimuli should she perceive? Should the man's movements be vigorous, deep, parallel to the vagina, oblique to it? What positions most benefit the stimulation of the deepest part of the vagina and the cervix? Should the emphasis be on partnership, sharing and communication during intercourse? How important is the interplay between the feminine and masculine? Should the woman focus on the perception of her sensations? Should she fantasize during sex? There are likely a wide range of answers to these questions. They vary from one woman to another and also within each woman depending on her hormonal cycle, her romantic relationship and her life in general. Future research will provide us with more information on this subject.

Symptomatology

The difficulty with prolonging intercourse, or premature ejaculation, may be primary (lifelong) or secondary (acquired). It is primary when it has been present since the first sexual experience with a partner. It is secondary when it occurs after a period of satisfying sexual functioning. It may also be chronic or intermittent, generalized (with the majority of partners and in most contexts) or situational (with specific partners or in particular contexts) (Meyers et al., 1983; *DSM-IV TR*, American Psychiatric Association, 2000).

The capacity to prolong the length of sexual activity extends along a continuum. Some men ejaculate at the sight of their partner undressing. Others ejaculate during foreplay following stimulation of their body or genital organs. There are individuals for whom ejaculation occurs at the moment of intromission of the penis inside the vagina. For a certain number, it takes place after a few pelvic thrusts. For others, ejaculation always comes shortly after the beginning of intercourse, whether this is 15 seconds, 20 seconds, 30 seconds, 1 minute, 1 minute and a half or 2 minutes (Jehu, 1979; Kaplan, 1974; Masters and Johnson, 1970). Finally, there are other men who succeed, with various degrees of ease, to last for as long as they desire.

Premature ejaculation, or the difficulty with prolonging intercourse, may occur in the absence (simple) or presence (complicated) of other sexual symptoms like erectile dysfunction or hypoactive sexual desire disorder for the man and vaginismus, dyspareunia, anorgasmia and hypoactive sexual desire disorder for the woman.

Some older individuals – in their forties – see their ability to extend the length of intercourse decline because of the onset of an erectile difficulty that is organic in origin. These men require greater stimulation to obtain an erection. Being already very excited when intercourse occurs, they no longer have any room to manoeuvre before reaching the level of excitement that triggers ejaculation, and they are precipitated towards it from the first coital movements.

The sexual interaction scenarios in which men who have trouble pursuing their lovemaking engage vary to some extent. Some refuse to be touched at all for fear of ejaculating before intercourse. Foreplay is therefore one-sided and only the woman receives tactile stimulation. Others, who present a little less difficulty, participate in foreplay and accept some form of stimulation avoiding, nonetheless, being stroked on the genitals. There exist as well a large proportion of men who intensely stimulate their partner during foreplay. When they feel she is close to orgasm, they proceed hurriedly towards intercourse. During coitus, they try to distract themselves by thinking of something else, biting their lips, pinching their skin, contracting the anal sphincter and so on. Finally, after a few in-and-out thrusts of the pelvis, they reach ejaculation to their great disappointment, leaving their partner unsatisfied (Masters and Johnson, 1970). Many are completely preoccupied by various fears such as losing their erection, not being able to prolong intercourse or displeasing their partner. In this way, they differ from men who succeed in lengthening the time of intercourse. In effect, the latter focus on the sexual stimuli they like as well as on the pleasure they feel and they have few anxiety-driven thoughts (Hartman et al., 2005).

Cognitive, emotional, behavioural and relational reactions to the duration of intercourse

Brief intercourse is not considered an annoyance or a problem by all men and women. In fact, there is not a correlation between the length of intercourse and felt dissatisfaction (Laumann et al., 1999; Grenier and Byers, 2001; Byers and Grenier, 2003; Rowland et al., 2007). Many couples who do not make intercourse last more than a minute are happy, and a number of couples who succeed in lasting beyond 5 minutes feel miserable. This observation is confirmed by the study of Steggall et al. (2008). While these researchers were testing a combination therapy for premature ejaculation, they made an interesting discovery. The relationship improvement they found amongst their subjects at the end of their study did not correlate with the length of intercourse. The success of the treatment did not depend on the duration of intercourse but on the reintroduction of intimacy. They concluded that the increment of the duration of intercourse should be only a part of the total therapeutic focus and that the ultimate goal of the treatment should not be brought down to a time-orientated figure but must also incorporate self-reported mutual enjoyment. However, current social changes promoting women's liberation and right to pleasure encourage the rise of expectations among women and support their dissatisfaction towards sexual relations that do not happen the way they would like, including the ones that they find not long enough (Segraves, 2006).

Once a person is dissatisfied with the length of intercourse, he or she may have other reactions. It is not rare, in fact, for the man battling with this problem to be disappointed with his performance, to depreciate himself, to blame himself for his inability to gratify a woman, to believe that he will never be able to find a solution to his dysfunction and to fear the reaction of his partner.

As for the woman, even if she has been cooperative and understanding at the beginning of the relationship, it may not take long for her to start experiencing frustration and discontent. She might derive little pleasure during intercourse and quickly develop a negative image of sexuality. She possibly will avoid touching her partner or moving for fear of exciting him too much. She may reproach him for not being able to relax, for having his mind elsewhere, or for adhering to repetitive sexual scripts. She may perhaps interpret the efforts made by the man to delay his ejaculation as a reluctance to let himself go and as a lack of interest in her. She may eventually blame him not only for completing intercourse too soon but also, from his sullen demeanour, for putting an end to sexual intimacy. Sometimes she may even become angry, convincing herself that he only thinks about his own pleasure and that he's taking advantage of her (Masters and Johnson, 1970; McCabe, 1997; Rowland et al., 2004; Althof, 2006; Revicki et al., 2008).

The man may react adversely to the woman's reactions and consequently exacerbate his own difficulties. He may become more anxious about his ability to satisfy his partner. This performance anxiety could lead him to ejaculate more rapidly, to suffer erection problems or to experience a decrease in sexual desire. He may even lose confidence in himself, feel hopeless, perform less well at work, become less healthy and be less happy in life. As for couples, a decrease of frequency of sexual intercourse and a deterioration of the relationship have been often observed. Sexuality, which was supposed to be a source of love and joy, turns into an area of disappointment and bitterness. The woman may engage in extra-marital relations to confirm her femininity or to obtain sexual satisfaction. Sometimes, this dysfunction leads to separation and divorce (Hastings, 1963; Kaplan, 1974; Jehu, 1979; Byers and Grenier, 2003; Patrick et al., 2005; Rowland et al., 2007).

There also exist other types of attitudes and behaviours. Some men are utterly egoistic and attempt to pass off their deficiencies as normal to their partners. As for women, they are not all demanding, hostile or protesters. Their reactions are extremely diverse. They could escape this condition, resign themselves to it, be subjected to it, endure it or to be content with it (Collier, 2006). Many, out of timidity, accept it in silence. Others who suffer from a sexual problem (decreased libido, pain with intercourse, aversion) are very happy that sexual relations remain brief (Metz and McCarthy, 2003).

As for single people, they may become reluctant to meet a new partner for fear of not measuring up and this may isolate them even more socially (Symonds et al., 2003).

Aetiology

A large number of hypotheses have been suggested to explain the onset and maintenance of the difficulty with prolonging intercourse or premature ejaculation. The review of the literature indicates, however, that most of the biological and psychological aetiologies put forward are not evidence-based or that attempts to confirm them have brought about conflicting results (Buvat, 2011). In the following sections, the main causes of the difficulty to delay the onset of ejaculation during intercourse proposed by different researchers will be presented and critiqued.

Organic causes

Pathologies and traumatisms

Medical disorders at the origin of the difficulty to extend the length of intercourse are rare (Segraves, 2006). Certain urological conditions (hyperesthesia of the gland, shortening of the frenulum) (Shapiro, 1943) and certain pathologies of the spinal cord (spina bifida) (Kaplan, 1974) could be causes of this dysfunction. Researchers report a high prevalence of chronic prostatitis among individuals unable to delay the onset of ejaculation (Screponi et al., 2001; Liang et al., 2004; Shamoul and Nashaar, 2005). Zorgniotti (1979) observed that men who experience shorter intercourse times have higher penile blood pressure than others.

However, he did not explain in which way this condition could trigger ejaculation. Pirke et al. (1979) investigated the functioning of the pituitary and testicular systems and did not succeed in establishing a link between these systems and the length of intercourse; men who ejaculate soon after the intromission of the penis inside the vagina possess the same testosterone and luteinizing hormone levels as those who make coitus last longer. Certain neurological disorders (spinal cord tumours, multiple sclerosis and tabes dorsalis) as well as various surgical procedures striking at nerves and nervous centres controlling ejaculation could lead to this problem (Meyer et al., 1983; Tollison and Adams, 1979).

Pasini (1997) cites childhood enuresis as a possible cause of the inability to prolong intercourse in adulthood. However, as early as 1943, Shapiro had demonstrated that out of 1,130 subjects suffering from premature ejaculation only 8 per cent had experienced enuresis. Malformations, anatomical particularities or physiological disorders in the partner (too narrow vulva, too thick hymen, absence of vaginal lubrication) have been mentioned as possible causes of rapid ejaculation (Abraham, 1967; Solano, 2000), but there has not been any scientific study to verify the validity of these hypotheses. As for the role of circumcision, Waldinger et al. (2005a), in a study carried out with 491 subjects, found no difference between circumcised and uncircumcised men in relation to the ability to extend the length of intercourse.

The struggle to prolong the duration of sexual activity was detected among men who had endured a cranial trauma (Simpson et al., 2003) or a spinal cord lesion (Kuhr et al., 1995) as well as among individuals suffering from hypogonadism (Holbrook and Cohen, 2003) and non-insulin-dependent diabetes (El-Sakka, 2003). However, according to Segraves (2006), the small sample size of the population studied just as the absence of control groups reduces the weight of these research findings to the mere title of hypotheses. Moreover, not all men who experience ejaculation occurring prematurely suffer from these trauma or illnesses.

Carani et al. (2005) examined 34 patients who were seeking treatment for a problem of hyperthyroidism. They noted that 50 per cent of these patients suffered from premature ejaculation. After treatment of their thyroid problem, the length of intercourse of these men increased on average from 2.4 minutes (± 2.1 minutes) to 4.0 minutes (± 2.0 minutes). These observations do not, however, correspond to those of Waldinger et al. (2005c). These researchers did not find any link between premature ejaculation and thyroid disorders among the 680 men with premature ejaculation whom they studied. The relationship between thyroid problems and premature ejaculation is therefore not simple. It would appear, on first view, that men with hyperthyroidism would have a higher tendency to ejaculate rapidly than individuals in good health. On the other hand, men who ejaculate prematurely do not seem to have any more thyroid problems than individuals in the general population. According to Waldinger et al. (2005c), additional research should be undertaken to clarify the correlation that exists between these two conditions.

According to Kaplan (1974, 1983), when difficulties with prolonging intercourse appear after a period of satisfying sexual functioning, we may suspect the presence of pathological organic factors, especially if these difficulties are not accompanied by major changes in the sex life of the individual. Godpodinoff (1989) observed, among the majority of his patients suffering from secondary premature ejaculation, the existence of various organic troubles such as diabetes, atherosclerosis or arterial hypertension. However, many of these patients also suffered from erectile difficulty. Under these circumstances, we could make the hypothesis that premature ejaculation in these men follows largely from an adaptation to an erectile problem caused by an organic disorder (premature ejaculation resulting from sexual overstimulation in order to develop or maintain an erection) rather than from a pathology in itself. In another connection, many men who have developed an organic erectile dysfunction learn to ejaculate rapidly before losing the little erection they have in order to adapt to this crippling situation (Kaplan, 1983). The advent of medications that support the physiology of the erection (IPDE5) now makes it possible to modify this practice.

Most researchers seem to agree that the majority of men who experience trouble prolonging intercourse are in good physical health and do not have any anatomical anomaly. The fact that sexological treatments (Semans, 1956; Masters and Johnson, 1970; Godpodinoff, 1989; De Sutter et al., 2002; de Carufel and Trudel, 2006; Kempeneers et al., 2012) garner high success rates, and this thanks uniquely to the acquisition of knowledge, techniques and strategies, confirms this observation.

Excessive rapidity of the ejaculatory reflex

Semans (1956) put forward the hypothesis that premature ejaculation is caused by excessive rapidity of the ejaculatory reflex. Several authors have attempted to verify this hypothesis. Vignoli (1978) and Godpodinoff (1989) reported a shorter latency of evoked response in the bulbocavernosus muscles among individuals with premature ejaculation than among subjects who prolong intercourse. The research by Colpi et al. (1986) refuted these results. This is not surprising knowing that even if the reflex of the bulbocavernosus muscles takes place very quickly, this does not mean that the ejaculatory reflex threshold is lower and that a lesser excitement is enough to trigger it. In addition, and above all, the first reflex of the ejaculatory process (emission reflex) does not include in any way the bulbocavernosus muscles. It only involves the epididymis, the vas deferens, the prostate and the seminal vesicles. The bulbocavernosus muscles do not come into play until the second ejaculatory reflex (the expulsion reflex) begins.

High sensitivity of the glans penis

For some authors, premature ejaculation could be caused by a high sensitivity of the glans penis (Hastings, 1963; Hong, 1984). Rowland et al. (1993) explored the penile sensitivity of premature ejaculators and men who were sexually functional. They discovered that the threshold of subjective perception of vibrotactile stimuli applied to the penis is the same among both groups. These researchers concluded, from the above-mentioned findings, that the difference in terms of the length of intercourse between men who ejaculate rapidly and those who do not cannot be attributed to a hypersensitivity of the receptors situated on the surface of the penis. Paick et al. (1998) used a vibrator to measure the sensitivity of glans, the shaft of the penis or the region of the frenulum of men with a short intercourse time and men with a longer one and did not observe any difference between the two groups of men. Van den Broucke et al. (2007) verified penile vibrotactile sensitivity by placing receptors on six penis surface areas of 58 men. They could not establish a correlation between the degree of sensitivity of the penis and the length of intercourse. In addition, Rowland (2005) remarked that men possessing low sensitivity of the genital receptors could attain ejaculation shortly after the beginning of intercourse.

The studies on excessive rapidity of the ejaculatory reflex and the investigations on hypersensitivity of the penis are inconclusive. Consequently, they cannot serve as a guide at the present time in the creation and development of new ways to improve the length of intercourse.

Lack of perception, control and strength of the perineum muscles

La Pera and Nicastro (1996) assume that the muscles of the perineum are involved in the control of the ejaculatory reflex. According to them, difficulty extending the length of intercourse is due to a lack of perception, control and strength of the perineal muscles. A man afflicted with this problem does not identify which muscles are involved in the mechanism of controlling the ejaculatory reflex, is not able to execute the correct movement and does not possess muscles strong enough to inhibit the ejaculatory reflex.

This hypothesis is incorrect for two reasons. Firstly, ejaculation is a reflex and, consequently, it cannot be controlled (neither provoked nor interrupted) voluntarily. Secondly, the perineal muscles are not at all involved in the first reflex of the ejaculatory process (emission reflex). This reflex is essentially the work of ducts and glands (efferent ducts of the testis, epididymis, vas deferens, seminal vesicles, prostate) over which a human being does not possess any power.

The only effect that exerting the muscles of the pelvis can have is to hinder the normal process of the expulsion reflex (second reflex of ejaculation) preventing the sperm from getting outside the penis. But as the first reflex of ejaculation has occurred, the man all the same loses his erection and can no longer continue intercourse.

Frequency of sexual activity

Spiess (1984) and Godpodinoff (1989) report that longer periods of abstinence are positively correlated with a shorter intercourse time. This finding is supported by research results by Grenier and Byers (2001). In their study, subjects who report having sexual relations more frequently mention being able to extend the length of intercourse longer. They also emphasize experiencing more control, being less concerned about the eventuality of ejaculating too soon and feeling more capable of determining the onset of their ejaculation.

Disturbance of serotonergic neurotransmission

From the observation that taking antidepressants contributes to delaying ejaculation, Waldinger et al. (2004) proposed the hypothesis that disturbances at the level of the serotonergic neurotransmission in specific areas of the central nervous system could be at the origin of the difficulty with prolonging intercourse over a minute. According to this group of researchers, this condition is caused either by a decreased central serotonergic neurotransmission, a 5-HT2C receptor hyposensitivity and/or a 5-HT1C hypersensitivity, or a combination of these factors. It would be genetic by nature and this would make the release threshold of the ejaculatory reflex lower. Waldinger and Schweitzer (2008) state that the serotonin dysregulation hypothesis may explain only a small percentage (2–5 per cent) of the difficulty with prolonging intercourse in the general population. Additionally, due to an absence of selective 5-HT1A and 5-HT2C receptor ligands for safe human usage, this hypothesis has so far not been confirmed (Waldinger, 2013). On top of that, the fact that the average duration of masturbation is the same among men, regardless of whether they can or cannot prolong the length of intercourse (Rowland et al., 2000), seriously undermines this hypothesis.

Genetic factors

For more than sixty years, scientists have been interested in the effects genetic factors have on a man's ability to prolong the duration of intercourse. As early as 1943, Shapiro hypothesized that premature ejaculation could have a hereditary component. In the 1990s, Waldinger et al. (1998d) indicated that relatives of patients with premature ejaculation showed an increased likelihood of ejaculating prematurely. However, Jern (2013) cautioned that the results obtained by Waldinger et al. (1998d) cannot be deemed conclusive. Basically, since family members live together to a greater extent than non-related individuals, resemblance could be caused not only by genetic factors but also by a shared environment. In an effort to distinguish the respective impact of genetic and environmental factors, Jern et al. (2009) explored the correlations between 228 pairs of identical twins, 225 pairs of fraternal twins, 349 pairs of non-twin biological male siblings and the fact of ejaculating prematurely; based on this study, Jern (2013) came to the conclusion that genetic factors play a role, but environmental factors contribute the "lion's share of the variance in premature ejaculation" (location 4,650 of 123,806).

Research on relatives set the stage for genetic studies. Based on their hypothesis that lifelong premature ejaculation (characterized by a persistent intravaginal ejaculation latency time (IELT) of less than 1 minute and an inability to delay ejaculation) is related to disturbances of central serotonin (5-hydroxytryptamine [5-HT]) neurotransmission and 5-HT receptor functioning, the group headed by

Waldinger suggested that the serotonin transporter gene-linked polymorphism (5-HTTLPR) is associated with significant effects on the intravaginal ejaculation latency time in men with lifelong premature ejaculation (Janssen et al., 2009). However, the results obtained by these researchers refuted their hypothesis as they did not find any significant differences in the 5-HTT polymorphism alleles and genotypes between 89 Dutch Caucasian men with lifelong premature ejaculation and 92 Dutch Caucasian controls. The distribution of the genotypes was respectively S 47 per cent, L 53 per cent/LL 29 per cent, SL 48 per cent, SS 22 per cent for the premature ejaculation group and S 48 per cent, L 52 per cent/LL 29 per cent, SL 45 per cent, SS 26 per cent for the control group. This data shows that there are genetic differences related to central serotonin neurotransmission between men, but that these differences are equally distributed amongst men who are not able to prolong intercourse for more than 1 minute ("short" IELT) and those who are ("normal" IELT). Yet in men with lifelong premature ejaculation, this group of researchers found a difference between LL, SL and SS genotypes in the geometric mean intravaginal ejaculatory latency time (IELT). The LL genotypes had shorter IELT (13.2 seconds) than the SS (26 seconds) and SL (25.3 seconds) genotypes. They concluded from this data that "the 5-HTTLPR polymorphism is associated with significant effects on the latency to ejaculate in men with lifelong PE" (p. 276). Even if these differences are statistically significant, they are nonetheless minimal and, as such, cannot be considered influential. Other reasons to disregard the conclusion drawn by Janssen et al. (2009) include the fact that other genotypes (SS and SL) are equally found in men with a shorter IELT and these men are also considered to be suffering from lifelong premature ejaculation. Furthermore, these researchers stated in the same article that "there were no significant differences in the 5-HTT polymorphism alleles and genotypes between 89 Dutch Caucasian men with LPE and 92 Dutch Caucasian controls" (p. 276). These results imply that even if the LL genotypes are associated with a shorter IELT in men who cannot prolong intercourse for more than 1 minute, these genotypes are also present in the same proportion in men who can prolong intercourse for more than 1 minute (control group) and do not prevent them in any way from doing so. Consequently, the LL genotypes, because they are (as other genotypes) generally distributed the same way in men, do not stand out as a causal factor for the difficulty with prolonging intercourse. But even more disturbing is that other studies have found results opposite to the ones reported by Janssen et al. (2009). In research done in Iran including 82 men with premature ejaculation and 82 men able to prolong intercourse, Safarinejad (2009) demonstrated, contrary to the research of Janssen et al. (2009), that the S/S genotype was significantly more prevalent among men with premature ejaculation than the L/L genotype. The results of Safarinejad (2009) were confirmed by an investigation carried out in Turkey by Ozbek et al. (2009), who found the same distribution of genotypes in 70 men with premature ejaculation and 70 men able to prolong intercourse. In research on the efficacy of an antidepressant (sertraline, a selective serotonin reuptake inhibitor), Safarinejad (2010) discovered that L allele subjects with lifelong PE reacted significantly better than S allele subjects. Finally, Jern et al. (2013) analysed the relation between the genotype of 1673 Finnish male twins and siblings of twins aged 18–45 and their answers to a questionnaire regarding ejaculatory function. They found no significant association between the 5-HTTLPR polymorphism and a self-report measure of ejaculation latency time or a composite variable measuring premature ejaculation. They discovered no difference in genotype frequencies between men who ejaculate in less than 1 minute, men who last more than 11 minutes and those who do not ejaculate during intercourse. Jern et al. (2013) concluded that their study, given the large sample size and multifactorial measures used (contrary to the other studies which had small numbers of subjects, showed contradictory results and suffered from methodological inconsistencies), indicates that the 5-HTTLPR polymorphism has a limited, if any, impact on ejaculatory function.

The major flaw of the research on genetic factors – which is seriously invalidating – is that it does not correlate the genetic parameters with the total length of sexual excitement (which evolves through foreplay and intercourse) but only with the length of sexual excitement occurring during intercourse (also called intravaginal ejaculatory latency time). Sexual excitement[1] is the only cause of ejaculation. No other factor can trigger ejaculation by itself.[2] All the factors involved in hastening the onset of ejaculation work in conjunction with sexual excitement. Since sexual excitement starts much before the beginning of intercourse, it is an enormous methodological mistake to neglect this fact and to study the relation between genetic factors and the last part of the course of sexual excitement instead of studying the relation between genetic factors and the total course of sexual excitement. In effect, if there were genetic factors that accelerate the progression of excitement, they would not wait until the beginning of intercourse to exert their influence. They would act as soon as sexual excitement begins, and men would therefore ejaculate within 1 minute after the start of foreplay if they were suffering from premature ejaculation. This is almost never the case. Genetic factors do not affect to such an extent (if they do at all) the course of excitement during foreplay or masturbation. Furthermore, these factors do not simply kick in to precipitate ejaculation when intercourse begins. The difference in the speed of the intensification of sexual excitement towards ejaculation that could occur between foreplay and intercourse is not due to a change in genetics that takes place when a man inserts his penis inside the vagina of his partner. It is mainly due to changes in sexological factors (like the start of continuous penile stimulation provided by the vagina or the need to use muscular contractions to effectuate penetration movements) and the way they are dealt with, as well as to psychological and/or relational factors interfering with the management of sexual excitement. In other words, the difference between the capacity to prolong the length of sexual excitement during foreplay and the capacity to do so during intercourse does not pertain to genetic factors. It relates to the application of sexual knowledge and skills that could be affected by psychological and relational conditions. Genetic factors would not be selective concerning the moment – during foreplay or intercourse – in which they influence the progression of sexual excitement towards ejaculation; the selection of a specific strategy or the way one uses one's body, on the contrary, will make a difference to the speed at which sexual excitement evolves towards ejaculation during foreplay or intercourse. If a man can prolong foreplay or masturbation more than intercourse, genetic factors have nothing to do with his shorter intercourse time (or IELT). On the other hand, knowledge of how to manage his sexual excitement during intercourse and his ability to do so play a crucial role.

To summarize, as sexual excitement is the cause of ejaculation and as it does not start at the beginning of intercourse but much before, the duration alone of sexual excitement during intercourse (or IELT) cannot be used to assert that organic factors influence the course of sexual excitement (or to assert that organic factors influence the speed at which sexual excitement intensifies to the point of triggering ejaculation, or to assert that organic factors are the cause of an ejaculation that happens earlier than desired, or to assert that organic factors are the cause of "premature ejaculation"). It is the total duration of sexual excitement (or total ejaculatory latency time (TELT)), which includes foreplay, that could indicate if any organic factor is playing a role in the way sexual excitement is evolving before ejaculation.

Since sexual excitement begins much before intercourse starts, it is essential that future research takes into account this aspect and explores the relationship between genetic factors – actually between all organic factors – and the totality of sexual excitement and not only the last part of it. As just noted, all factors that contribute to quicken the onset of ejaculation do so in conjunction with sexual excitement. Intercourse, including all its particular components, is one of these factors. The manner in which the different factors (genetic, traumatic, pathological, psychological, relational and sexological, including the unfolding of intercourse) are interacting with sexual excitement must be established and the effects they have on it must be distinguished from each other. The way genetic factors interact with sexual excitement should also be assessed in different situations other than intercourse, such as masturbation, manual stimulation from the partner, fellatio and so on. Finally, it is important to stress once again that intercourse, with all its sexological (personal and interactional) ingredients, is a very powerful factor affecting the course of sexual excitement and, consequently, the moment ejaculation is reached.

Despite the conclusion of Jern et al. (2013) and the major flaw that afflicts current research on genetic factors, there is still reason to believe that genetic differences exert some type of influence on the onset of ejaculation. This effect – which would be rather small – would be most noticeable when a man does not possess the skills and the knowledge necessary to manage his sexual excitement. This is what research by Janssen et al. (2009), Safarinejad (2009) and Ozbek et al. (2009) tends to reveal. However, as soon as a man has the information and the ability to postpone the onset of his ejaculation, he can prolong intercourse (have a longer IELT) no matter what his genetic background is. This is confirmed by the study of Janssen et al. (2009), which found that men who do and do not prolong intercourse have the same genotypes. The genotype influence, if it exists, is then overridden by effective behaviour and knowledge. This is clearly observed in less demanding situations than intercourse – like foreplay, oral sex or masturbation – where almost all men (without much technique) can easily prolong the length of their sexual excitement without reaching ejaculation. This observation is validated by the research of Rowland et al. (2000), which shows that the average length of masturbation is the same for all men (4.4 minutes), regardless of their capacity to prolong intercourse for more than 1 minute or not, and irrespective of their genetic constitution. It is also confirmed by the research of Strassberg et al. (1987), which reveals that men having a mean IELT of 1.9 minutes display a masturbatory time of 3.4 minutes. In addition, according to Segraves (2006), even if it were true that genetics induce interindividual differences, they do not prevent men from acquiring through learning effective ways to overcome their supposedly hereditary tendency and extend the length of intercourse.

To conclude, there are probably some genetic factors that contribute to rendering the management of sexual excitement a little bit more difficult to achieve, but only to a small degree, and only for a limited number of men. Furthermore, these factors, for the most part, can be surmounted through learning. On the other hand, for the few men who do not benefit much from sex therapy (excluding the cases where psychological factors like anxiety or relational factors like a partner's lack of cooperation play a critical role), it is plausible to imagine that their physiology is constrained by some biological parameters (including genetic factors), but these parameters remain to be discovered.

Medication

Assalian (1994) reports that several medications interfere with the ejaculatory process (thioridazine, chlorpromazine, chlordiazepoxide, perphenazine, trifluoperazine, reserpine, butyrophenones, monoamine oxidase inhibitors, guanethidine, phenoxybenzamine, clomipramine, fluoxetine). Some of these medications delay the arrival of ejaculation (i.e. clomipramine, fluoxetine) but others may accelerate it. The dosage should also be taken into account. At certain doses the same medication retards the onset of ejaculation, at other doses it speeds it up. Similar accelerating effects can be produced by stimulants or toxics such as iodine, bismuth and potassium hydroxide (Abraham, G., 1967) or drugs like amphetamines, cocaine, amyl nitrite and certain hallucinogens (Paradis and Lafond, 1990).

The majority of men who seek treatment for difficulty with prolonging intercourse do not take any medication or drugs. It is therefore clear that the consumption of medications and drugs explains only a minority of rapid ejaculations. It is advisable, however, to take this into account in the anamnesis of patients.

Sexological causes

Sexological causes relate specifically to sexual factors that interfere with the sexual functioning of individuals. Due to a lack of knowledge on the subject of sexuality, there was until recently a tendency to regard sexual difficulties as symptoms of psychological or organic problems. It simply could not be imagined that sexual causes existed.

Before beginning an overview of sexological causes, the male sexual excitement and sexual emotional curves will be described. These curves provide a framework for analysing the sexological factors that generate and heighten sexual excitement. With this knowledge, it will become possible to understand why properly managing sexual excitement prevents ejaculation from occurring too early.

The sexual excitement curve

Sexual excitement is a neurological reaction that arises following an effective external or internal sexual stimulation. It consists of a series of neural impulses resulting from the stimulation of nerve endings of the target organs as well as the involvement (provoked by a chemical-physiological activation and a cognitive activity) of specific cerebral centres. These impulses vary in quantity and intensity and in turn lead to physiological reactions such as the erection of the penis, increased heart rate, elevation of blood pressure, acceleration of the breathing rate, augmentation of muscle tension and ejaculation. The evolution of sexual excitement may be transposed visually with the aid of a curve on which intensity is shown on the ordinate and duration on the abscissa. Due to particularities inherent in any sexual experience, each curve has its own pattern. Figures 1.1, 1.2 and 1.3 reproduce the course followed by the excitement of three different men.[3]

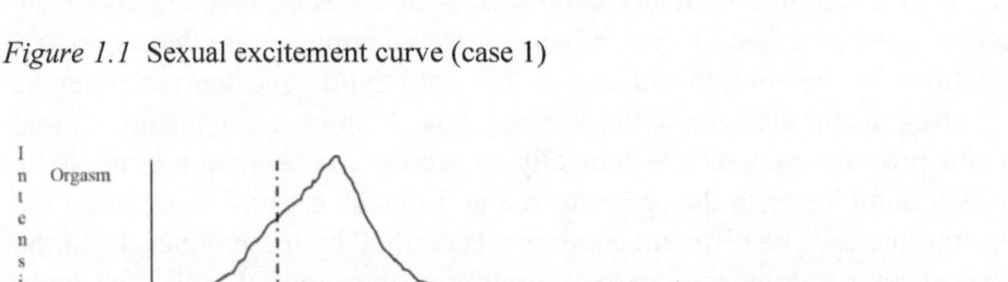

Figure 1.1 Sexual excitement curve (case 1)

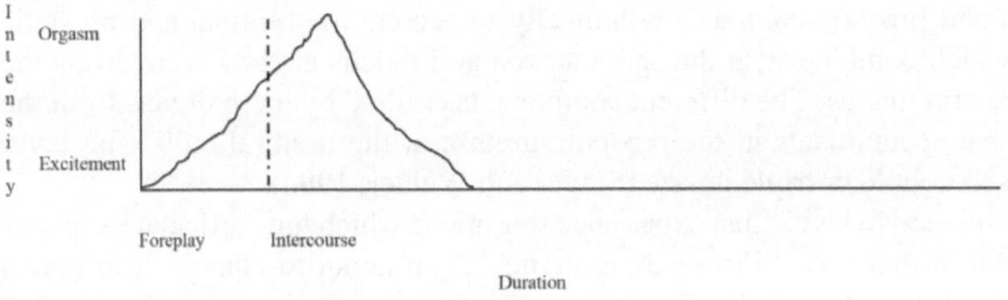

Figure 1.2 Sexual excitement curve (case 2)

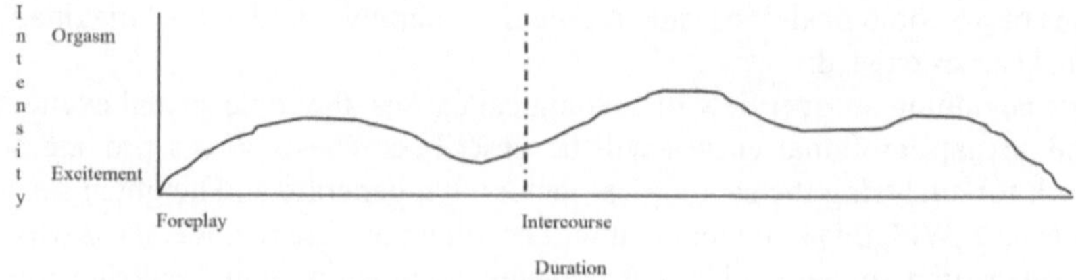

Figure 1.3 Sexual excitement curve (case 3)

We may see that the first man extended the duration of intercourse. The second ejaculated soon after intromission. The third prolonged intercourse without reaching orgasm.[4] As instructive as they are, these curves do not give us much information about what actually happened during these sexual activities. At the very most, they tell us about the duration and intensity of the sexual excitement.[5] In order to gather more clues from the male sexual excitement curve, I divided it into four zones. This division is realized on the basis of the physiological reactions that occur during the complete male sexual response cycle and which were mainly described by Masters and Johnson (1966). I will begin this presentation with a description of the fourth zone, that of ejaculation, because it is, by its reflex nature, the actual source of the difficulty with prolonging intercourse.

THE FOURTH ZONE: THE ZONE OF EJACULATION

Ejaculation is assured by the action of the cerebral and spinal centres, which form a highly coordinated network. The sympathetic, parasympathetic and somatic nervous systems, activated by diverse sexual stimuli, act synergistically to prompt the physiological occurrences of the ejaculatory response. Ejaculation consists of two phases, the emission and the expulsion phase (Figure 1.4). These two phases are reflexes and take place in succession (Benson, 1988). When sexual excitement becomes sufficiently intense, the emission reflex is triggered. This reflex manifests itself through involuntary contractions of the accessory organs of the reproductive system. Efferent sympathetic nervous impulses produce peristaltic contractions of the smooth muscles of the epididymis and the vas deferens thereby starting the progression of the spermatozoa. At the same time, the seminal vesicles and prostate contract rhythmically to secrete the seminal and prostatic fluids, which combine with the spermatozoa and mucus already secreted by the bulbourethral glands. The different components emitted by these organs form the semen that accumulates in the prostatic urethra at the urethral bulb. The latter expands to double or triple in size (Singer and Weiner, 1994).

On a subjective level, men experience sensations which they articulate in popular speech in this way: "I'm ready to come", "I'm about to come", "I'm gonna explode", "I'm coming". There is not anything apparent (the semen has not yet been expelled out of the penis), but they know that ejaculation has been released

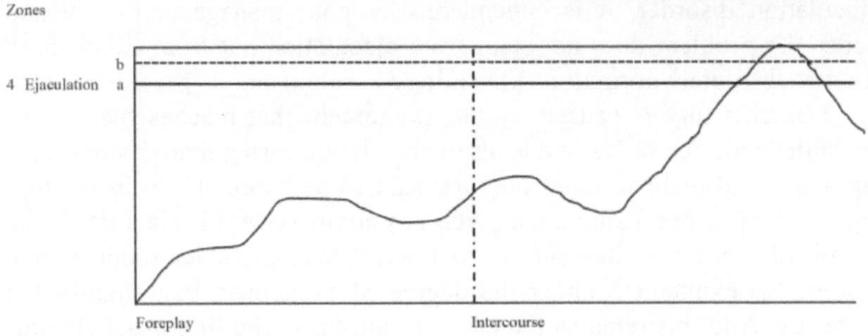

Figure 1.4 Zone 4: The zone of ejaculation

Zone 4: The ejaculation zone (a: emission reflex or point of no return; b: expulsion reflex).

and it is impossible to stop it. They experience a feeling of irresistibility called "ejaculatory inevitability". This feeling is justified because once these contractions are triggered they cannot be stopped or delayed. They are reflexes and consequently independent of the will.

Once the urethral bulb is distended enough by the accumulation of sperm, the expulsion phase begins. A series of reflex contractions occur involving the urethral bulb and the muscles of the perineum. The seminal fluid is then propelled from the prostatic urethra into the penile urethra, and then outside of the urinary meatus. The urethral sphincter, already contracted during the emission reflex, prevents the sperm from flowing towards the bladder and causing a retrograde ejaculation. Just like the contractions of the emission phase, the contractions of the expulsion phase are reflexes (Benson, 1988). These contractions allow for the release of physiological and emotional tensions and constitute a source of immense pleasure for the majority of men (Masters and Johnson, 1966).

Sexologists call the moment when the man attains the level of excitement (threshold) that sets off the emission reflex the "point of no return". This very eloquent expression signifies that the man can no longer return to lower excitement levels, neither avoid ejaculation. Excitement is too high, the threshold of the emission reflex is reached, ejaculation begins to take place and its unfolding continues until the end, no matter what he attempts to do.[6]

We find in many articles published in medical and sexological reviews the assertion that the difficulty to extend the length of intercourse is caused by a lack of control over the ejaculatory reflex or over ejaculation. This notion is antinomic because a reflex, by definition, cannot be the object of voluntary control. Moreover, the anatomical structures that contract during the first reflex of ejaculation (emission reflex) are ducts (epididymis, vas deferens . . .) and glands (prostate, seminal vesicles . . .) over which a man cannot in any way exercise voluntary control. When the emission reflex occurs, the erection is destined to disappear and intercourse to end. Irrespective of the means used, ejaculation cannot be stopped once it has been released.

In fact, the difficulty with prolonging the duration of intercourse is not due to an ejaculation disorder. It is engendered by poor management of sexual excitement. The problem does not stem from ejaculation but from excitement. Ejaculation is absolutely normal; its physiology is sound and its processes occur naturally. The difficulty is caused by the excitement that reaches the release threshold of the emission reflex and leads to ejaculation earlier than desired. This reality applies to all men, whether they are said to be "normal" or "premature ejaculators". There is not a single man who has control over his ejaculation; he only has control over his excitement. If a man wants to lengthen intercourse time, he must keep his excitement under the degree of excitement that triggers the emission reflex. And this remains the case, during his entire life, in all circumstances and with all partners.

THE THIRD ZONE: THE ZONE OF EJACULATORY IMMINENCE

The third zone – that of ejaculatory imminence – is situated just below the ejaculation zone (Figure 1.5). At this stage, a minute rise in excitement caused by the slightest increase of stimulation releases ejaculation (Masters and Johnson, 1966). During coitus, when the man's sexual excitement carries him to the beginning of this stage, he or his partner needs only to execute two or three additional pelvic thrusts for him to immediately reach the point of no return. In a sense, it is a danger zone for couples who want to prolong the length of intercourse because, at this point, a tiny surge in excitement will trigger the ejaculation reflex.

The zone of ejaculatory imminence is easily identifiable. When a man enters this zone, precise physiological reactions occur at the level of his genital organs and warn him – if he pays just little attention to them – of the proximity of the ejaculatory reflex. The testicles rise closer to the body, the penis becomes firmer and the muscles of the perineum contract stronger (Masters and Johnson, 1966). Some men feel quivers along the penis shaft; others feel like their glans will

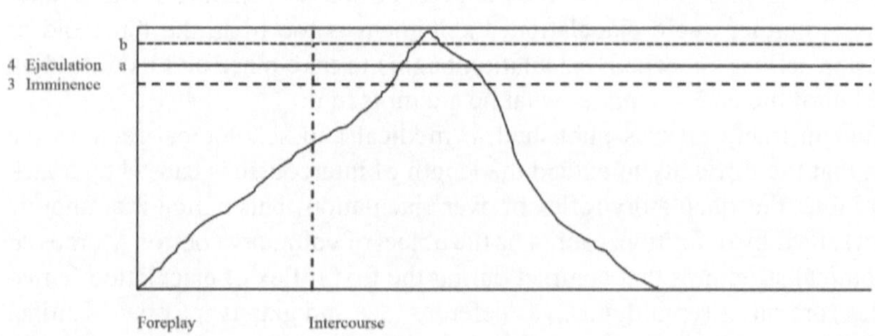

Figure 1.5 Zone 3: The zone of ejaculatory imminence

Zone 3: The ejaculatory imminence zone. Zone 4: The ejaculation zone (a: emission reflex or point of no return; b: expulsion reflex).

explode. It is up to each individual to identify the sensations that occur in their genitals at this moment and to react accordingly.

Many men would like to pursue intercourse at these soaring heights of excitement because they derive such intense sexual pleasure. Unfortunately, it is very difficult to navigate at high levels of excitement and impossible to do so within the zone of ejaculatory imminence. When a man enters this zone, his excitement heads in but two directions: up or down. It cannot be maintained at this degree of intensity. If he continues to receive stimulation, he will automatically advance towards ejaculation. If he wants to distance himself from the point of no return, he has to interrupt all stimulation and apply the emergency techniques that can be found in the sixth session of the sexual excitement management programme for the difficulty with prolonging intercourse described in the third part of this book (Figure 1.6). If he wishes to carry on inside the ejaculatory imminence zone, he will proceed quickly towards ejaculation (Figure 1.7).

Actually, the sensations and the pleasure experienced inside the ejaculatory imminence zone may be what certain men and Tantra practitioners call an "orgasm without ejaculation". If this is the case, it means that these men reach a high level of excitement and pleasure and that they bring these down before reaching the ejaculation zone. They do not control their ejaculation, they just do not reach it. If this is not the case, it is difficult to agree with this assertion ("orgasm without ejaculation") because the proponents of the capacity to achieve orgasm without ejaculating do not define what they call orgasm. They do not describe its cognitive-emotional components or its physiological-corporeal elements. It then becomes impossible to know if these very few men have had an orgasm without ejaculation by controlling their ejaculation or just do or feel something else. But as in functional sex therapy, an orgasm is a physiological discharge (following an increase in sexual excitement) which is experienced with pleasure (in the case of the man, an ejaculation felt with pleasure). It becomes difficult to understand how one of these components (discharge or pleasure) can still be called an orgasm

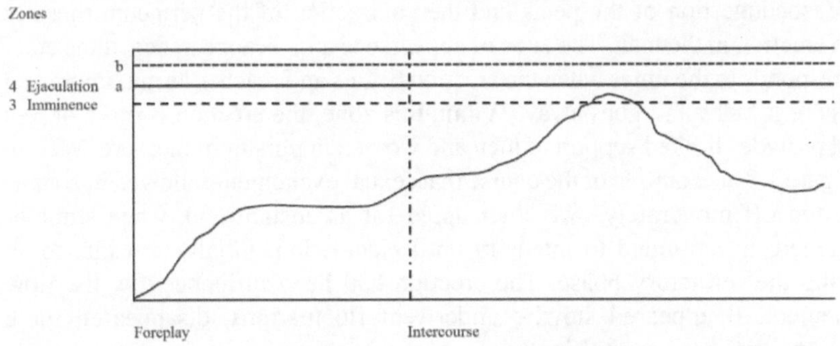

Figure 1.6 An example of management of sexual excitement inside the zone of ejaculatory imminence

Zone 3: The ejaculatory imminence zone. Zone 4: The ejaculation zone (a: emission reflex or point of no return; b: expulsion reflex).

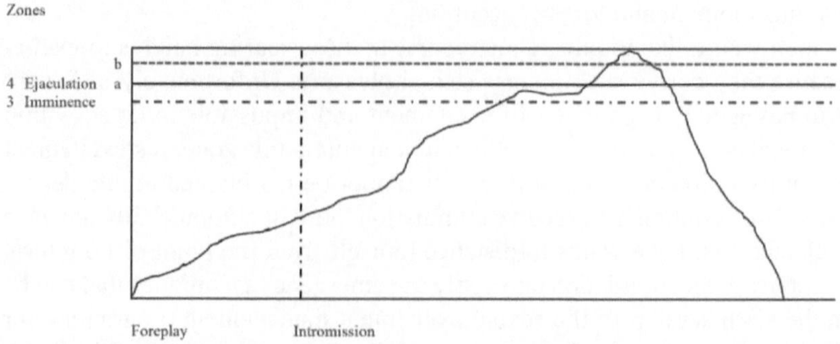

Figure 1.7 An example of a failed attempt to prolong the length of intercourse inside the zone of ejaculatory imminence

Zone 3: The ejaculatory imminence zone. Zone 4: The ejaculation zone (a: emission reflex or point of no return; b: expulsion reflex).

when it is dissociated from the other. It is either a discharge without pleasure or a climax of pleasure without discharge.[7] This discussion brings us back to the fact that ejaculation is a reflex process and that it cannot be deliberately controlled.

We will now look at the first zone. It is described before the second zone to facilitate the understanding of this presentation.

THE FIRST ZONE: THE ZONE OF APPEARANCE AND DISAPPEARANCE OF THE ERECTION

Any perceived stimulus (internal or external), codified as erotic and appreciated sensually, generates sexual reactions. Among these reactions, we note an increase in heart rate, a rise in blood pressure, accelerated breathing, vasocongestives response (influx of blood flow to the genitals in particular and some other parts of the body), a reaction of sudation and an intensification of myotonic activity (muscular contractions). Vasocongestion of the penis and the contraction of the perineum muscles cause an erection in the man. The zone of appearance and disappearance of the erection corresponds to the times when the erection begins and reaches its maximum and those where it fades and goes away. Within this zone, the erection is more or less firm and provides limited support to men and women in pursuit of pleasure. We can see in Figure 1.8 an example of the course that sexual excitement followed in zone 1.

It started off moderately, was interrupted for an instant and, when stimulation resumed, it continued to intensify until ejaculation. Finally, it came to an end during the refractory phase. The erection had been influenced by the flow of excitement. It appeared slowly, underwent fluctuations, disappeared for a moment, and then returned to finally dissipate after ejaculation.

The level of appearance and disappearance of the erection zone is not fixed. It varies according to circumstances, age and state of health. For example, during times of extreme fatigue, following excessive consumption of alcohol or after a first ejaculation (during the refractory period[8]), the level of the zone of appearance

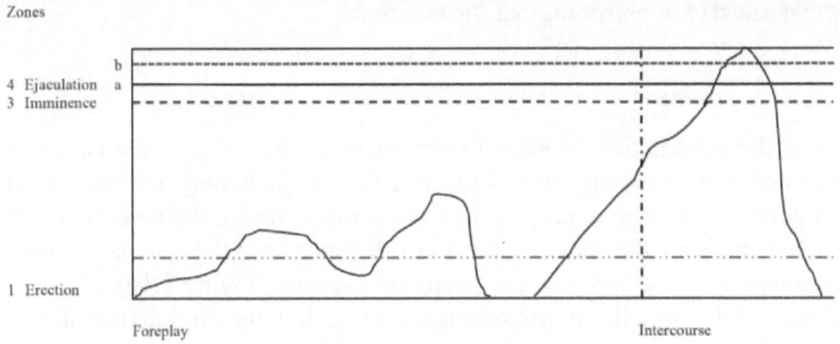

Figure 1.8 Zone 1: The zone of appearance and disappearance of the erection

Zone 1: The appearance and disappearance of the erection zone. Zone 3: The ejaculatory imminence zone. Zone 4: The ejaculation zone (a: emission reflex or point of no return; b: expulsion reflex).

and disappearance of the erection is located much higher. Diabetes, because of the neurological and vascular impairment it instigates, produces the same effect. And finally the aging process, due to the modifications it induces, has an impact on erections, which become longer to achieve, less rigid, more difficult to retain and easier to lose. In this context, the man requires more stimulation and excitement to reach erection. This becomes a problem when he needs to be very excited to obtain an erection sufficiently firm for intromission. At this moment, he no longer has any room for manoeuvre to manage his excitement. He is already almost in the zone of ejaculatory imminence when he gets his erection. The addition of stimulation that intromission of the penis inside the vagina causes, along with the hike in excitement that ensues, do not give him any respite and lead him rapidly to ejaculation. He experiences therefore an ejaculation that appears earlier than desired secondary to an erectile disorder (Figure 1.9). The most appropriate

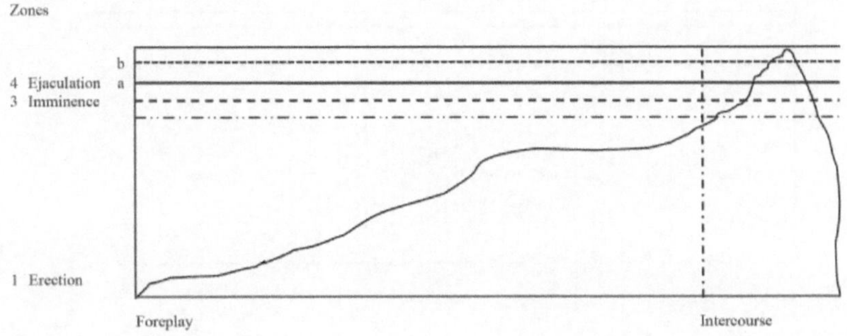

Figure 1.9 Rise of the level of the zone of the appearance and disappearance of the erection

Zone 1: The appearance and disappearance of the erection zone. Zone 3: The ejaculatory imminence zone. Zone 4: The ejaculation zone (a: emission reflex or point of no return; b: expulsion reflex).

solution at the present time for this type of dysfunction resides in taking medication (IPDE5) that assists the physiology of the erection.

THE SECOND ZONE: THE ZONE OF THE MODULATION OF SEXUAL EXCITEMENT

The zone of the modulation of sexual excitement begins when the erection is established and ends with the entry into the zone of ejaculatory imminence. It is the best zone in which to manage sexual excitement. Inside the modulation of sexual excitement zone, the man can stay a safe distance from the ejaculation zone while maintaining a good erection and obtaining pleasure (Figure 1.10).

In the case of the inability to prolong intercourse, it is the modulation of sexual excitement that is not done properly. We see in Figure 1.11 that, as soon as

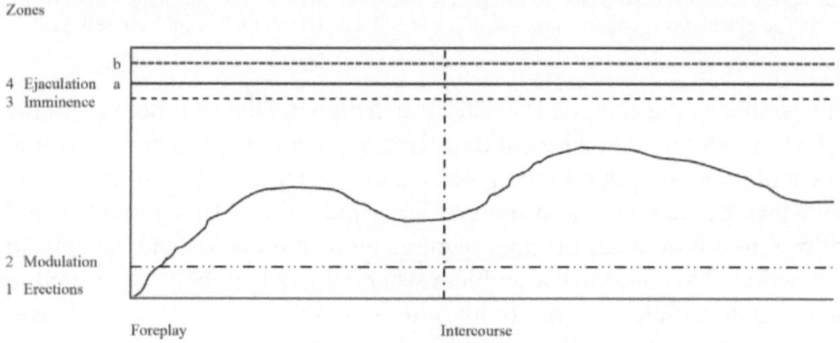

Figure 1.10 Zone 2: The zone of the modulation of sexual excitement

Zone 1: The appearance and disappearance of the erection zone. Zone 2: The modulation of sexual excitement zone. Zone 3: The ejaculatory imminence zone. Zone 4: The ejaculation zone (a: emission reflex or point of no return; b: expulsion reflex).

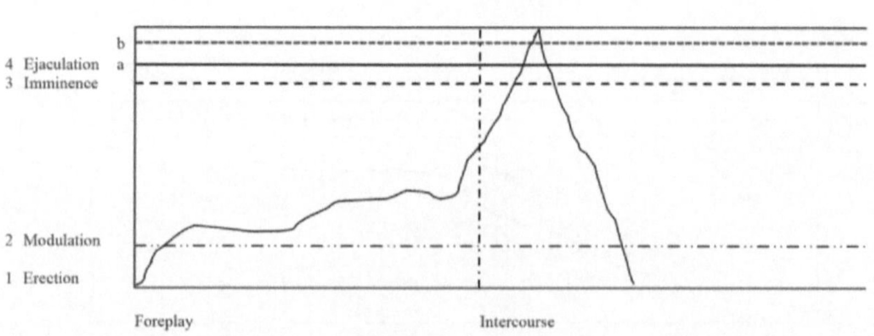

Figure 1.11 Curve of a case of difficulty with prolonging the length of intercourse

Zone 1: The appearance and disappearance of the erection zone. Zone 2: The modulation of sexual excitement zone. Zone 3: The ejaculatory imminence zone. Zone 4: The ejaculation zone (a: emission reflex or point of no return; b: expulsion reflex).

intromission approaches, excitement soars and heads straight towards the zone of ejaculatory imminence and then to that of ejaculation.[9]

The zone of the modulation of sexual excitement offers enormous potential from an erotological point of view. Within this zone, it is possible to experience a wide range of sexual emotions and amorous feelings. It grants the time and freedom necessary to express tenderness, display sensuality, show affection, desire, be excited, divulge innermost feelings, have fun, let go, be passionate, display manliness, share fantasies, enjoy the presence of one's partner, complement one another, share and love. It encourages variety and experimentation, expression and discovery, dialogue and contact. Figure 1.12 provides an example of a complete sexual response cycle where the man modulated his excitement.

The sexual emotional curve

There is a sexual emotional activation concomitant to the sexual physiological activation. This activation – which is also involuntary – includes emotions such as sexual attraction, desire, pleasure or satisfaction. This activation can also be portrayed graphically (Figure 1.13).

Sexual emotions are impressions, moods, desires, longings, drive, stirrings and pleasure of a sexual nature experienced by a person. They are sought by people in their sex life. They are essential elements of sexual functioning equal to obtaining the neurophysiological excitatory response. Their absence, low frequency or opposing sides (like sexual aversion, shame or disgust) are very often a source of significant distress.

I insist on the use of the word sexual to distinguish sexual emotional activations from other emotional activations – sentimental and affectionate among others – which also take place during sexual activity. When this distinction is not

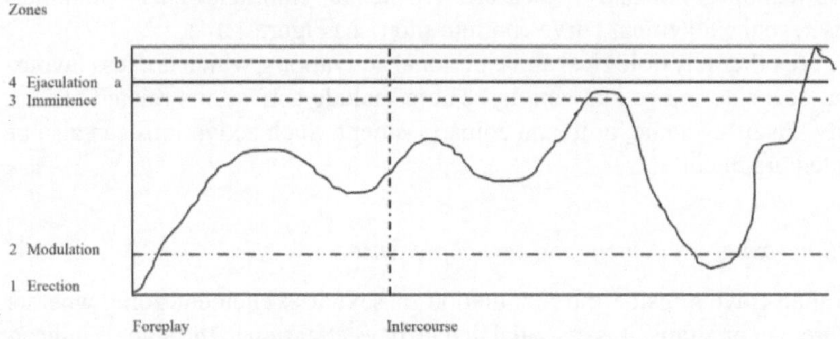

Figure 1.12 Example of a sexual response cycle taking place inside the four zones of the male sexual excitement curve

Zone 1: The appearance and disappearance of the erection zone. Zone 2: The modulation of sexual excitement zone. Zone 3: The ejaculatory imminence zone. Zone 4: The ejaculation zone (a: emission reflex or point of no return; b: expulsion reflex).

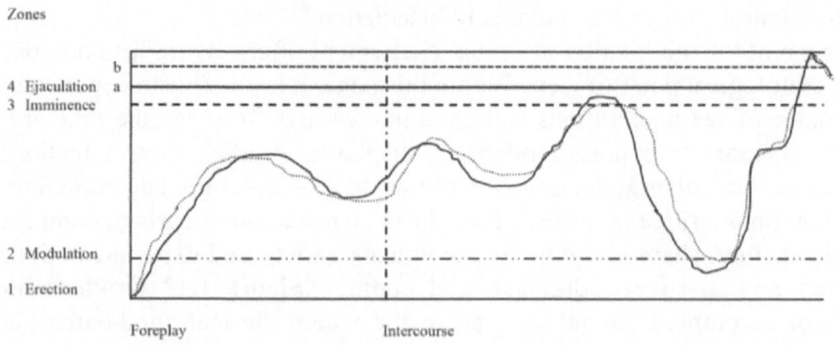

Figure 1.13 Example of a sexual response cycle including physiological and emotional activations taking place inside the four zones of the male sexual excitement curve

Zone 1: The appearance and disappearance of the erection zone. Zone 2: The modulation of sexual excitement zone. Zone 3: The ejaculatory imminence zone. Zone 4: The ejaculation zone (a: emission reflex or point of no return; b: expulsion reflex). Solid line: sexual physiological activation; dashed line: sexual emotional activation.

made, considerable confusion ensues during the diagnosis and treatment of several sexual dysfunctions.

It could be assumed that the curve of sexual pleasure automatically follows that of sexual excitement, but this isn't always the case. In fact, sexual emotional activation and sexual physiological activation don't always go hand in hand during sexual activities. Take for example a man who doesn't possess the ability to prolong the duration of intercourse. His excitement propels him towards ejaculation from the start of coitus. Distraught by this forceful reaction and worrying about the eventuality of negative relational consequences, he tenses his entire body to stop its progression. He doesn't savour the present moment and the emotion he is feeling is not that of pleasure. His sexual emotional curve plummets while his sexual excitement curve continues to rise (Figure 1.14).

There are other physiological and emotional activations, which are less favourable, that occur during sexual activity. These include activations related to fear, insecurity, disgust, shame, guilt and embarrassment. Such activations can also be represented graphically.

Modulating sexual excitement and sexual pleasure

When a man travels inside the modulation of sexual excitement zone, whether during foreplay or coitus, it is essential that he pays attention to the signals indicating that his excitement is climbing. These signals include the following reactions and changes: rise in muscular tension (buttocks, perineum, abdomen, arms, legs and face), heightening and acceleration of breathing, reduction in the range and increase in the speed of pelvic thrusts, greater focus on a particular sexual stimulus, intensifying of sexual sensations and escalation of pleasure.

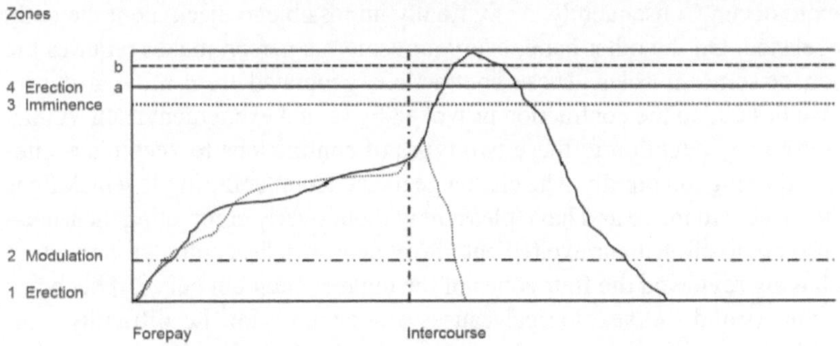

Figure 1.14 Example of dissociation between the sexual excitement curve and the sexual pleasure curve

Zone 1: The appearance and disappearance of the erection zone. Zone 2: The modulation of sexual excitement zone. Zone 3: The ejaculatory imminence zone. Zone 4: The ejaculation zone (a: emission reflex or point of no return; b: expulsion reflex). Solid line: sexual physiological activation; dashed line: sexual emotional activation.

There are two major types of method for modulating the flow of sexual excitement and keeping it under the level that releases ejaculation, which is to say under the threshold of the ejaculatory reflex. The first entails managing the quantity and intensity of stimulation the man receives. In general, when stimulation intensifies, whether it is visual, tactile, sonant, cognitive or other, excitement rises. When it diminishes, excitement descends. The man must therefore remain conscious of the height of his excitement and be careful not to receive or not to bring about by himself (by the speed of his pelvic thrusts, for example) too much stimulation. On top of that, as increase of sexual pleasure often provokes an escalation of sexual excitement, he must also be aware of the intensity of the pleasure he is experiencing when he receives stimulation in order not to let himself overwhelmed by this pleasure and lose control of his excitement. For her part, the woman may pay close attention to her partner's corporal reactions and reduce the intensity of exchanges when it becomes necessary.

The second method is aimed at reversing the physiological reactions caused by sexual excitement. Of these physiological reactions, only breathing and mytonia (muscular tension) are accessible to the will. Heart rate, blood pressure, sudation and vasocongestion cannot be controlled voluntarily. When a man becomes sexually excited, his muscles contract at the same time as his breathing quickens and becomes more thoracic. These reactions are normal and enable sexual excitement to escalate and for ejaculation to occur. They are caused by sexual excitement and, in turn, they enable it to increase. To lower his sexual excitement, a man must reverse these reactions, which is to say he must reduce the intensity of his muscular contractions, slow down his respiratory rhythm and breathe from his abdomen. To summarize, sexual excitement generates muscular contractions as well as elevates and accelerates breathing. The release of these contractions and the return to slow and deep abdominal breathing diminishes excitement. It is necessary for the muscular tension created by sexual excitement to increase in order for the ejaculation reflex to occur. Consequently, it is virtually impossible to ejaculate if the body is totally relaxed. On the other hand, every movement a person makes requires the contraction of some muscles. These contractions generated from moving during sexual activities add to the contraction provoked by sexual excitement itself. A man must therefore pay attention to these two types of contractions to keep his excitement from climbing too rapidly. The challenge men encounter during lovemaking is not only to be able to move and have pleasure without overly contracting their muscles but also not to allow their excitement make their muscles contract too much.

After having reviewed the four zones of the male excitement curve, it becomes easier to understand the sexological causes associated with the difficulty with extending the length of intercourse. But before going any further, it is important to keep in mind that the cause of ejaculation is nothing other than sexual excitement. Spontaneous ejaculation (triggered without excitement generated by internal or external sexual stimulation) besides nocturnal emissions, ejaculations provoked by certain medications (selective noradrenaline reuptake inhibitor, neuroleptic) or ejaculations happening during intense periods of anxiety, occurs very rarely. A man does not just ejaculate while walking down the street or watching sports on television. Neither can emotions like anger, fear or sadness make a man automatically ejaculate. The same applies for diseases, traumatisms and genetic factors. In fact, it has never been reported that a pathological condition can provoke instant ejaculation like a cold can make somebody sneeze, for example. A man will not ejaculate, apart from a few exceptional cases arising during episodes of extreme anxiety (Redmond et al., 1983), unless he is sexually excited. His ejaculation takes place when his excitement mounts and reaches the degree of intensity (threshold) that triggers the emission reflex. If the rise of excitement is not managed and it progresses rapidly, the chances are very high that ejaculation will occur earlier than desired and that one or both members of the couple will be dissatisfied.[10]

Sexological factors promoting the rise of sexual excitement

We will now take a look at the factors that permit sexual excitement to build and reach the zone of ejaculation. Knowledge of these factors provides the man with the possibility to better manage his sexual excitement and to delay the arrival of his ejaculation. These factors have been grouped into three categories: the presence of stimuli, the focalization on a particular stimulus and a way to use one's body characterized by rapidity, tonicity and/or globality of movements.

THE PRESENCE OF STIMULI

Stimuli arise from the context, the partner or the individual himself. In order to cause sexual excitement they must be perceived by the man, codified as erotic and appreciated.[11] Stimuli stemming from the context, that is to say the surroundings, the situation and the atmosphere generally play a less important role for the man than for the woman. On the other hand, those emitted by his partner – whether it is her physical appearance, her touch, her pelvic thrusts or her expressions – hold a preponderant place in the creation of his sexual excitement. As for those brought on by the man himself, these principally involve fantasies, the meaning he gives to the romantic encounter and the way he views his partner, as well as the pleasure he derives from his movements and from his muscular tensions. When the quantity and intensity of these stimuli increase, excitement intensifies and progresses normally towards ejaculation. However, if the stimulation escalates rapidly, the progression of excitement could be too fast and lead to an ejaculation that happens before it is desired. This could also be the case if an overstimulation happens. There are several sexological causes of sexual overstimulation. Here are the principal ones:

1. The man who carries out rapid and vigorous movements of intercourse from the beginning of intercourse, in the hope of giving his partner an orgasm before ejaculating himself, obtains such a high stimulation that he ejaculates sooner than he would like.
2. The woman who moves quickly and with intensity in order to achieve orgasm before her partner ejaculates overstimulates him and causes the rapid rise of his excitement and the arrival of his ejaculation.
3. The man who prefers post-ejaculatory satisfaction over the pleasure accompanying sexual excitement will proceed promptly towards ejaculation, even if he tries to convince himself that he would like to prolong the duration of his lovemaking.
4. The woman who believes that the progression of her sexual excitement should steadily climb will demand uninterrupted stimulation from her partner. This overactivity will in general become too great for the man and will hasten the arrival of his ejaculation (Crépault and Desjardins, 1978).
5. The man who believes that a woman only derives sexual pleasure when she is penetrated vigorously and without stopping imposes upon himself conditions incompatible with the adequate management of his excitement.
6. The man who likes the sensations procured by very high levels of excitement tends to seek intense stimulation. Unfortunately for him, it is impossible to carry on for a long time in the upper level of the zone of the modulation of sexual excitement and even less so in the zone of ejaculatory imminence, without ejaculating.
7. Some men idealize their partner to such a degree that in spite of themselves they transform her into a hyper-stimulus. They develop very strong emotional, sentimental and excitatory charges and, as they do not know how to modulate their sexual excitement very well, they ejaculate earlier than they desire.

FOCALIZATION ON A PARTICULAR STIMULUS

When sexual excitement reaches a certain level, focusing on particular stimuli will increase it dramatically. These stimuli vary from one person to another. It could be the vagina's warmth for one, the sight of breasts for another, the partner's facial expressions for a third and so on (Chatton, 2008). In general, men tend to objectify the female body, select specific stimuli and pay close attention to them. But this focalization on preferred stimuli, combined with the corporeal movement which were described further below, drives excitement at a dizzying speed towards the threshold of the ejaculatory reflex.

If in addition to focusing on specific erotic stimuli, the man is not attuned to the bodily signs that indicate the intensity of his excitement, he may be certain that without knowing it his excitement will continue to soar to heights where there is no longer any possibility of stopping it from reaching the ejaculation zone. Moreover, we find within the sexological literature that the non-perception of sensations that accompany the rise of sexual excitement is hypothesized as a cause of the difficulty with prolonging the length of intercourse (Kaplan, 1989). When a man does not perceive these sensations, he does not have any reference point and has no idea to what degree his excitement has progressed. If ejaculation was not a physiological reflex process impossible to control, the man would not have to concern himself with these sensations to postpone his ejaculation.

To counter the effect of focalization, many resort to what is called cognitive distraction. They try to concentrate on something else in order not to perceive the stimuli coming from their partner and not to become overly stimulated. This technique is not effective, as mentioned above, and we will see in more detail why this is the case in the eighth session of the third part of this book.

GLOBAL, RAPID, HYPERTONIC AND LOW-AMPLITUDE PHYSICAL MOVEMENTS

The manner in which a man moves during sexual relations has considerable influence over the flow of his sexual excitement. The following ways of moving lead to a rapid rise in excitement and the arrival of ejaculation:

1. Performing thrusting movements by moving the trunk as a single unit (without separating the pelvis from the torso).
2. Moving the pelvis speedily.
3. Moving continuously, maintaining a regular pace, without slowing down or making any pauses.
4. Accelerating the speed of movements.
5. Executing in-and-out thrusts of small amplitude.
6. Strongly contracting muscles and more particularly the buttocks, abdominals, perineum muscles, leg muscles (by squeezing the thighs, extending the legs) and the arm and hand muscles (while firmly grasping one's partner, for example).
7. Breathing high into the chest, while pulling in the abdomen.
8. Breathing rapidly.
9. Holding one's breath and keeping the air under pressure in the rib cage.

When a man's body movement combines all of the characteristics which have just been listed (globality, rapidity, intensity and low amplitude of movement), it lends itself to the creation of considerable muscular tension. This muscular tension supports and enhances sexual excitement and causes it to quickly peak towards ejaculation. There is a close relationship between the way in which a man uses his body and the course of his sexual excitement. It is worth mentioning that only one of these ways of moving is enough to lead him to discharge. It should also be remembered that these bodily movements are normal. They are part of the different types of movements used by a man when he takes part in sexual activities. Difficulties only arise when both members of the couple want to prolong intercourse and the various features of these movements make ejaculation appear earlier than they wish.

We find the same hypertonia in the following situations:

1 When a man contracts his buttock and perineum muscles because he believes this is how an erection is obtained and maintained.
2 When a man contracts all of his muscles to prevent ejaculation from occurring at the very moment he enters into the zone of ejaculatory imminence.
3 When a man assumes a position that requires the use of several muscles, such as the one where he is on top of his partner.

The behaviours just mentioned create muscular tension that adds to the muscular tension already brought on by excitement. This build-up of tension benefits the rise of excitement and the arrival of ejaculation.

The analysis we just made regarding the movements, behaviours and strategies that increase excitement and provoke ejaculation leads us to the observation that, in the vast majority of cases, the difficulty with prolonging the duration of coitus is not a pathology nor the result of a physical, emotional or marital disorder. It derives from poor management of sexual excitement, itself caused by a lack of information and training. On the contrary, the difficulty with extending the length of intercourse can itself be found at the source of sexual performance anxiety, lack of confidence in oneself, marital problems and depression.

OTHER SEXOLOGICAL FACTORS

There are other sexological factors that make it more difficult to manage sexual excitement inside the modulation zone. Among those encountered most frequently, we find the conditions surrounding initial sexual experiences, ejaculatory frequency, attitude towards sexual tension and masturbatory mode.

The conditions under which the first sexual experiences took place often contribute to forming habits that persist and which determine the way a man behaves during subsequent sexual relations. The adolescent who masturbated speedily to avoid being surprised by his parents or who complied with the demands of a prostitute, who urged him to hurry, learned how to act to hasten the arrival of ejaculation (Masters and Johnson, 1966). If he does not change, often due to a lack of knowledge, his manner of proceeding, he will retain a corporal movement that will continue to cause him to ejaculate quickly.

Moreover, abstinence makes it harder to manage sexual excitement. After a period of ejaculatory deprivation, physiology imposes its ardour and enhances the build-up of excitement. Men who do not ejaculate as often as their sexual appetite demands experience greater difficulty managing their excitement with the resumption of sexual activity (Grenier and Byers, 2001). This physiological constraint persists until they ejaculate as frequently as their body requires.

A man's attitude towards sexuality has a significant influence over the course of his sexual excitement. For Crépault and Desjardins (1978), individuals who fail to prolong the length of intercourse envision the dynamic of sexual excitement as oriented solely towards the discharge of tension and consider less stimulating the erotic and sensory dimensions of the erection itself. They conceive the rise of sexual excitement towards orgasm as a rapid dynamic. For many of them, this attitude developed from the earliest masturbatory sessions and was maintained during initial sexual relations, even in the absence of constraining circumstances. Crépault and Desjardins (1978) also noted that men who ejaculate soon after the beginning of intercourse tend to associate the intromission of the penis inside the vagina with the culmination of excitement, that is to say with ejaculation. The vagina's warmth is therefore a trigger for them. Furthermore, this trigger factor also makes itself present in their masturbatory fantasies. In all these cases, we observe the creation of conditions extremely conducive to the steady and rapid surge of excitement.

There are even some men who view sexual tension as something to get rid of rather than something to appreciate. They have often learned to masturbate quickly, without pause, while performing fast moves to reach a rapid release of their sexual tensions. They behave somewhat like those who prefer to eat fast and alleviate their hunger rather than to take the time to sit at a table and enjoy a meal. Their motivation is more extrinsic (to please their partner) than intrinsic (to diversify their pleasures). Through this vision of sexuality and masturbatory style, they have registered in their body ways to stimulate themselves and react to sexual excitement that are totally incompatible with the prolonged management of sexual excitement during intercourse.

This analysis confirms that sexological factors are always, with the exception of a few rare cases of organic origin, the primary cause of the difficulty with prolonging the length of intercourse. If intercourse occurs quicker than expected, it is because sexual excitement is not adequately regulated. However, we must not forget that there are a multitude of psychological and relational factors which interfere with the capacity to manage sexual excitement in a functional manner. If, due to ignorance, the role of these factors has been overvalued in the past, one should not, by means of reaction, underestimate them today.

Psychological causes

Psychological causes that can impair good management of sexual excitement may be grouped into three categories: anxiety, alexithymia and unconscious intrapsychic conflicts.

Anxiety

Several authors postulate a link between anxiety and premature ejaculation (Wolpe, 1973; Zilbergeld, 1992; Assalian, 1994; Dunn et al., 1999; Corona, 2006). However, Lazarus (1971) indicates that treating anxiety does not bring any conclusive results in the improvement of premature ejaculation. Tollison and Adams (1979) feel that the link between anxiety and premature ejaculation is not clearly established. According to them, anxiety may be a cause in some cases, and in others, not. Beck and Barlow (1984) recommend not confusing general anxiety with anxiety related to sexuality. They believe that only the latter type of anxiety could contribute to quick ejaculation. This would be the case in men who ejaculate too fast and end up becoming anxious whenever approaching sexual relations in general and intercourse in particular. They would be afraid of frustrating their partner and would fear her reactions (sadness, withdrawal, blame, threats, ridicule in the presence of others, rejection, relationship break-up . . .).

The results of studies by Rowland and his collaborators are in line with the hypotheses of Beck and Barlow. Indeed, these researchers have shown that men who ejaculate rapidly are more anxious than others during sexual activities; they also have greater difficulty achieving and maintaining an erection and their heart rate is more elevated (Rowland et al., 1996; Rowland et al., 2000). Following these observations, Rowland (2005) infers that a change in the relationship between the autonomous nervous processes involved in erection and ejaculation could accelerate the arrival of ejaculation. Normally, the parasympathetic nervous system dominates at the start of the sexual response cycle and ensures the onset of erection. Then, when the individual becomes sufficiently excited, the sympathetic nervous system takes over and prompts ejaculation. Among men who ejaculate prematurely, the transition from the parasympathetic to the sympathetic could be altered by anxiety. This emotion is known to activate the sympathetic system and the latter may in this way become too stimulated and enter into play sooner than expected. The premature activation of the sympathetic nervous system could be held responsible for the acceleration of the heart rate, the weakness of erections and the rapidity of ejaculation. Indeed, increased heart rate, provoked by the sympathetic system, is a recognized consequence of anxiety; it is part of the adaptation to danger and the onset of the fight or flight response. In addition, as the sympathetic system is also the antagonist of the parasympathetic, it may be at the source of weaker erections. Finally, sympathetic activation caused by anxiety could add up to sympathetic activation generated by sexual excitement. This addition may in turn cause the release of ejaculation, even though sexual excitement has not yet reached the ejaculatory reflex threshold. This hypothesis could be confirmed by the fact that spontaneous ejaculations are reported to occur during episodes of intense anxiety (Redmond et al., 1983). It could also explain why a high proportion (47.4 per cent) of men suffering from social phobia ejaculate soon after the beginning of intercourse (Figueira et al., 2001).

Anxiety could also influence the arrival of ejaculation by means of three other mechanisms. First of all, the fear of failure or of frustrating his partner causes, like any other fear, changes in the man's body. He breathes higher and quicker.

He contracts several groups of muscles, such as those of the jaw, abdomen, chest, neck, face and inner thighs (Coretti et al., 2006). These muscular contractions join those caused by sexual excitement and facilitate the occurrence of ejaculation. Secondly, anxiety-driven thoughts distract the individual. They invade his mind and divert his attention from what he must do to manage his sexual excitement, namely to perceive the signals indicating the rise of his excitement and apply management strategies and techniques to this excitement. Finally, anxiety renders it quite impossible to read the signals indicative of the levels of sexual excitement. In fact, as anxiety stimulates the sympathetic nervous system in the same way as sexual excitement, the latter may become activated enough to trigger ejaculation without the man being extremely excited. Consequently, body signals indicating high levels of excitement do not appear (precisely because excitement is not high enough) and the man has no access to any normal bodily points of reference telling him that he is approaching ejaculation.

The sex therapist who, after detecting vague anxieties in his patient, immediately attributes the difficulty of the latter to these anxieties, more often than not commits an error. It is important to examine whether these anxieties interfere in some way with the actual regulation of sexual excitement. Do they create a significant activation of the sympathetic nervous system during sexual activities? Do they generate a considerable amount of muscular tension? Do they prevent him from paying attention to the signals indicative of his excitement levels? If this is the case, the clinician could put forward the hypothesis that anxiety is impeding his patient from managing his excitement. In general, anxieties that hinder sexual response do not have any bearing on the everyday subjects of life like work, finances or family life. They encompass instead sex-specific problems such as the apprehension of not having a firm enough erection, the fear of ejaculating too soon or the worry of displeasing one's partner.

However, identifying these anxieties is not sufficient in itself. It must also be established whether the man knows how to manage his sexual excitement. Indeed, if the therapist treats the anxiety but the patient does not possess the knowledge and skills necessary to regulate his excitement, the latter will fail to prolong the duration of his sexual relations.

Alexithymia

Alexithymia is a cognitive and affective disorder characterized by a difficulty in identifying and describing emotions and bodily sensations as well as by a propensity to be focused on the external world (externally oriented cognitive style) rather than on the internal world. Michetti et al. (2007) compared 100 consecutive outpatients with lifelong premature ejaculation with a control group of 100 male volunteers. They observed in patients with premature ejaculation significantly higher scores of alexithymia than in the control group. They also found a positive correlation between the severity of premature ejaculation and the level of alexithymia. Moreover, they noticed the highest correlation between an externally oriented cognitive style and the severity of premature ejaculation.

The results of Michetti et al. (2007) are in line with the hypothesis of Kaplan (1989), which states that the non-perception of bodily sensations associated with the rise of sexual excitement is at the source of premature ejaculation.

More studies are needed to confirm these findings, but at first glance they look promising in that body awareness and inner consciousness are primordial factors in the proper management of sexual excitement.

Unconscious intrapsychic conflicts

Psychoanalytic theory postulates that premature ejaculation is a symptom of unconscious intrapsychic conflicts. Stekel (1927), Bergler (1950), London (1957), Salzman (1972) and Stanley (1981) put forward that a man afflicted with this sexual difficulty would harbour in his unconscious mind intense sadistic feelings towards women. These affects would lead him to ejaculate quickly in order to sully and deprive his female partner of pleasure. This sadistic attitude towards women would originate during the urethral stage of psychosexual development and would relate to the dynamic that has been established between the mother and child at that time. It would result in ambivalence towards women that would translate into the symptom of premature ejaculation. This symptom would permit a man to symbolically avenge his mother by depriving his partner of sexual gratification. It would also allow him to retain his emotional equilibrium by keeping his sadistic impulses repressed. Abraham (1967) adds to this sadistic tendency a masochistic component which would be conveyed by a desire on the part of a man to punish himself by restricting or spoiling his own pleasure.

These hypotheses are very interesting. However, they were formed on the basis of analysis of a few cases and consequently it would be impossible to generalize their postulates to all men who ejaculate earlier than they would like. In addition, they do not take into account the individuals who possess the same type of personality, but who have no trouble delaying the arrival of their ejaculation.

For her part, Kaplan (1989), who is a psychoanalyst herself, reports that the majority of men who have difficulty prolonging the length of intercourse do not suffer from any apparent neurosis or any personality disorder, and she therefore believes that unconscious intrapsychic conflicts do not play a causal role. Besides, the fact that the capacity to prolong intercourse can be easily increased through very simple training makes it highly unlikely that problems reputed to be so severe and so deep are at the root of this disorder.

But the harshest criticism that could be made against these psychoanalytic hypotheses is that they are not easily verifiable. The gap between psychoanalytic theoretical constructions and observable reality is so wide that these hypotheses can neither be proven nor refuted by scientific research (Segraves, 2006). Moreover, analytical treatment, regardless of its length, does not procure results, to the point that modern psychoanalysts have renounced it and refer men who cannot prolong intercourse to sex therapists.

If psychodynamic factors ever play a role, it would be – as in the case of anxiety and marital problems – indirectly. These factors would interfere with the ability to manage sexual excitement, which would allow intensification of excitement and, as a result, a release of ejaculation earlier than desired. But before evaluating the eventuality of this interference, it is essential to verify if a man has the knowledge, techniques and strategies to manage his sexual excitement.

Relational causes

Sexual dysfunctions are viewed within marital therapies as the result of interactions between both members of the couple. A sexual dysfunction is born when spouses try to work out a relationship problem by using a solution which is at the origin of the very symptom which is the sexual disorder. This symptom, or this sexual dysfunction, persists in so far as it is regularly reinforced during exchanges between the man and the woman who need it in order to avoid dealing with bigger problems (Gentry, 1978). According to El Féki (2007), the symptom remains because it has a function in the system that is the couple. Conflicts of interest, power struggles, hatred towards the spouse, marital discord and revenge are all elements that could make the management of sexual excitement more difficult for a man (Polonsky, 2000). Some women express their hostility towards their husband by willingly causing his ejaculation. To do so, they move energetically at crucial moments and make their husband ejaculate quickly despite the desire of the latter to prolong intercourse (Jehu, 1979). Then, they rebuke him for thinking only of himself and for not caring about their pleasure. For his part, Sager, quoted by Kaplan (1974), hypothesizes that the man would perceive the woman's request to delay his ejaculation as an attempt on her part to dominate him. His shortening of intercourse would therefore represent a symbolic act of rebellion against a wife hungry for control.

On another hand, Levine (1975) notes that there are women who, by their conduct, trigger the rapid termination of intercourse. Their goal is to reduce to a minimum the length of intercourse which, for them, is a source of anxiety. At that moment, the sooner a man ejaculates, the less they have to endure this unpleasant feeling.

The criticism we could make of the systemic hypothesis is that if without doubt the couple's negative interactions could bring on the spouse's premature ejaculation, they are not the only causes of this dysfunction. Perelman (1980) and Zilbergeld (1992) mention in fact that although marriage therapy improves the couple's relationship, it generally does not have an effect on the moment of ejaculation unless the sexual problem is treated through sexological means. In addition, none of the 36 couples selected for research conducted by de Carufel and Trudel (2006) on the effectiveness of the functional sex therapy treatment for the difficulty with prolonging intercourse suffered from marital distress (this was a selection criterion for participating in the study). This finding demonstrates that a couple may not be able to prolong their sexual encounters while still being functional on the marital sphere. Finally, Astbury-Ward (2002) claims that if a conflicting relationship could contribute to a sexual difficulty, the reverse is also true: a sexual difficulty could create conducive conditions for the development of marital disharmony. At this point, the marital difficulty does not participate in the initiation of the sexual problem but appears as a consequence of the way the partners respond to this sexual problem and can be, as a reaction, involved in its perpetuation.

As in the case of anxiety, it is important to assess whether the marital conflict impairs the management of excitement during sexual relations. If it does not, we cannot consider it a causal factor of the difficulty with prolonging intercourse.

Theoretical and clinical considerations with regard to psychological and relational causes

This review of psychological and relational factors reveals that they can play a major role in the aetiology of the difficulty with prolonging intercourse. However, the sex therapist should always look first for the cause of a brief intercourse within the sexual functioning of the man and his partner. Following this, he could examine the other areas of his patient's life and analyse the links between psychological and relational factors and sexual functioning. If not, he will always find psychological, relational or monetary problems (which every human being has for that matter) and will assume these are the problems that shorten the duration of coitus. And he will do so without even knowing how his patient behaves sexually. But reality is different. Two-thirds of men do not present any major difficulties managing their excitement. Even so a good number of them experience all kinds of problems. That being said, the contrary is also true. Many men who do not succeed at effectively extending their sexual relations do not in addition encounter any particular troubles in other areas of their life. The individuals unable to prolong the length of intercourse – one must not forget that they constitute close to 30 per cent of all men – display a phenomenal variety of personalities, intellectual capacities, levels of emotional intelligence, ethnic origins, economic profiles, marital situations and life experiences. This variety is such that we cannot identify a common factor leading to shorter-than-desired intercourse apart from the way they manage their sexual excitement.

Metz and McCarthy (2003) cite in their book the following list of factors as possible causes of premature ejaculation: work shift/work schedule, partner's illness, professional stress, financial troubles, family problems, presence of parents in the household, dilapidated housing, lack of privacy, sexual orientation, lack of interpersonal skills, demanding partner, dependent personality, unrealistic expectations, differing needs of the couple, marital dissatisfaction and infidelity. This list has been presented in order to warn practitioners against any drifting of this sort. It is easy to conclude, from reading assumptions so numerous and disparate, that these authors do not know much about the way human beings function sexually. As a result of a lack of sexological understanding, they fall back on their field of expertise, in this case, psychology. None of these factors can be the direct cause of the difficulty with prolonging intercourse. They can only harm the management of sexual excitement. And it is insufficient management that is at the root of the heightening of excitement and, as a consequence, the onset of ejaculation. We should recall that an enormous number of men manage their sexual excitement and control its rise despite being afflicted with, like most people, flaws or problems such as those mentioned by Metz and McCarthy.

Erectile disorders and premature ejaculation

Several authors (Bricaire and Dreyfus-Moreau, 1964; Caprio, 1968; Pasini, 1997) consider that many premature ejaculations are in fact the result of an erectile disorder, whether physiological or psychological in origin. They indicate that the man either hurries to ejaculate before losing his erection or subconsciously sets out to ejaculate quickly in order to lose an erection that has appeared unexpectedly. Nevertheless, Rowland et al. (1997) did not observe any erectile difference between a sample of men who ejaculated prematurely and a control group. On the contrary, results from the survey conducted by Porst et al. (2007) revealed that 32 per cent of men with premature ejaculation also suffer from erectile dysfunction. Yet Poudat and Jarrousse (1992), as well as Cawer (1998), maintain that impotence may sometimes be the consequence of premature ejaculation. These two hypotheses seem plausible. Certain individuals "overstimulate" and "overexcite" themselves in order to strengthen a weak erection and as a consequence ejaculate rapidly. Others, inversely, react badly to their inability to extend the duration of sexual activities; they think dismal thoughts and pay less attention to sexual stimuli, which leads to an erectile disorder. Actually, the link between erectile disorders and premature ejaculation might be viewed in seven ways.

1 There are men who ejaculate prematurely and have absolutely no erectile difficulty. These represent the majority of cases.
2 Some men ejaculate prematurely and also exhibit an erectile disorder without either of these problems being related. They have always ejaculated rapidly, and subsequently developed an erection problem for medical and/or psychological reasons independent of their difficulty with extending the length of their sexual activities.
3 There are men who at the beginning of their sexual life do not ejaculate prematurely, but their progressive erectile difficulties create the tendency to ejaculate earlier and earlier. This problem most commonly occurs among older men. In order to get a difficult to obtain erection, they overstimulate themselves by using every stimuli to which they have access (touching their partner, looking at her, using sexual fantasies, making faster thrusting movements and so on). Consequently, they become more excited and this surplus of excitement contributes to strengthening their erection. However, at the same time, this surplus of excitement may bring about their ejaculation sooner than desired. In this case, the rapidity of ejaculation is secondary to an emerging erectile dysfunction. Moreover, according to Jannini (2011), these men may find it easier and less humiliating to ejaculate sooner than their partner would like them to because "they were too excited by her" than to admit that they

have an erectile problem. They may decide to ejaculate prematurely in order to avoid revealing their difficulty in maintaining a rigid erection and therefore to escape facing the relational turmoil that an erectile disorder could entail.

4 Like Porto (2008), I have observed that numerous men avoid perceiving sexual stimuli for fear of becoming overly excited and ejaculating prematurely. By diverting their attention away from genital sensations, caresses, erotic thoughts and visual stimuli, which are at the origin of sexual excitement, they succeed in maintaining low levels of sexual excitement. However, since sexual excitement is what causes an erection, and in this case it is not very high, erectile difficulties can ensue. These men are caught in a trap. In trying to delay their ejaculation, they reduce their perception of stimuli which provokes a decrease of excitement and consequently causes their erection to diminish. Conversely, in trying to get an erection, they focus on sexual stimuli which then increases their sexual excitement and consequently leads them to ejaculation. This happens because they do not know how to properly manage their sexual excitement.

5 Many men who routinely ejaculate too fast put themselves down and thus tend to suffer from a lack of self-confidence. They have developed such an intense performance anxiety in relation to intercourse and are so uneasy with women that they have lost their erectile capacity. During sexual relations, they cannot stop worrying and they hardly even perceive the stimuli emanating from their partner. An erection obviously cannot materialize under such conditions.

6 Some men will refer to themselves in consultation as being impotent, meaning that they are "impotent" to satisfy their partner because they cannot last long enough during intercourse to give her an orgasm with thrusting movements of the penis. Otherwise, they do not have problems with their erection apart from the normal fact that they lose it after ejaculation. Obviously, they do not suffer from an erectile disorder but from the difficulty with prolonging intercourse for as long as they desire.

7 According to Jannini (2011), some patients who are unable to extend the length of intercourse articulate their complaint as an erectile disorder because penile detumescence occurs rapidly after ejaculation. The last two cases exemplify the fact that the clinician must be vigilant so as to avoid a misdiagnosis and the initiation of a treatment based on false premises.

The differential diagnosis between the difficulty with delaying ejaculation during intercourse and an erectile disorder must be reached early on. Concerning the timing and order of the therapeutic intervention, the American Urological Association recommends in its guidelines on the pharmacologic management of premature ejaculation (Montague et al., 2004) avoiding psychological and pharmacological treatments for patients with difficulty postponing ejaculation when they present an erectile dysfunction at the same time. The erectile disorder needs to be treated first. This means that it is essential for a patient to be able to achieve a satisfactory erection and not be concerned about getting or losing it before trying to manage his sexual excitement and prolong intercourse.

Theoretical and clinical considerations with regard to the causes of premature ejaculation or the difficulty with prolonging intercourse

The prematurity of ejaculation can be considered as either the reflection of a difficulty to extend the duration of sexual activities (usually intercourse) without ejaculating, or the indication of a lack of desire of one of the partners to prolong these activities.

The difficulty with extending the duration of sexual activities (usually intercourse) without ejaculating is the result of the inability to manage sexual excitement in the necessary way to keep its intensity under the level that triggers the ejaculatory reflex. This management is contingent on the regulation of the quantity and the intensity of endogenous and exogenous sexual stimulations a man receives. It also depends on a man's capacity to handle his bodily reactions provoked by sexual excitement, as well as on the manner in which he moves, uses his muscles and breathes during sex. The management of sexual excitement could also be rendered more difficult by the way the woman moves sexually, the sexual positions adopted, the anxiety associated with sexual activities, and an ejaculatory frequency inferior to the man's physiological needs. The fact that the duration of masturbation for men who ejaculate shortly after the beginning of coitus is the same as that for men who succeed in lengthening the time of intercourse, and the observation that treatments for premature ejaculation based on training are very effective, suggests that constitutional factors do not play a preponderant role in the aetiology of this sexual dysfunction. Among these factors, the most cited are penile sensitivity, the rapidity of the evoked potential of the bulbocavernosus muscle, serotonergic neurotransmission and genetic factors. As for the diverse pathologies put forward, the most prone to precipitate the onset of ejaculation, mainly in cases of acquired premature ejaculation, are hyperthyroidism and prostatic inflammation. That being said, research has still to establish a cause and effect link between these pathologies and premature ejaculation, as well as explain how they would precipitate the arrival of ejaculation.

One partner's lack of desire to extend the duration of sexual activities could obviously be at the origin of an ejaculation deemed too soon for the other partner. The man who does not want to or no longer wants to continue lovemaking will ejaculate when he feels like it, without taking into consideration his partner's wishes. This produces premature ejaculation for the woman, but not for the man. On the other hand, the woman who does not want to engage in the sexual relation could make the man ejaculate despite his desire to continue. In this case, there is premature ejaculation for the man, but not for the woman.

As discussed earlier, the words we use can influence the way we think about a phenomenon. Although the term "premature" signifies that an event occurs before the moment it is due (for example, premature fruits refer to fruits picked before they are ripe in order to be able to transport them) or before the moment it is considered appropriate (for example, a premature launching indicates that a new type of car is introduced onto the market before the population is ready to buy it), the association of "premature" and "ejaculation" has led many scientists to view "premature ejaculation" as a physiological entity on its own and to consider it as a pathological condition related to the physiology of ejaculation rather than a dissatisfaction with the duration of sexual activities (an ejaculation that happens earlier than the man or the woman desires it). For example, a group of researchers (Waldinger et al., 2005; Waldinger and Schweitzer, 2006) go as far as to describe the fact of ejaculating most of the time in less than a minute after the intromission of the penis inside the vagina as a "neurobiological aberrant phenomenon". This connotation is erroneous for two reasons. The first is that there is no relationship between the moment of ejaculation and its physiology. Ejaculation, irrespective of the moment it happens, is always the same. It appears after the erection is complete (among young and healthy subjects), its deployment in two phases occurs according to established biological programming and the ejaculate is normal. The ejaculatory process would be pathological if its unfolding was incompatible with the biology of reproduction or if it engendered one or several of these consequences: attack on anatomical integrity, hindrance to physiological functioning, threats to the survival of the organism, pain or sickness. This is obviously not the case. Consequently, the moment when ejaculation occurs does not make it a neurobiological aberrant phenomenon, even if it takes place very soon after the beginning of coitus and even if some people react emotionally and behaviourally very badly to this situation.

The second reason is that sexual excitement[12] is the one and only cause of ejaculation. There is no such illness that could make a man ejaculate like a cold makes him sneeze, gastroenteritis makes him vomit or an allergy causes a rash. It is the same for genetic factors; these do not on their own make a man ejaculate when he is watching a football game on television, for example. Any organic condition that exerts an effect on the onset of ejaculation does it in conjunction with sexual excitement, not by itself.[13] That said, since sexual excitement is what leads to ejaculation and because organic conditions that could influence the arrival of ejaculation would interact with sexual excitement, it is the total duration of the excitement phase that must be measured in order to evaluate the presence of an organic disorder and not only the duration of the excitement phase from the beginning of intercourse to ejaculation (or IELT). Excitement is what brings on ejaculation, and it does not just start to build at the moment when the penis is inserted inside the vagina. It begins way before (for a man to be able to penetrate his partner he needs to have an erection and to have an erection he needs to be sexually excited). Actually, excitement develops as soon as the man perceives and takes pleasure in sexual stimuli (this could be from the initiation of foreplay or even earlier). It heightens over time and when it becomes sufficiently intense it triggers the ejaculatory reflex whether there is insertion of the penis inside the vagina or not.

Another point to consider is that the nature of sexual excitement is always the same, irrespective of the type of external stimulation (manual, oral, vaginal or anal) applied to the penis. A man does not suddenly become equipped with a special neurophysiology of sexual excitement when he receives stimulation from the vaginal walls. Therefore, knowing that excitement is the cause of ejaculation, that it begins before intercourse, and that the neurophysiology of excitement is the same before and after intromission of the penis in the vagina, intercourse (or IELT) lasting less than a minute does not give any particular indication of the state of health of the neurobiology leading to ejaculation and of the ejaculatory process itself. We noted earlier that if a man wants to prolong the duration of his sexual activities – whatever the type – he must manage his sexual excitement and maintain it below the level that triggers the ejaculatory reflex. We are also aware that it is much more difficult to manage excitement during intercourse than during other forms of stimulation (due to the intensity and continuity of vaginal stimulation, the emotional involvement, the symbolic connotations, the movements, the muscular tension, the positions, the man and woman's physical activity, the efforts to please one's partner, and so on).

It is evident from these observations that excitement and the moment when it culminates do not determine the normality or abnormality of the ejaculatory process. These two reactions are distinct and the ejaculatory process follows the same neurophysiological mechanisms, whether excitement sky-rockets or ripples, whether it reaches its peak after 30 seconds or 30 minutes. Ejaculation is caused by sexual excitement when it becomes intense enough. The release of ejaculation depends on excitement, but not its characteristics or the way it happens. To base one's arguments on the length of intercourse (or IELT) in order to assert that an ejaculation is a "neurobiological aberrant phenomenon" proves to be a serious theoretical and methodological mistake. As we have just seen, among subjects in good health, ejaculation is normal even if they ejaculate shortly after they penetrate their partner. Also, in view of the fact that excitement is the cause of ejaculation, it is the total duration of excitement (from its emergence, which occurs during foreplay or even before, to ejaculation) – and not only the duration of excitement during intercourse – that must be measured to determine if there is an organic problem. The cause of ejaculation occurring soon after the start of intercourse (following foreplay of a certain length of time) resides in the management of sexual excitement and not in an organic defect or pathology of the physiology of either ejaculation or sexual excitement. Likewise, the criterion that makes it possible to determine if, after a certain period of foreplay, intercourse ends too soon as a result of the inopportune arrival of ejaculation is not a physiological norm but a personal desire.

Again, the words we use to describe a phenomenon influence our understanding of it. In the case of the expression "premature ejaculation", if we drop the word "premature", a totally new perspective is gained. Only the word "ejaculation" remains. We can then ask ourselves questions such as "When is ejaculation happening?" "Are the man and the woman happy about the moment of its occurrence?" "Are there any biological, psychological, relational or sexological factors (intercourse with all that it entails being the major factor) that make the management of sexual excitement more challenging?" This perspective implies that there is no such reality as "premature ejaculation", but only ejaculations that take place after various durations of excitement and whose occurrence may be influenced by diverse factors.

None of the above excludes the fact that the moment of arrival of ejaculation may be influenced by organic factors that are traumatic, pathological or constitutional in nature. These factors would act to accelerate the rise of excitement or lower the ejaculatory reflex threshold to the point where ejaculation would take place rapidly after the beginning of the excitement phase. This hypothesis would be plausible in the following cases: the duration of the excitement period is brief;[14] it does not vary regardless of the source of stimulation (the individual himself, the partner), the type of external stimulation (manual, oral, vaginal or anal), the positions adopted or the management techniques utilized; it cannot be modified by a sexological treatment based on training. If this was the case, we could instead use the term "early ejaculation" to describe this condition. The term "premature ejaculation" would be reserved for an ejaculation occurring before a man or woman desires it (an early ejaculation could be considered premature or not, depending on the point of view of the individuals involved). The length of intercourse (the intravaginal ejaculatory latency time or IELT) is not an indicator in establishing the organicity of an early ejaculation. This is because sexual excitement, which is the cause of ejaculation, begins to build the moment stimulation is enjoyed by the man, which generally takes place much before the beginning of intercourse. If there was any biological aberration at play, it would trigger ejaculation right from the start of the excitement phase. It would not wait for the insertion of the penis inside the vagina in order to manifest itself. When the duration of the excitement phase is long, however, there are not any strong, abnormal organic factors involved in the inception of ejaculation, even when the intercourse time is short. To conclude, it is not the duration of coitus that indicates if the onset of ejaculation is influenced by an overwhelming pathology, traumatism or constitutional trait, but rather the total duration of the excitement period. Cases of early ejaculation are rare and up until now their study has been hindered because they have been lumped in with cases of ejaculation that occurs shortly (generally less than 1 minute) after the beginning of intercourse.

The following graphs help us better understand the methodological error that consists of measuring, in order to detect an organicity, the duration of the excitement phase from the intromission of the penis inside the vagina (length of intercourse or intravaginal ejaculatory latency time, Figure 1.15) instead of from the moment when excitement really begins to grow (total ejaculatory latency time, Figure 1.16). Figure 1.16 enables us to observe that sexual excitement begins to develop prior to coitus. If there was organicity this would have affected the course of excitement and led to ejaculation during foreplay, as we see in Figure 1.17.

Cases of early ejaculation are extremely scarce and in reality organic factors are not very influential. Moreover, according to Segraves (2006), even if it were true that genetics create interindividual differences, they do not prevent men from acquiring through learning effective ways to overcome their hereditary tendency and prolong the length of intercourse.

To summarize, the only cause of ejaculation is sexual excitement. All other factors are not causative of ejaculation. They are either facilitative of the intensification of excitement which leads to ejaculation (like sexual stimulation, muscular

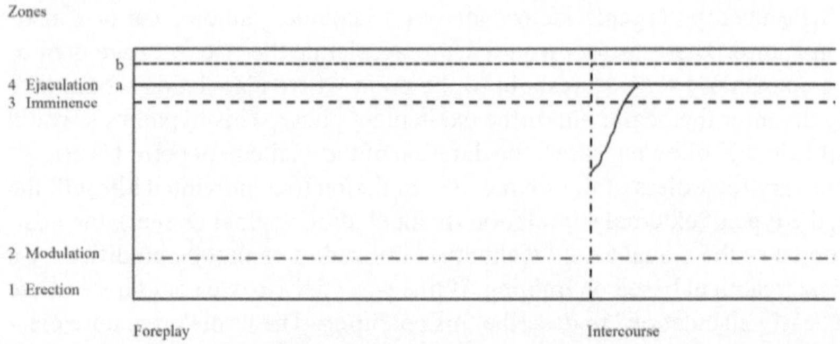

Figure 1.15 Example of a measure of the excitement phase from the start of intercourse until the beginning of ejaculation (intravaginal ejaculatory latency time)

Zone 1: The appearance and disappearance of the erection zone. Zone 2: The modulation of sexual excitement zone. Zone 3: The ejaculatory imminence zone. Zone 4: The ejaculation zone (a: emission reflex or point of no return; b: expulsion reflex).

contractions or yet to be confirmed organic factors), inductive of the lowering of the ejaculatory reflex threshold (like yet to be discovered organic factors) or interruptive of the management of sexual excitement (like psychological or relational factors). Ejaculation happens following sexual excitement produced by sexual stimulation. The way in which sexual excitement evolves and the speed at which it reaches the intensity that triggers the ejaculatory reflex is essentially determined by sexological factors. These encompass the quantity and the intensity of internal and external stimuli and the manner in which a man deals with his body reactions stemming from this stimulation. The handling of these sexological factors – sexual

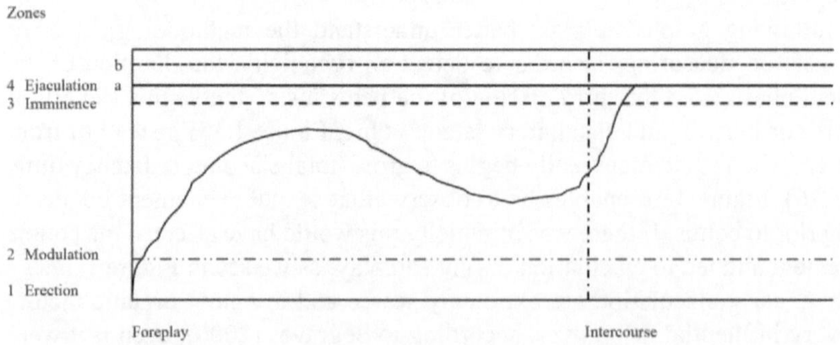

Figure 1.16 Measure of the excitement phase of the same sexual activity as in Figure 1.15 but, this time, from the start of foreplay until the beginning of ejaculation (total ejaculatory latency time)

Zone 1: The appearance and disappearance of the erection zone. Zone 2: The modulation of sexual excitement zone. Zone 3: The ejaculatory imminence zone. Zone 4: The ejaculation zone (a: emission reflex or point of no return; b: expulsion reflex).

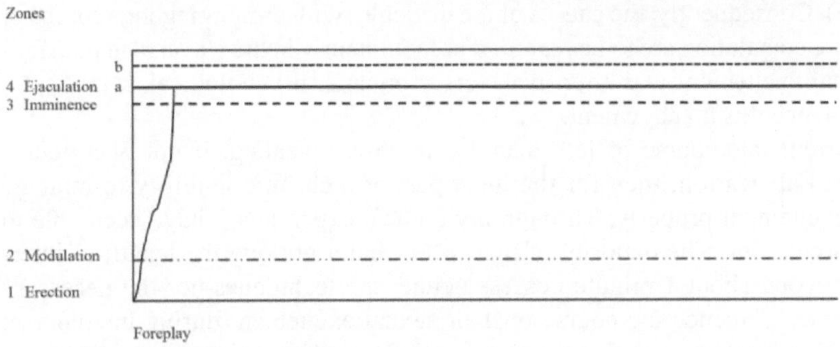

Figure 1.17 Example of a measure of the excitement phase from the start of foreplay until the beginning of ejaculation (total ejaculatory latency time) in the case of an early ejaculation where it was impossible to have intercourse because of the brevity of the excitement phase

Zone 1: The appearance and disappearance of the erection zone. Zone 2: The modulation of sexual excitement zone. Zone 3: The ejaculatory imminence zone. Zone 4: The ejaculation zone (a: emission reflex or point of no return; b: expulsion reflex).

stimulation and body reactions – is called the "management of sexual excitement" and rests on knowledge about sex, copulative strategies, attitude towards sensuality and corporeal skills. This management can be influenced, to an extent that we do not know but which is minor and concerns only few men, by organic (genetic, sympathetic, pathological, pharmacological or traumatic) factors. These factors make the management of sexual excitement somewhat more difficult by either slightly speeding up the progression of sexual excitement or lowering the ejaculatory reflex threshold. It is important not to forget that these organic factors also include normal constitutive (genetic) factors. These normal constitutive factors would foster the acceleration of sexual excitement during intercourse and pertain predominantly to the ways in which a man moves his body and contracts his muscles when he is involved in executing the sexual act. Some men could have a normal, more active–reactive neuro-muscular system than others. They can act and react more quickly and more intensely than other men. During masturbation or foreplay, this neuro-muscular quality does not come into play much because their body is not fully involved and stimulation is more easily controlled. During intercourse, however, the stimulation is continuous and their body is completely involved in the act. This neuro-muscular promptitude, which is certainly an asset in other aspects of life, could then create an obstacle to the prolongation of intercourse. This observation should incite us to look not only at pathological factors during the investigation of a sexual difficulty but also at healthy qualities which used inappropriately could hinder the sexual functioning of men and women. This is especially true when it comes to the difficulty with prolonging intercourse or premature ejaculation. The management of sexual excitement is also influenced by positive and negative psychological factors (e.g emotional well-being, anxiety) and positive and negative relational factors (e.g. interpersonal harmony, power struggle). Consequently, the causes of the difficulty with prolonging intercourse or premature ejaculation are to be regarded predominantly in the way a man manages his sexual excitement and after in factors – organic, psychological, relational – that influence this management.

Recurrent intercourse of less than 1 minute is revealing, if not of a neurobiological aberration, then for the most part of a chronic inability to manage sexual excitement properly. Through my clinical experience I have been able to isolate a constant. The majority of men who cannot prolong the length of intercourse beyond about 1 minute possess neither the techniques nor the necessary strategies to influence the course of their sexual excitement during intercourse. This lack of control over their excitement hastens them towards ejaculation in spite of themselves. Those who can extend coitus beyond more or less 2 minutes have generally acquired the knowledge and skills that allow them to manage their excitement and to pursue their lovemaking much longer. A grey area exists between 1 and 2 minutes where we come across individuals who master some processes, but not well enough to act as they please with regard to the evolution of their sexual excitement.

As for research aimed at discovering a pathological length of intercourse at the root of emotional or relational distress, they are destined to failure from the outset. Between the objective reality (duration of sexual activity) and the subjective response (satisfaction/dissatisfaction) that follows, there is always a cognitive processing of information[15] that comes into play. This cognitive processing of objective reality, influenced by personal variables and cultural factors, determines the subjective response, which in this case extends on a continuum ranging from satisfaction to dissatisfaction. In other words, an intercourse time of 3 minutes, for example, is and will always be considered by some as satisfactory and by others as unsatisfactory.

Consequently, since events are not the cause of people's emotions but rather their cognitive processing of these events, it becomes illusory to hope to discover objective realities accompanied with subjective reactions and to declare that these are universal sexopsychiatric pathologies (in this case premature ejaculation). In other words, it is futile to search for an intercourse time judged to be unsatisfactory and to qualify it as dysfunctional (or premature) for all.

Although there is technically no specified length of intercourse that can generate dissatisfaction (or satisfaction), dissatisfaction tends, in many of our current cultures, to increase with the brevity of intercourse. One of the reasons for this dissatisfaction may come from the focus we have placed over the past thirty years in the western world on personal growth and fulfilment. The compulsive quest for happiness that stems from this encourages multiplying demands on the spouse and does not promote tolerance towards things that do not go the way somebody hopes.

Dissatisfaction with the length of intercourse and the partner's accompanying reactions explain neither the emotional nor the relational distresses of the individual. Here as well, cognitive factors (attitude, interpretation, acceptance, rejection) play a central role in creating the anger, anxiety or depression a man and a woman experience following their sexual frustration and their spouse's reaction. For example, a man who mentally beats himself up because he barely lasted "x" minutes and who constantly puts himself down because his companion is disinterested in sex for the very reason that she does not like this "short duration" creates, through his internal monologue, the cause of his own depressive state. He could choose to react in a very different manner and in a more constructive one in the face of his current shortcoming and his partner's reaction to it. Consequently, due to their reactive nature, emotional and relational strains or distress are not valid criteria to confirm that an ejaculation is premature. This is explained by the fact that individuals' reactions (emotional and behavioural) towards a reality do not define the nature of this reality. They only accompany it.

For all these reasons, it is a waste of time to think that one could discover a definition to reconcile an objective physiological response and a subjective emotional response. In other words, it is illusory to imagine that one could succeed in developing a definition that associates a precise duration of intercourse and a given reaction of dissatisfaction. A clear distinction must be made between the duration of a sexual activity and the reaction towards the duration of this activity. This is why I suggest the use of two definitions. The first, "early ejaculation", describes an objective condition. It designates an ejaculation that occurs soon after (less than 1 minute) the start of the excitement phase (not after the beginning of intercourse) and in which its arrival is precipitated by one or several organic factors (pathological, traumatic or constitutive). The second, "premature ejaculation", signals a subjective condition. It can be defined in the clinical context as an ejaculation that takes place earlier than a man or woman desires. This definition applies regardless of the duration of the excitement phase which precedes ejaculation, and regardless of the factors – organic, cognitive, behavioural or relational – that facilitate its appearance (for example, rapid activity of the sympathetic nervous system, flawed knowledge, inadequate bodily movement, demands of the partner and so on). Therefore no length of intercourse, because it is arbitrary, and no emotional or relational distress, because it is irrelevant, can be used as criteria to define premature ejaculation. That being said, I prefer by far to use the expression "difficulty with prolonging intercourse" for the reasons explained in the introduction to this book.

Treatments

There are several treatments for the difficulty with prolonging intercourse or premature ejaculation. They are presented here in relation to the causes that have been described in the previous section.

Treatments focused on organic causes

Medical and surgical treatments

The descriptions of medical and surgical treatments for different urological, neurological and systemic pathologies which may be at the origin of the difficulty with prolonging intercourse, or premature ejaculation, go beyond the scope of this book. The interested reader is therefore encouraged to refer to material specializing in this subject.

Treatments intended to decrease penile sensitivity

Procedures with the goal of reducing sensitivity to penile stimuli are grouped into three categories. The first consists of ways to diminish vaginal stimulation, such as the use of condoms or limiting the amplitude of the in-and-out thrusts of the penis inside the vagina (Hastings, 1963). No conclusion can be drawn about the effectiveness of these procedures as there has not been any research carried out on them.

The second category of methods aims to lower the excitability of the receptor organs of the glans penis by applying a cutaneous anaesthetic, either as a cream (Aycock, 1949; Damrau, 1963; Berkovitch et al., 1995; Xin et al., 1997) or spray (Dinsmore et al., 2006). A lidocaine-prilocaine cream formulation increased the average intercourse time from 1.49 to 8.45 minutes among a group of 42 men (Busato and Galindo, 2004).

The procedure for the use of anaesthetic creams is as follows: the man must first apply a thin layer of cream to the glans penis and up to half an inch lower on the shaft of the penis. Next, he must place a condom on the penis for 10 to 20 minutes so as not to rub the cream off onto clothing and to be able to move freely. Lastly, he may either keep the condom on, or remove it and wash the penis to wipe away all traces of the cream, before proceeding to have sexual relations.

Anaesthetic products have positive and negative aspects. They are generally effective and easy to use, requiring minimal effort on one's part, and do not cost very much. On the other hand, there are problems with dosing: the man can apply too much cream (which causes a numbness of the glans and could provoke an erectile problem) or not enough (which impairs the efficacy of the product) (Althoff et al., 2010). The woman could suffer vaginal anaesthesia and become momentarily incapable of reaching orgasm if the procedure explained in the paragraph above is not followed properly and the cream comes into contact with her genital organs (Sharlip, 2006). Several men report difficulty obtaining a full erection. Those who achieve an erection lose it 30 to 45 minutes after the application of the product (Hawton, 1988; Atikeler et al., 2002). For others, it becomes impossible to reach ejaculation (Koos Slob et al. 2006).

The third practice resides in blocking the afferent impulse originating from the dorsal, lateral and glanular aspects of the penis by selective resection of the dorsal nerve of the penis. In a study conducted by Zhang et al. (2012), the length of intercourse was increased from 1.1 minutes to 3.8 minutes after the surgical procedure, whereas the post-operative results were not significantly improved for the control group. Authors report that erectile function was not affected, but do not mention to what extent penile sensitivity was lost and how the subjects reacted to this.

The treatments aimed at strengthening the perineum muscles

La Pera and Nicastro (1996) developed a programme aimed at increasing the perception, control and strength of the muscles of the perineum. The hypothesis behind this programme was that a man who cannot manage to prolong the length of intercourse is incapable of controlling the ejaculatory reflex due to a lack of control and strength of his perineal musculature.

The rehabilitation protocol is drawn from methods used to treat faecal and urinary incontinence. It comprises physical therapy (physiotherapy) of the pelvic floor, electrostimulation and biofeedback.

The authors report that 11 out of the 18 subjects who participated in this research acquired control over their ejaculation and have been cured. Unfortunately, they do not clearly indicate what "to be cured" means. Neither do they say what this represents in terms of length of intercourse and satisfaction with the means of control used.

It was explained in the section pertaining to aetiology that it is impossible to control the ejaculatory reflex. It was also indicated that it is preferable for a man to relax his muscles rather than contract them in order to decrease sexual excitement and distance himself from the ejaculatory reflex. Consequently, although La Pera and Nicastro's hypothesis is not plausible but their programme seems to have some merits, we might consider the factors behind this success. The most likely reason is that the men who managed to last longer contracted their perineal muscles well before reaching the zone of ejaculatory imminence and then relaxed them, allowing their sexual excitement to decline. If this muscular relaxation was also accompanied by a halt in the movements of penetration, it resulted in a significant interruption of stimulation. Excitement therefore dropped even lower and these men distanced themselves further from the zone of the ejaculatory reflex.

Pharmacological treatments

BENZODIAZEPINES

Munjack and Crocker (1986) and Segraves (1987) each state a case where there has been improvement in ejaculatory latency by taking benzodiazepines. However, these are isolated cases and no generalization can be established from these explorations.

ALPHA BLOCKERS

Shilon et al. (1984) studied the effect of the administration of the medication phenoxybenzamine, an a-adrenergic blocking agent, on ejaculatory latency. Out of nine patients, seven obtained good results and one, excellent. The most significant side effect noted, however, was the absence of sperm in the ejaculate (aspermia). Other side effects associated with taking alpha blockers include diarrhoea, nausea, vomiting, headaches, orthostatic hypotension, palpitations and cutaneous rash on the face and trunk (Boutot, 1991). In terms of methodology, these authors do not define operationally what constitutes "good" or "excellent" results, therefore diminishing the impact of their study and preventing any comparison with the results of other research.

BETA BLOCKERS

Cooper and Magnus (1984) administered beta blockers to 12 men. The results were negative. In addition, as these drugs cause erection problems, their use is contraindicated in the treatment of the difficulty with prolonging the duration of sexual activities.

ANTIDEPRESSANTS

The idea of using antidepressants to improve the length of intercourse derives from the clinical observation that as a side effect these substances delayed ejaculation in people suffering from depression. Several authors (Eaton, 1973; Porto, 1981; Assalian, 1988; Segraves et al., 1993; Strasberg et al., 1999; Rowland et al., 2001b) report that the use of clomipramine, a tricyclic antidepressant, is effective in delaying the moment of arrival of ejaculation. Results from clinical studies reveal increases in the length of intercourse up to six times (daily intake of 12.5–50 mg of clomipramine) in contrast with four times observed with on-demand use (identical dosage) taken 4–6 hours before sexual intercourse (Waldinger et al., 2004b). In addition, Segraves et al. (1993) mention that the libido, the synchronization of the moment of ejaculation, the quality of ejaculations and overall sexual satisfaction increased significantly among individuals to whom they had administered this medication. Among the side effects, however, they noted the presence of nausea, dizziness, diarrhoea and erectile difficulties. Another major downside stems from the fact that the effect of clomipramine only lasts for as long as the medication is taken (Assalian, 1988; Boutot, 1991).

More recently, we have witnessed the introduction of a new class of antidepressants – the selective serotonin reuptake inhibitors (SSRIs) – which also have the side effect of delaying the onset of ejaculation. Studies carried out by different groups of researchers demonstrated that the following drugs are able to prolong the length of intercourse: citalopram (20–40 mg/day: twofold increase), fluoxetine (20–40 mg/day: fivefold increase), sertraline (50–200 mg/day: fivefold increase) and paroxetine (10–40 mg/day: sevenfold increase) (Ludovico et al., 1996; Waldinger et al., 1998c; Kim and Keun, 1998; Yilmaz et al., 1999). These medications take effect fully after a period of 4 to 6 weeks of daily use (Waldinger and Olivier, 2004c). They have little effect when taken occasionally (McMahon and Touma, 1999a; Waldinger et al., 2004a). The most potent of these antidepressants, paroxetine, increases the length of intercourse sevenfold (Waldinger et al., 1998c), which is quite remarkable at first glance. However, when we analyse the results obtained by these researchers, we realize that this seven-fold increase in the length of coitus is only of interest for men who already present an elevated duration time. Indeed, Waldinger et al. (1998c) report that the group of their subjects with an average of 14 seconds at the outset only succeeds, after six weeks of daily use of paroxetine, in carrying out intercourse of 1 minute and 32 seconds. Such a small duration, even if it is seven times greater than the former duration and statistically significant, is regarded as unsatisfactory by a large majority of men and women. To date, SSRIs are prescribed off-label. In many countries, the regulatory authorities strongly advise against prescribing a medication for indications other than the ones for which it has been approved or licensed (i.e. off-label). This limits the scope of treatments available to the practitioner.

A new medication, dapoxetine (structurally linked to fluoxetine), has recently been developed. It is the first SSRI created specifically for treating difficulty with prolonging the length of intercourse (Pryor et al., 2006). Taken on demand, it is effective from the first dose and shows an increase of 2.5- and 3.0-fold respectively for dosage of 30 mg and 60 mg. However, as dapoxetine has only 40 per cent of the strength of paroxetine and taking into account the adverse reactions it may cause, Waldinger et al. (2006) question the effectiveness of this drug. Moreover, it has only been approved in a few countries (Althof et al., 2010).

Between 10 and 60 per cent of men who use SSRI-class antidepressants report experiencing undesirable sexual side effects, namely the loss of erections, a decrease in sexual desire, ejaculation troubles and a reduction in sexual satisfaction (Waldinger et al., 1998; Montejo-Gonzalez et al., 1997). These unpleasant sexual effects could make the use of antidepressants unsuitable for increasing the length of intercourse for a certain number of men (Barnes and Eardley, 2007).

SSRIs class antidepressants equally entail other side effects such as neurological troubles, psychiatric disorders, dermatologic reactions, fluctuations in body weight, anxiety, headache, fainting, nausea, drowsiness, diarrhoea, fatigue, dizziness and weight gain with the risk of developing type-2 diabetes mellitus (Rosen et al., 1999; Hiemke and Hartter, 2000; Rowland et al., 2004; Waldinger et al., 2004; Fava et al., 2000; Williams et al., 2006). An overdose or interaction with drugs that increase serotonergic activity in the central nervous system could also lead to serotonin syndrome. This syndrome includes severe and persistent symptoms such as myoclonia, hyperreflexia, excessive perspiration, chills, coordination problems and certain mental disorders (Lane and Baldwin, 1997). Recent data indicate that SSRI-class antidepressants could increase impulsive tendencies and suicidal behaviour in certain patients (Healey and Whitaker, 2003; Riley and Segraves, 2005). It is important to note that cessation of these antidepressants should be gradual so as to avoid withdrawal symptoms (McMahon et al., 2004). These symptoms include lethargy, agitation, insomnia, headache, dizziness, nausea and gait instability (Haddad, 1998; Tamam and Ozpoyraz, 2002).

The efficacy of antidepressants in prolonging the length of intercourse diminishes and disappears two to three days after their discontinuation (Waldinger et al., 1998c). They do not therefore change in any way the physiology of the human being. They just alter it for the period of their usage.

NARCOTIC ANALGESIC

Tramadol, a centrally acting opioid receptor agonist, which is medically approved as an analgesic, has been subjected to research to verify its utility in postponing the arrival of ejaculation during intercourse. A dosage of 25 mg on-demand 1–2 hours before sexual intercourse brought up an increase from 1.17 minutes at baseline to 7.39 minutes after treatment (Salem et al., 2008). Dyspepsia (indigestion) and somnolence were the most common side effects observed. Due to its potent sedating and analgesic properties, tramadol may reduce vigilance and, therefore, decrease patients' working capabilities. Moreover, a chronic tramadol intake is associated with a risk of addiction. Altogether, these dangers suggest that the prescription of tramadol should be limited to rare occasions (Porst, 2011).

PHOSPHODIESTERASE TYPE 5 INHIBITORS

Although they were developed to treat erectile dysfunction, phosphodiesterase-5 inhibitors (PDE-5i) (sildenafil, vardenafil, tadalafil) have been used to increase the length of intercourse (Ekmekcioglu et al., 2005). They have also been administered in combination with SSRI-class antidepressants (Chen et al., 2003; Salonia et al., 2002). Although positive outcomes have been reported by these researchers, a systematic analysis of 14 studies on the PDE-5i treatment of premature ejaculation done by McMahon et al. (2006) revealed that 13 of the 14 studies reviewed failed to fulfil the evidence-based medicine criteria for drug trial design. The authors stated that the results of these inadequately designed researches were unreliable. Moreover, a double blind, placebo-controlled study demonstrated that phosphodiesterase-5 inhibitors had no effect on the capacity to prolong the duration of coitus, even if they were associated with greater self-confidence and greater sexual satisfaction (McMahon et al., 2005). These conflicting results reveal the need for further large, randomized, double-blind, placebo-controlled studies before being able to declare on the effectiveness of phosphodiesterase-5 inhibitors for men with the difficulty to extend the length of intercourse (Chen, 2011).

On the other hand, the prescription of PDE-5i – combined with sexological, psychological and/or relational intervention – is the treatment of choice when the difficulty to extend the length of intercourse is secondary to an erectile disorder. This is especially the case when, with age or a progressive pathological condition, the erection becomes more difficult to obtain and maintain. In this particular instance, the man needs to get more excited – by hyperstimulating himself physically, visually or cognitively – for the penis to become sufficiently rigid to penetrate and to execute the thrusting movements inside the vagina. However, as the excitement rises, the margin between the degree of excitement necessary to have a sufficiently rigid erection and the degree of excitement triggering the ejaculation narrows dramatically, a man does not have the necessary space to manoeuver and ejaculates often earlier than desired. He is then caught between two evils: frustrating his partner by not having a rigid erection and therefore looking unmanly, or frustrating his partner by ejaculating too early and appearing "too enthusiastic", selfish or, even worst, sexually incompetent. Since most men fear and despise their partner's emotional, verbal and behavioural reactions following the loss of their erection more than after an ejaculation that appears earlier than desired, their preference is to ejaculate too soon by rushing intercourse over not having an erection rigid and lengthy enough to fully pursue the sexual activities. In these cases, the use of a PDE-5i is appropriate to re-establish the erectile functionality and get rid of the need for intense excitement to provide an adequate erection. Nevertheless, this reinstated erectile functionality will not create the capacity to prolong intercourse more than it was feasible before the appearance of the erectile dysfunction. Specific interventions aimed at increasing the length of intercourse will be required.

PROSTAGLANDIN E-1 INJECTION

Tordjman (1989) developed a two-step treatment. The first consists of in vitro deconditioning under hypnosis carried out on the couple. The second involves in vivo deconditioning using a prostaglandin E-1 injection inside the corpus cavernosum of the penis. This researcher reports having obtained a success rate in 17 cases out of 20. However, he does not provide any data on the duration of coitus before ejaculation occurs. We therefore do not know if the man continues to ejaculate rapidly but could, as a result of prostaglandin E-1, maintain his erection and carry on the in-and-out thrusts inside the vagina or if he can really postpone the moment of arrival of his ejaculation.

On a methodological level, Tordjman's research presents serious flaws. He did not use a control group. He does not indicate how he selected his subjects. He does not describe his experimental protocol and he did not measure the length of intercourse. The only evaluations he made focus on the sexual satisfaction of the couple and on the degree of anguish experienced. Consequently, his study could be considered as exploratory and no conclusions could be drawn for the moment.

Now, from a medical point of view, the contraindications associated with the use of prostaglandin E-1 injections stem from their invasive nature and from their possible iatrogenic effect. These injections are only suitable for highly-motivated individuals or for those who have failed with other therapies (Boutot, 1991).

Theoretical and clinical considerations with regard to pharmacological treatments

Several authors express caution against the abusive use of pharmacological products in treating the difficulty with prolonging intercourse. McCarthy (1994) considers that offering a medical solution to a multidimensional problem, comprising behavioural, emotional and relational aspects, involves the risk of promising a quick and easy cure without taking into account the essential factors, which are the psychological and marital dimensions. For Boutot (1989), premature ejaculation cannot be remedied with the simple absorption of a chemical substance; drug intervention should fall within the broader scope of a therapy that includes in-depth treatment. As for Assalian (1994, 2005), he maintains that a pharmacological intervention is indispensable in the following cases: the individual failed a sexological therapy, he faces a divorce because of this dysfunction or he has suicidal tendencies related to this difficulty. In the case of men who have not succeeded in sexological therapy, he hypothesizes that these men have a constitutionally hypersensitive sympathetic nervous system. This hypersensitivity would prevent them from establishing the difference between ejaculatory imminence and ejaculation itself and/or leads to a discharge of the sympathetic nervous system as soon as it is activated. Strassberg et al. (1990), for their part, use the expression "somatic vulnerability" to describe this condition. Thus, for individuals who have not made any marked progress following a sexological therapy, who are unable to extend the duration of masturbation and who do not have any serious psychological or relational problems, a pharmacological intervention accompanied by sexual education might prove the solution of choice. For my part, I believe that it is necessary to inform patients on the positive and negative aspects of the diverse possible solutions and let them decide on the option to adopt. However, it is important not to lose sight of their intention, which is, very often, to give more pleasure to their partner. In order to help them achieve this goal, the practitioner must ensure that their lovemaking techniques are well suited to the characteristics of female eroticism.

Ideally, the best medication for prolonging the length of intercourse should possess the following characteristics: a) on-demand efficacy or works when taken occasionally (does not necessitate treatment that stretches over several weeks before inducing changes); b) fast acting (does not require a period of more than one hour to take effect); c) does not negatively affect sexual functioning (decreased desire, loss of erection, absent orgasm); d) does not cause unpleasant side effects (nausea, diarrhoea, dizziness, fatigue, drowsiness and so on). Such a medication, in addition to extending the length of intercourse, would give a man the opportunity to increase his self-confidence. However, it would not improve personal and relationship intimacy skills gained through an education in eroticism. A man could think he knows everything about the art of love and continue to believe that long and vigorous coital movements are the essential ingredients of sexual contentment for women. He would therefore forsake his first goal, which is to satisfy his partner sexually and emotionally.

Psychological treatments

Systematic desensitization

Wolpe (1973) believes that anxiety could be at the origin of the difficulty with prolonging the length of intercourse. His hypothesis is based upon the fact that both anxiety and ejaculation depend on the sympathetic nervous system. The suggested therapeutic method is systematic desensitization, which is reputed to be effective in the treatment of anxiety. After learning a relaxation technique for a few weeks, the patient constructs a hierarchy of eight progressive anxiety-generating situations related to his problem. In the next session, the therapist makes the patient relax; then the patient imagines the first situation as he continues to relax himself. When he succeeds in imagining the first situation while maintaining himself in a state of relaxation, he moves on to the next one. He progresses in this manner until the most distressing situation of the hierarchy no longer provokes any anxiety (Wolpe, 1958). Ince (1973), Kraft and Al-Issa (1968) as well as Obler (1973) reveal having successfully treated this difficulty with the help of systematic desensitization. However, none of them used control groups or objective measures of the different variables. As for Lazarus (1971), he notes that the technique obtains rather disappointing results. Considering these contradictory findings, we could assume that systematic desensitization is effective when the difficulty to extend the length of intercourse is caused by anxiety but it is of little help in the absence of this factor.

Psychoanalysis

Ejaculating soon after the beginning of intercourse is considered within the psychoanalytic model as the consequence of a feeling of hostility towards women. The treatment goal is to lead the patient to become aware of his unresolved Oedipal conflicts (Fenichel, 1945). The techniques used include free association and transference analysis. The patient is asked to speak about his memories, dreams, thoughts, fantasies, bodily sensations and affects, as they come into his mind, even if they seem banal, embarrassing or shocking to him. This deep exploration is facilitated by the use of open-ended questions, interpretation of resistances and the analysis of transference. Transference resurfaces conflicts and fantasies and allows the patient to re-experience feelings, object relationships and defences of the past and the present moment in an intense way (Meyer et al., 1983). Once the patient becomes aware of his unresolved Oedipal conflicts and departs from his sadistic urges towards women, his difficulty with prolonging intercourse is supposed to disappear (Fenichel, 1945).

The results obtained from psychoanalytic treatments are disappointing (Kaplan, 1974; Marmor, 1976). In addition, psychoanalysis's method of investigation, because of the non-standardization of treatment, the variation of the problems dealt with (personal history of diverse patients) and the absence of objective measures, is not scientific in nature and determines neither the magnitude of the results obtained nor the therapeutic ingredients that provoked them. Finally, we can even ask ourselves whether the basic hypothesis of the psychoanalytic approach is valid when we know that treatments based on the pause (stop and start procedure) (Semans, 1956), the squeeze technique (Masters and Johnson, 1970) or the management of sexual tension (de Carufel and Trudel, 2006), which do not in any way address the clients' subconscious, bring about excellent results.

Relational treatments

Systemic couple therapy

Systemic therapy views the difficulty with prolonging intercourse as the result of relational dynamics between the spouses. This type of therapy is therefore helpful for countering the adverse effects caused by the couple's negative interactions. The therapist takes great care to change the behaviours that are unconsciously used by the marital partners and that have the effect of perpetuating the symptom which is the difficulty with prolonging intercourse (Weakland et al., 1974). He focuses on the present circumstances and on the functional value of the symptom. Suggesting to the patient that he continue his dysfunctional behaviour constitutes the most important therapeutic intervention of this type of treatment. This technique, called "paradoxical injunction" or "symptom prescription", consists, in the case of the difficulty with prolonging intercourse, of increasing the frequency of brief intercourse. The man can then realize that he has the ability to act on his symptomatic behaviour and that change is possible (Gentry, 1978).

Kaplan (1974) is of the opinion that couples therapy, although it can improve the marital relationship in general, has little effect on the ability to prolong the length of intercourse. According to her, there is no doubt that the spouses' unpleasant and stressful interactions is at the origin of this dysfunction. However, she believes the difficulty with prolonging intercourse can only be treated by the use of specific techniques. Zilbergeld (1992) and Perelman (1980) fully agree. They feel that marriage therapy has little effect on the ability to extend the length of coitus and also recommend using specific techniques to solve this problem.

Given the detrimental effects that marital conflicts may have on sexual functioning, many authors advise properly evaluating the couple dynamic in the management of patients. This assessment covers the interactions prior to and following the onset of the sexual difficulty, each one's ability to commit to the relationship, and the sexual history of the marital partners (past and current relationships, beliefs and expectations, sexual activities and so on) (Schnarch, 1997; Mrdjenovich et al., 2004).

Sexological treatments

Techniques aimed at reducing the attention paid to erotic stimuli

There are three types of technique intended to reduce the allocation of attention to erotic stimuli. The first consists of occupying the mind with non-sexual matters until the woman reaches orgasm (Hastings, 1963). These matters could be thinking about a round of golf, doing multiplications, recalling an unpleasant memory and so on. The second resides in contracting the anal sphincter as hard as possible and concentrating on keeping it contracted while continuing intercourse (Kinsey et al., 1948). The third comprises a variety of bodily manoeuvres such as pinching the skin, biting the tongue or squinting the eyes (Assalian, 1994; Hastings, 1963).

Clinical reports on the methods destined to reduce the attention allotted to erotic stimuli reveal disappointing results (Aycock, 1949; Hastings, 1963; Marmor, 1976). In addition, these practices are of dubious quality. The man who has to think of something else, who contracts the anal sphincter, who avoids being touched or who bites his lips during sexual relations is not creating a very erotic atmosphere, either for himself or for his partner. Finally, all these diversion tactics prevent the man from focusing on his bodily reactions indicating his sexual excitement levels and thus impede him in effectively managing his sexual excitement.

The "stop and start" technique

Semans (1956) proposed the hypothesis that the difficulty with prolonging intercourse is caused by an excessive rapidity of the ejaculatory reflex. The method he developed – the "stop and start" technique – aims to lead the man to better support the summation of stimuli and thus delay the triggering of the ejaculation reflex. According to this method, the woman stimulates the man's penis until he feels the forewarning sensations of ejaculatory inevitability. She then stops all stimulation until these sensations disappear. The process is repeated. Once the patient is capable of withstanding indefinitely this type of extra-vaginal stimulation using a lubricant, he may then expect to take part in sexual relations without ejaculating prematurely. The eight cases that Semans treated in this way improved the length of intercourse. Unfortunately, the author does not provide any objective data enabling evaluation of the actual progress of his subjects. Neither did he use a control group or carry out any follow-up. Finally, the very limited number of subjects studied precludes all generalization.

Zilbergeld (1975) indicates having used, with men without a partner, the "stop and start" technique in combination with relaxation, assertiveness and self-expression techniques as well as with sexual information. The "stop and start" technique was applied within the context of masturbatory practices. Subsequently, the subjects engaged in the same masturbatory activities, but used a lubricant to simulate vaginal sensations and increase the level of difficulty. Without giving precise figures, Zilbergeld mentions that the majority of subjects had longer intercourse than before the treatment. The instruments of measurement employed were self-reports by the subjects. The absence of objective measures, pre-test and a control group constitute a serious impediment to the internal and external validity of this research. In addition, the use of techniques as heterogeneous as relaxation, assertiveness, self-expression and the "stop and start" technique make it impossible to determine exactly what could have provoked the change. The conclusions that may be drawn from this study are therefore very limited.

Jern (2014) tested a small, handheld battery-powered vibrating stimulation device as a variation of the "stop and start" technique. During each masturbation exercise, participants were instructed to stimulate themselves close to ejaculation, then stop until the sensations of impending orgasm diminished. This was repeated three times per session. The fourth time, men were allowed to ejaculate.

The programme was comprised of three sessions a week over six weeks. The participants saw their mean ejaculatory latency time increase from 87.91 seconds before treatment to 201.78 seconds after a six-month follow-up period. These results are encouraging. However, as there were only 11 participants in the study, more research is needed to come to a clear conclusion.

Treatments aimed at increasing the perception of sensations preceding the ejaculatory reflex

Kaplan (1974) considers that the difficulty with prolonging the length of intercourse is caused by a non-perception of erotic sensations leading up to the ejaculatory reflex. The central element of the treatment consists of getting the man to concentrate in a continuous way on his pre-orgasmic sensations and to avoid being distracted by the components of sexual interaction with his partner. To this key element, Kaplan adds communication techniques between the married couple. If it proves necessary, she also deals with issues related to treatment resistance presented by the man or the woman.

In order to guide the man to perceive the sensations which precede the ejaculatory reflex, Kaplan (1989) employs a variation of the "stop-start" technique developed by Semans (1956). In the first session, the couple engages in foreplay, and then the man lies on his back while his partner stimulates his penis manually or orally. The man therefore concentrates exclusively on the sensations coming from his penis. He does not try to give pleasure to his partner because this preoccupation could make him lose his concentration. In addition, it is advised that he not let himself be invaded by any thoughts whatsoever that could distract him from his erotic sensations. As soon as he perceives the sensations indicative of the arrival of ejaculation, he asks his partner to stop stimulating him. These sensations then disappear within a few seconds. Before the erection is lost, the spouse resumes the stimulation. This technique is practised three times. On the fourth time, the man may ejaculate. The couple is also encouraged to expand their sensual repertoire.

During the second session, the man places his hand on that of his partner's and guides it in an exploration of different speeds, pressures and caresses. In the following sessions, the couple uses a lubricant in order to create the sensations most similar to those encountered inside the vagina.

After three to six sessions, the man is supposed to have gained some control over his excitement. From this moment on, the couple may proceed to coitus. This is done in the position where the man is lying flat on his back and the woman is sitting on him. The woman inserts the penis in her vagina, and then waits until the man signals her to begin moving her pelvis. He directs the movement of the woman's pelvis with the help of his hands. Once again, when the man feels that ejaculation is imminent, he tells his partner and she stops all stimulation. They remain motionless until the sensations subside. This activity is repeated three more times and, on the fourth time, the man is allowed to ejaculate. During the following session, the man begins to move his pelvis. When the couple has acquired some control in this position, they move on to the side position. The treatment ends with the successful application of the pause in the position where the man is on top of the woman. The "stop-start" exercises must be performed at a frequency of once every two weeks after the end of the treatment.

Kaplan (1989) reports success rates of 80 per cent with this treatment. In addition, most of the patients she treated acquire, according to her words, permanent mastery. She did not, however, use a control group or carry out objective measures of the length of intercourse.

The use Kaplan (1989) made of Semans' (1956) technique appears to achieve good results. We do not know, however, how the man learns, if he ever does, to postpone the moment of arrival of his ejaculation when he engages sexually with his partner, that is to say when he is no longer exclusively focused on the sensations in his penis but is also attuned to her reactions.

The reconditioning of the sexual response

Masters and Johnson (1970) attribute the acquisition of the difficulty with prolonging the length of intercourse to the conditioning associated with initial sexual experiences. In order to reverse the effects of this conditioning and to modify the sexual habits developed by the couple as a reaction to this dysfunction, they created a multi-modality therapeutic intervention programme. This places emphasis on the exploration of sexual pleasuring, the development of effective communication, the acquisition of knowledge about sexuality and training in the squeeze technique. Here are the key highlights of this treatment:

SEXUAL EDUCATION

Sexual education covers the anatomy of the genital organs and the physiology of the male and female sexual response. It also includes information concerning the causes of the difficulty with prolonging intercourse and its consequences on the couple's sexual and conjugal life. Finally, it deals with the expectations and sexual behaviours of the spouses as well as the myths and illusions they harbour regarding sexuality.

COMMUNICATION TRAINING AND SENSATE FOCUS

Within the approach developed by Masters and Johnson (1970), the conjugal relationship, and not the individual members of the couple, is the patient. Consequently, an important part of the treatment is devoted to establishing appropriate behavioural patterns for the sexual functioning of the couple as an interacting entity. To reach that goal, Masters and Johnson developed the sensate focus procedure in which the man and the woman learn to give and to receive touch strictly for pleasure and without obligation of performance.

The sensate focus exercises take place in an intimate and non-stressful atmosphere. The marital partners are nude. One spouse acts as the giver and the other acts as the receiver. The giver has the task of touching, caressing or massaging the receiver with the goal of providing him/her pleasure. During the first stage, which comprises two sessions, sexual touching of the breasts and genital organs is prohibited; there is no sexual stimulation and no particular state of excitement is supposed to be achieved. The receiver applies himself/herself to perceiving the sensations the giver is creating without feeling obliged to perform, without having to explain his/her preferences or without worrying about reciprocating the pleasure he/she has just received. The giver could, in addition to pleasuring the receiver, surrender to the pleasure he/she feels when touching and watching him or her react. If sexual excitement does occur, the couple is instructed not to proceed to intercourse in order to prevent performance anxiety. When the exercise is finished, the members of the couple reverse roles. It is recommended that talking is reduced to a minimum during the sensate focus sessions because it can detract from the awareness of physical sensations. However, the partner being touched can let his or her partner know, either verbally or non-verbally, if any touch is uncomfortable. They are also encouraged to share their values, attitudes and sexual desires with each other after the session is completed.

The second stage is devoted to developing a system of communication between the spouses. This system of communication includes verbal and non-verbal elements that allow the couple to articulate their impressions, reactions and sexual preferences. The receiver is invited to guide the giver by placing his/her hand on top of his/her hand and indicating his/her preferences in terms of areas to stimulate, pressures to apply or ways to touch. Masters and Johnson mention that these non-verbal messages are better conveyed in such a way that the person being touched does not take over full control, but simply adds some extra input to the touching. During this stage, the members of the couple could introduce the stimulation of breasts and genital organs. However, they must do so in the context of pleasure and sensual enjoyment, without imposing upon themselves any form of performance demand.

In the next stage, instead of taking turns touching each other, the couple is instructed to try some mutual touching. The purpose of this exercise is to practise a more natural form of physical interaction, and to help each partner shift attention to his/her partner's body and away from watching his/her own response. Couples are reminded that no matter how sexually excited they feel, intercourse is still prohibited.

THE SQUEEZE TECHNIQUE

The "squeeze" technique, which is derived from the "stop and start" technique developed by Semans (1956), is the key therapeutic modality of Masters and Johnson's programme. The couple, after completing the sessions on sensate focus, moves to training in this technique. The woman stimulates the man's penis until he obtains an erection. As soon as the erection is complete, she places her thumb on the frenulum and her index and middle fingers on both sides of the coronal ridge of the glans penis. She applies pressure for 3 to 4 seconds. The man loses at this very moment his urge to ejaculate. He could also experience a loss of erection of about 10 per cent to 30 per cent. After an interval of 15 to 30 seconds, the woman repeats the same procedure. During the first session, alternating between stimulation and the squeeze technique is practised five times. The goal of this exercise is to help the man recognize the levels of excitement he is able to maintain indefinitely without ejaculating.

The next step incorporates intercourse. To start, the couple performs two or three manual stimulations followed by the squeeze technique. Then, the man lies on his back and the woman proceeds to intromission of the penis in the vagina. She remains motionless in this position. When the man feels his excitement approaching the point-of-no-return, she withdraws and squeezes the penis. This sequence is repeated three or four times.

During the following step, the man executes pelvic thrusts while the woman remains motionless. After that, the woman can also move her pelvis. The final phase is for the couple to have sexual relations in the side position. During all these steps, the spouses are counselled to employ the squeeze technique to contain the man's excitement within the limits that permit him to postpone his ejaculation.

Masters and Johnson (1970) advise the spouses to use the squeeze technique for a period of six to twelve months after the end of the programme. They also recommend that they engage in foreplay prior to proceeding to intercourse. Lastly, they insist on the fact that reasonable control could only be gained when the couple participates in sexual activities on a regular basis.

The results obtained by Masters and Johnson (1970) are excellent. Of the 186 men whom they treated, 182, that is to say 97.8 per cent, increased the length of intercourse at the end of the treatment. Among the factors that contributed to this high success rate is the fact that the patients were carefully selected. They were referred by a professional source and did not present any major psychopathology. More than half had already gone through psychotherapy before beginning the programme and most were more educated than the general population.

Among Masters and Johnson's methodological strengths, we note the utilization of a large number of subjects, the description of the therapeutic ingredients, the use of two therapists and a follow-up period of five years. As for the weaknesses, they include a bias in the selection of the subjects, the lack of a control group and the use of non-structured interviews during the follow-up period to assess the subjects' progress. But the lack of objective measures to determine the length of intercourse remains the most significant shortcoming in Masters and Johnson's research. In fact, the criterion which they employed to determine the success of their therapy is the "reversal of the basic symptomatology". A success criterion this vague holds very little scientific or clinical value. First, we do not know what the symptoms were for each individual at the outset. Second, we are unaware of the exact nature of the subjects' sexual functioning after the treatment and, third, we do not have any statistics to draw comparisons with the results from other therapies. Moreover, the absence of means to verify the intervention of the authors, who were both the originators of the treatments and the experimenters of this research, undermines the validity of this study.

Other researchers have tried to find out if it is possible to obtain the same results as Masters and Johnson (1970) by using the same techniques as them, but by modifying the therapeutic format. We know that the therapeutic format employed by Masters and Johnson is very particular. It requires the presence of both partners, takes place over an intensive two-week period and demands that the treatment is led by a male–female co-therapy team. Tanner (1973) successfully treated two couples whereby one of the partners was psychotic. Leiblum et al. (1976) formed groups of couples and treated them over a period of 12 weeks. Golden et al. (1978) also treated couples in groups, but over a period of 10 weeks. The results these researchers achieved compare to those of Masters and Johnson (1970). However, they neither used control groups nor carried out objective measures of the therapeutic gains. Lowe and Mikulas (1975) employed bibliotherapy to treat premature ejaculation; the 10 men in their study all improved the length of intercourse. Zeiss (1978) also made use of written material to help couples improve the man's capacity. On the other hand, the treatment programme he formulated involved the use of both the pause and penile compression. The results obtained by Zeiss are excellent; in addition, he measured objectively the diverse variables that he studied, and this before and after the administration of the treatment. Furthermore, in a well-designed study, de Carufel and Trudel (2006) verified the efficacy of the clinical application of Zeiss's (1978) treatment (which includes sexual education, communication techniques, sensate focus as well as the pause and squeeze techniques) by utilizing an objective measure of the length of intercourse. The couples in this study had on average increased the duration of coitus from 56.8 seconds to 7 minutes 52 seconds and maintained these gains at follow-up (three months after termination of treatment). In fact, the only research that did not give results as good as Masters and Johnson's (1970) is that of Zeiss (1978). In this research, the men took part in group therapy and they had to communicate to their partner at home the information received during the sessions. It appears therefore that a very important variable in the therapeutic format of Masters and Johnson's (1970) programme is the woman's presence at the time of the therapeutic meetings.

Long-term studies reveal that most individuals who went through treatment for premature ejaculation of the same type as Masters and Johnson have a tendency to lose, with the passage of time, the gains achieved over the course of the therapy. Hawton and Catalan (1986) highlight that only a third of their patients who developed the ability to prolong intercourse retained this capacity three years after the end of the treatment. DeAmicis et al. (1985) point out that almost all their clients' therapeutic acquisitions (apart from sexual satisfaction) had disappeared after a period of three years. Grenier and Byers (1992) propose the hypothesis that this diminished ability to prolong intercourse could be attributed to diverse factors such as a drop in the couple's motivation, the onset of other sexual problems within the couple or a modification of attraction by the partners for one another.

One hypothesis that would explain a regression this generalized would be that it is easy to lose learned techniques. This loss occurs more easily if the couples experience a somewhat prolonged interruption in their sexual activities, if they do not have the opportunity to regularly put into practice the learned techniques or if they adopt new sexual behaviours promoting the acquisition of wrong techniques. Actually, we see the same erosion of skills and knowledge in most activities – like in golf or foreign language acquisition, for example – when they are not practised regularly and properly. There is no magic solution to improving one's sexual competence. Like any other endeavour, sexological changes need to be applied in order to remain effective. Contrary to certain authors who assert that sexological treatments are ineffective because of the fact that with time some patients lose their acquired ability to delay ejaculation, it should be emphasized that these treatments are effective but that their techniques require practice and fine tuning.

Relapse prevention programmes based on behavioural, cognitive and relationship strategies have, however, been developed and could be put into practice by couples without the need for them to re-consult with their therapist (McCarthy, 1993).

The major downside of Masters and Johnson's (1970) programme resides in the anti-erotic nature of the squeeze technique. This technique requires interrupting the flow of the sexual encounter and applying a gesture contrary to the mood that prevails during amorous exchanges. This method is even more paradoxical since the sensate focus exercises that precede the application of the squeeze technique are intended to get the couple to create an erotic atmosphere based on shared excitement and pleasure. When the woman withdraws and compresses the man's penis, she causes an interval completely cut off from the sexual act. The spouses therefore alternate between an erotic atmosphere and a therapeutic atmosphere. This way of doing things differs significantly from Semans' (1956) technique where the couple simply stops, without necessarily interrupting the erotic exchanges.

The modulation of sexual excitement

Desjardins (2007) and Crépault and Desjardins (1978) consider that the difficulty with prolonging the length of intercourse is dependent on the attitude that consists of envisaging the excitement rise as a fast dynamic. The proposed treatment is intended to expand the man's awareness of his sexual excitement and to teach him how to modulate it, that is to say how to increase and decrease its intensity. To begin, the man explores the dimensions of his sexual excitement through masturbation, without concerning himself with having to satisfy his partner in any immediate context. With the help of masturbation, the man learns to perceive his sexual excitement and to identify the phenomena preceding the imminence of ejaculation. He also develops the ability to modulate his sexual excitement and to use fantasies associated with intercourse.

Next, the man is encouraged to let himself go to receiving slow caresses, overall as well as on the genitals, in a state of tonic relaxation so as to become aware of his sexual excitement. The couple is also advised to refrain from intercourse for a while in order to allow the man to rediscover the pleasure of being in erection and to stay in tune with his excitement.

Finally, the man is led to enhance his erotic behaviour by diffusing his sexual tension from the genital organs throughout his body. To do this, he can widen his gaze, vary the rhythm of his movements, breathe more deeply, thrust his pelvis and relax his buttock muscles.

Desjardins (2007) does not provide results concerning the effectiveness of his treatment, nor does he describe his research procedure. In fact, his findings stem from clinical explorations and not experimental research. Analysis of this treatment reveals that an important place is dedicated to the acquisition of erotic knowledge and skills by the man. However, there is no mention of the role that the woman can play in improving or maintaining this condition.

Theoretic and clinical considerations with regard to sexological treatments

Sexological treatments are very effective. They help couples increase the duration of coitus and enjoy more satisfying sexual activities. Their success rests on the acquisition of knowledge, the refinement of the perception of bodily signals indicative of the rise of excitement, the development of sensuality and the mastery of skills (communication, assertiveness, sexual expression, movement and breathing). Here, the therapist's work compares in part to that of a teacher. Eroticism becomes the subject of learning and sexual satisfaction results from education.

Sexological treatments have been enriched over the last thirty years with elements of cognitive-behavioural therapy. There are now cognitive-behavioural sex therapies (Poudat and Jarousse, 1992; McCabe, 2001; Dintrans, 2004; El Feki, 2007). These therapies merge the contributions, among others, of Masters and Johnson and those of cognitive-behavioural therapy. Functional behaviour analysis, relaxation, and cognitive reframing and restructuring are used together with sexual education, communication training, sensate focus and the squeeze technique to treat the difficulty with prolonging intercourse and the anxiety that could accompany it.

It appears, therefore, in light of the excellent results obtained by sexological therapies that these contribute to the improvement of an individual's sex life. It is hoped that these discoveries will constitute a source of inspiration and motivation for researchers and will thus enable fundamental sexology and sex therapy to progress.

The sexual excitement management programme for difficulty with prolonging intercourse

The sexual excitement management programme for difficulty with prolonging intercourse, which is presented in its entirety in the third part of this book, is also a sexological treatment. It was created at the Department of Psychology at the Université du Québec in Montreal by de Carufel in collaboration with Desjardins and Trudel, then associate director and director of the author's doctoral thesis. Later, it was tested within research conducted at the Université du Québec in

Montreal (de Carufel, 1996) and at the Université de Louvain-la-Neuve (De Sutter, 2001). It was also the subject of a sex-therapeutic novel (de Carufel and De Sutter, 2001), of publications in international scientific journals (De Sutter et al., 2002; de Carufel and Trudel, 2006) and of a book (de Carufel, 2009).

This treatment falls within the functional sex therapy elaborated over the last twenty years by de Carufel (1990, 1996, 2001, 2006, 2007). Functional sex therapy is drawn from multiple sources. It includes contributions derived from character analysis (Reich, 1942, 1972), bioenergy (Lowen, 1975), sex therapy (Masters and Johnson, 1966, 1970), neurolinguistic programming (Bandler and Grinder, 1975), the sexo-corporeal approach (Desjardins, 1986), mindfulness (Didonna, 2009) and cognitive-behavioural therapies, as well as Oriental erotological teachings (Taoism, Kama Sutra) and corporeal arts (mime, dance).

Functional sex therapy is based on the sexual functionality model developed by de Carufel. This model integrates all of the physiological, emotional, cognitive and behavioural components of healthy and proper human sexual functioning. It gives therapists a frame of reference for evaluating the sexual functioning of their patients. It also allows them to develop effective tools to treat the many different male and female sexual disorders. Functional sex therapy takes into account the biological, personal, relational and social dimensions of sexuality and places emphasis on acquiring knowledge, learning new skills, personal autonomization, harmonization inside the couple and responsibilization of individuals. The theoretical foundations of functional sex therapy will be presented in a forthcoming book.

The sexual excitement management programme for the difficulty with prolonging intercourse was the subject of a very important study with experimental research protocols, control groups, operationalization of variables and objective measures of the length of intercourse using a stopwatch in pre-test, post-test and follow-up phases (de Carufel and Trudel, 2006). This study was presented as the best research of all time within the field of psychosocial interventions for premature ejaculation in a review of the scientific literature done by Melnik et al. (2011) for the Cochrane Collaboration, an international not-for-profit organization preparing, maintaining and promoting the accessibility of systematic reviews of the effects of health care. In this study, the sexual excitement management programme for the difficulty with prolonging intercourse was applied to 18 couples recruited in the greater region of Montreal in Canada. Mean duration of intercourse increased from 42.5 seconds to 7 minutes 48 seconds. This intercourse time is superior to that obtained – 4 minutes 55 seconds – after taking SSRI-class antidepressants (Waldinger et al., 1998c). It is also just as high as the mean IELTs – 8 minutes 4 seconds – of men in the general population of five countries studied by Waldinger et al. (2005b). Finally, it is similar to the average length of intercourse – 8 minutes (Fisher, 1973) – that women require to reach orgasm.

The men and women who completed the sexual excitement management programme were very satisfied with the treatment and the results. The women reported having achieved orgasm more frequently during intercourse. Both members of the couple saw their sexual and marital satisfaction increase. The therapeutic gains were maintained into the follow-up period, which took place three months after the end of the treatment.

The sexual excitement management programme for the difficulty with prolonging intercourse has several advantages for both clinicians and patients. First, it is based on a deep understanding of male sexual functioning. Second, it is described in a very detailed and comprehensive manner. Third, the techniques are not mechanical and do not interrupt the course of sexual activities as is the case with Masters and Johnson's squeeze technique; they integrate with sexual activities and promote interactions between both partners, which has the effect of improving the quality of the erotic and loving experience during foreplay and intercourse. Fourth, the woman does not have to intervene technically with her partner in order for him to manage his sexual excitement; she is not required to squeeze his penis, pull his testicles or push his perineum. Fifth, contrary to traditional treatments which require the participation of both partners, the sexual excitement management programme for the difficulty with prolonging intercourse may be undertaken by men on their own. Sixth, the treatment duration is short and its implementation is flexible; it runs over 12 sessions and may be followed for a period ranging from three to 36 weeks. Finally, experimental research and clinical observations show that its effects extend to other areas of life.

The full version of the sexual excitement management programme for the difficulty with prolonging intercourse is described in the third part of this book.

Treatment guidelines

The guidelines presented here will help the clinician decide what types of intervention will be the most appropriate to provide based on the results of the evaluation and the patient's preferences. These interventions can be grouped into sex therapies and pharmacological treatments. The sex therapies include the Masters and Johnson's programme (1970), Kaplan's treatment (1974), Zeiss and Zeiss's model (1978), cognitive behavioural sex therapy, Desjardins's sexocorporeal approach (2007), Kempeneers et al.'s self-help booklet (2012) and the sexual excitement management programme for the difficulty with prolonging intercourse (de Carufel, 2006). Pharmacotherapy comprises topical anaesthetic agents, antidepressants, narcotic analgesic (tramadol) and dapoxetine (Priligy, available in certain countries).

1 If ejaculation always occurs within 1 minute regardless of the type of stimulation (sexual thoughts, visual stimulation, masturbation, manual stimulation, oral stimulation, vaginal stimulation) or the sexual excitement management techniques and strategies a man uses, we can suspect that the onset of ejaculation is influenced by a pathology, traumatism or constitutional trait. These factors would hasten sexual excitement or lower the ejaculatory reflex threshold to an extent that ejaculation would take place very shortly (less than 1 minute) after the beginning of the excitement phase. This impossibility to

manage sexual excitement is extremely rare or purely hypothetical (see section titled *Theoretical and clinical considerations with regard to the causes of premature ejaculation or the difficulty with prolonging intercourse*). The therapeutic approach would include pharmacotherapy and sex therapy.

2 If the difficulty with prolonging intercourse is due to a lack of knowledge, skills and strategies pertaining to the management of sexual excitement – which is what one encounters in most lifelong cases – the best option is sex therapy. However, if the patient is not interested in learning, is not thrilled with what he has to do to modulate his sexual excitement, cannot afford the cost of the treatment or is facing pressure from his partner (such as the threat of her leaving him), pharmacotherapy is the best solution.

3 If the man possesses the knowledge, skills and strategies required to manage his sexual excitement but cannot put these to use because of organic, psychological or relational problems – which is what one usually sees when a man was able to prolong intercourse in the past but is now unable to do so – medical, psychological or marital interventions are the recommended treatments. This includes particular treatments for erectile dysfunction.

4 If sex therapy does not bring about the desired results, pharmacotherapy could be proposed.

5 If pharmacotherapy fails to help the patient, sex therapy could be suggested.

6 Short-term pharmacological support could be used at the beginning of sex therapy to facilitate the learning of the sexological information and techniques.

7 Short-term pharmacological support could be used at the same time as psychological or marital therapy to facilitate changes and help patients regain confidence, ease and serenity.

8 Specific sexological, psychological and/or marital interventions could complement pharmacotherapy.

Notes

1 This point will be developed at length in the sub-sections *Sexological causes* and *Theoretical and clinical considerations with regard to the causes of premature ejaculation or the difficulty with prolonging intercourse* in the *Aetiology* section.

2 There is no organic condition – genetic, traumatic or pathological – that makes a man ejaculate like a cold can make him sneeze or an allergy can give him a rash. The only exception, and this is according to anecdotal reports, may be episodes of extremely intense anxiety.

3 These curves have been provided by our patients. We often ask the latter to self-report the course of their excitement after having participated in a sexual activity and we then discuss with them how this activity unfolded.

4 An orgasm is a spasmodic physiological discharge which follows an increase in sexual excitement (ejaculation in the case of the man) and that is experienced with pleasure. It is important to note that there are physiological discharges that are not experienced with pleasure. Some individuals are so disappointed in themselves when they ejaculate too soon that they do not pay attention to the spasms of discharge and do not savour them. In other cases, it proves physiologically impossible to take pleasure in these discharges. Indeed, some men tense their muscles so hard when they become excited that the ejaculatory spasms may barely be noticed and consequently cannot be enjoyed.

5 The reader will have remarked that these curves differ from the sexual excitement curve described by Masters and Johnson (1966).
6 The significance of avoiding ejaculation is evidently to prevent the subsequent loss of erection. This loss of erection prevents continuing intercourse and satisfying the partner with the in-and-out movements of the penis inside the vagina, whereby lies the entire difficulty with prolonging the duration of intercourse.
7 This should not be confused with a dry orgasm where there is a discharge without expulsion of semen outside of the penis because the semen is entering the bladder (retrograde ejaculation) or there is no or very little semen due, for example, to a prostatectomy, genetic abnormalities of the reproductive system, certain medications used to treat high blood pressure, enlarged prostate, and mood disorders.
8 The duration of this phase differs with age and individuals.
9 The informed reader will notice the removal of the phase known as the 'plateau' that Masters and Johnson had included in their graph representing the human sexual response cycle. This has been done in this way for two reasons. The first is that this phase does not consist of any different physiological reactions – only more intense ones – than those observed during the precedent phase (excitement). The second is that the term "plateau" describes very badly an array of reactions subject to such large variations of intensity.
10 There are ways in our day and age to promote and enhance sexual harmony within the couple. If the woman requires prolonged stimulation, it is possible to a certain extent to help her to achieve orgasm more quickly. If it is the man who is having trouble extending the length of intercourse, he could be provided with the information and skills that will give him the capacity to manage the course of his excitement. However, as the woman's sexuality rests upon a myriad of factors, among them emotional factors, that are more extensive and complex than those of the man, and seeing as these factors are difficult to understand at this time, it is easier for the man to delay the onset of his ejaculation than for the woman to accelerate the arrival of her orgasm.
11 Unlike other stimuli, stimuli applied to the genital organs do not have to be perceived and savoured to create sexual excitement. By means of a neural network of reflex loops originating from the genital organs to the spinal cord and then returning from the spinal cord to the genital organs, the sexual excitement response could develop without cognitive processes intervening. This is why the strategy consisting of thinking about something else during intercourse does not work. Even if the man neither perceives nor enjoys any erotic stimuli at all, his genital organs will not be any less stimulated and excitement continues to build despite this mental, emotional and relational disconnect.
12 Sexual excitement is the neurophysiological response to a sexual stimulation. It generates for its part physiological changes such as erection, increase in heart rate, increase in muscular tension and ejaculation.
13 The only exception could be anxiety. According to certain anecdotal reports, anxiety on its own may during very intense episodes provoke ejaculation.
14 Scientific research has not yet determined this duration.
15 The cognitive processing described here consists of an evaluation and interpretation of the duration of intercourse. This processing is carried out based on knowledge, attitudes, points of view, values, desires, memories and so on.

2 Clinical assessment

Introduction

The clinical assessment in sexology consists of two parts. The aim of the first is to identify the presence of sexual disorders, estimate their severity, determine their causes and discover their consequences. The second aims to highlight the sexual assets and strengths of the patients as well as to determine their personal and relational erotic potential. Obtaining this information is critical in order to develop suitable and effective treatments. It is known that assessment is an essential step in all health sectors. However, it proves to be crucial in sexology where the same symptoms could be caused by a wide variety of biological, sexological, psychological and relational factors.

The clinical assessment for premature ejaculation or the difficulty with prolonging intercourse is carried out in two steps. The first takes place at the very beginning of consultations and assists in making the diagnosis. It includes the history of the disorder, the standard medical examination, the sexological medical examination and, when necessary, complementary medical examinations to screen for endocrine and urological risk factors (Jannini et al., 2011). The history of the complaint is taken by the sex therapist and the instruments of privilege used are the face-to-face interview and observation of the patients' body language. There are also a lot of questionnaires for assessing the emotions, cognitions, physiology and behaviour of the patients. When answered directly by the patient, however, this type of instrument tends to coerce his reality into predetermined categories instead of giving access to his life experience the way it really is. It is preferable for the therapist to keep these questions in mind, to ask them of his patient, to clarify them if necessary and to deepen his investigation beginning from the answers he receives and the reactions he observes. These questionnaires are actually more fitting for research than for therapy, where they serve mainly as guidelines. A few questionnaires deal specifically with the difficulty to manage sexual excitement and prolong the length of intercourse (premature ejaculation). The most important are the Arabic Index of Premature Ejaculation (Arafa and Shamboul, 2007), the Chinese Index of Premature Ejaculation (Yuan et al., 2004), the Premature Ejaculation Profile (Patrick et al., 2009), the Index of Premature Ejaculation (Althof et al., 2007) and the Premature Ejaculation Diagnostic Tool (Symonds et al., 2007). These questionnaires are useful for assessing such aspects as erectile function, sexual desire, intravaginal ejaculation latency, patient satisfaction, partner satisfaction and psychological distress. However, they should not be used to determine the presence or absence of a difficulty with prolonging intercourse (premature ejaculation) because they are based on erroneous definitions of this dysfunction. In reality, the criteria on which these definitions have been established are wrong. The most common among these is the length of intercourse (intravaginal ejaculation latency time). As we have seen in the *Definitions* section of the previous chapter, this criterion is absolutely arbitrary (even when one professes that it relies on evidence-based data). The second one is the occurrence or not of psychological or relational distress to assert that there is a difficulty with prolonging intercourse (premature ejaculation). This criterion is invalid because a reaction to a phenomenon does not determine the presence or the absence of this phenomenon (for example, if a person is not concerned about her diabetes, it does not mean that she does not have diabetes; the same applies in the case of the difficulty to manage sexual excitement, or premature ejaculation). Thirdly, some questions attempt to evaluate the control the man has over his ejaculation. These questions are completely useless as they do not recognize that ejaculation is a reflex process and that can in no way be subjected to voluntary control. Finally, some questions aim to establish the "impact" or "effects" of the difficulty with prolonging intercourse (premature ejaculation) on the man, the woman and the relationship. These questions reflect a poor understanding of psychological processes by their authors since they attribute emotions to events rather than to the way people react cognitively to these events, as cognitive therapy explains in great depth. Aside from these shortcomings, these questionnaires can indeed help the clinician pursue his investigation given that they cover several aspects of the patients' sexual functioning and provide information about the severity of the problems they are struggling with and the intensity of their reactions to these problems.

The medical examinations are performed by a physician specializing in sexology. The European Association of Urology's guidelines recommend that a complete andrological assessment should be performed at the initial visit on the man exhibiting signs of difficulty with prolonging the length of intercourse (Hatzimouratidis et al., 2010); a description of this assessment exceeds the scope of this book.

The second step of the assessment takes place throughout the therapy. In fact, at each of the twelve treatment sessions, the patients receive information on sexuality and perform bodily exercises. The discussions that follow the information provided are used to examine the patients' knowledge, beliefs, aspirations, sexual functioning and management strategies. The exercises, for their part, provide an opportunity to observe the patients' bodily movement and assess their physical abilities. From this data, the therapist proposes hypotheses concerning the way the patients move their body during sexual activities, discusses these with them and adjusts his interventions if necessary.

When a couple seeks consultation, both spouses are seen together, then separately. Booking individual meetings lets each spouse disclose certain facts and express certain feelings that they would do with difficulty, or not at all, in the other's presence. In addition, there are aspects of human functioning that are personal in nature. For the sake of efficiency and out of respect for the person, the clinical assessment should take this point into account.

The interview

After introducing himself and greeting the patient (or the couple), the therapist begins the interview by gathering general information. He obtains biographical data, verifies the health status, conducts an overview of professional, psychological, marital and family functioning, and inquires about the reasons for the consultation. While compiling this information, he gradually forms a therapeutic alliance with the patient. The therapist adjusts himself to the way in which the patient reacts, and the order of topics he deals with varies depending on the direction the meeting takes. He remains, however, directive and ensures that he obtains all the necessary information to establish the diagnosis. This part of the interview enables the therapist to identify the reason for the consultation.

Several eventualities can then present themselves to the therapist. He may be confronted with a situation in which one spouse feels that ejaculation occurs too quickly while the other does not want intercourse to be extended further. The course of action to take in this case is to uncover the motives behind each spouse's wish (personal insecurity, hypersexuality, sexual aversion, hypoactive sexual disorder and so on) and then to work accordingly. For example, when confronted with an uncomplicated disparity of interest, the therapist could help the couple find common ground so as to maximize the satisfaction of each partner (this might involve helping them increase the length of intercourse, seek compromise, change their sexual practice and so on) or simply accept this divergence.

The therapist may also find himself in the presence of an individual seeking therapy on his own who is fearful of being unable to satisfy his partner because he "only" lasts 45 minutes. Again, it is important to go over the grounds underlying this complaint. Is there a fear of not being normal, a wish to please the partner, a delusional disorder? In the first eventuality, reassurance based on the presentation of statistics about statistically normal duration might be sufficient. In the last one, a psychiatric referral would be the logical option. If the desire to satisfy the partner predominates, the therapist could encourage the patient to engage in a dialogue with his female companion in order for him to get to know her better. Obtaining an answer to the following two questions would provide a good start: What elements of their romantic and sexual interactions does she enjoy and desire to keep? What are the aspects she likes least and wishes to change? The knowledge acquired will tell the man which course of action to maintain and which behaviours to modify. If the man has made the changes requested by his partner yet she is still dissatisfied, but this time due to her own sexual functioning, she could, alone or accompanied by her mate, initiate a therapeutic process.

There are times when the therapist must decide whether to focus his interventions on the man or on the woman when it is the latter who is not reaching orgasm during sexual relations. Certainly, the woman's achievement of orgasm does not solely depend on the length of intercourse. However, if all the sexual factors related to the context and the partner are deemed satisfactory by the woman and appropriate by the therapist, it must be determined whether or not the length of intercourse or the factors related to the woman are the cause of her anorgasmia. To help make the decision, the therapist could use the temporal cursor (Figure 2.1). This small instrument provides a visual aid to decide whether to focus treatment on the man or the woman. By sliding the cursor along the intercourse length continuum and then stopping it on the exact moment when ejaculation usually occurs, the therapist sees the length of time that intercourse lasts. The closer the cursor approaches zero, the more the treatment should focus on the management (by the man and the woman) of the man's sexual excitement. The further it moves away from zero, the more the treatment should centre on the development of the woman's and man's ability to make the woman obtain orgasm. It goes without saying that if the length of intercourse is approximately 8 minutes (which is the average time required by women to achieve orgasm) specific therapeutic options intended for each of the partners could only be beneficial.

Most of the time, however, the therapist receives a man alone whose partner is complaining that the length of intercourse is too short (or who fears that his partner, even if she did not tell him, is dissatisfied with the length of coitus) and who in fact ejaculates almost immediately after intromission of the penis inside the vagina. Sometimes, the therapist will see some men in which ejaculation occurs before insertion (ejaculatio ante portas); nevertheless, even though these men are unable to proceed with intercourse for the moment, the clinical investigation and the treatment remain the same for them.

The last part of the interview assesses the man and woman's sexual functioning (personal and relational). It covers the physiological, cognitive, emotional and behavioural factors involved in this functioning. During this assessment, the therapist investigates the history of the patients' sexual life, with an emphasis on the difficulty with prolonging intercourse. He evaluates the man's erectile capacity and the nature and the strength of his sexual desires. He analyses the couple's sexual interactions and how they communicate with each other. Finally,

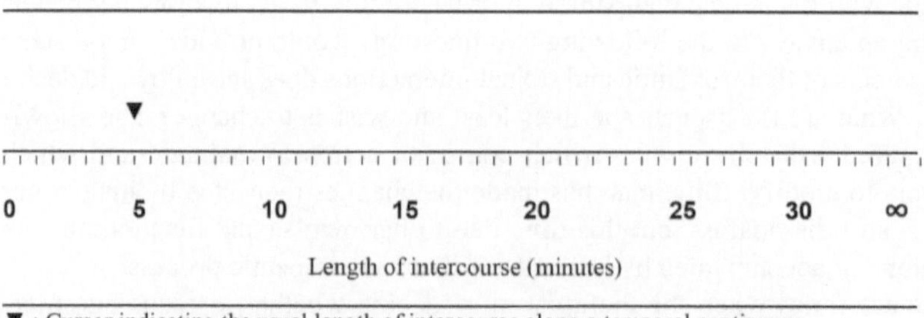

Figure 2.1 The temporal cursor

he explores each spouse's reactions with respect to their sex life, gauges their satisfaction and identifies their motivation to change. If necessary, he also examines in more depth the psychological and relational functioning in order to determine if these exert any influence on the sexual functioning of each spouse. A multitude of variables could have an impact on the onset and perpetuation of the difficulty with prolonging intercourse. In addition, the reactions associated with it could be so severe as to lead to the termination of the couple's relationship. It is therefore essential to carefully assess all of the variables associated with this sexual dysfunction in order to remedy it in the most complete and most satisfactory manner possible.

Below, you will find the interview protocol for conducting a clinical assessment of the man (whether he seeks therapy alone or accompanied) and the woman. This protocol is built from information contained in the first and third chapters of this book. It is a flexible investigative instrument. I therefore encourage the therapist to draw upon his intuition and creativity during its use. This involves, among other things, determining the order of the various topics to be investigated and deciding which issues will be raised in the presence of both partners and which will be dealt with in the individual sessions.

The interview protocol outlined below is presented with detailed explanations and precise references for each variable to be explored. However, it should be kept in mind that it has been developed above all as a guideline. The therapist may always add or subtract to it based on his knowledge, feelings and clinical experience.

The interview protocol

Introductions

- Greet the patient warmly and with empathy
- Introductions
- Invite the patient to sit down
- Engage in casual conversation if the atmosphere lends itself to this (briefly talking about matters of little significance – whether or not it was difficult to find the office, the weather or other topics – can help establish the relationship between the therapist and the patient).

General information

Gathering general information helps obtain necessary data and avoid raising the subject of sexuality too abruptly.

Identification

- Name
- Address

- Telephone number
- Age
- Education
- Occupation
- Marital status
- Children.

Health status

- Pathologies
- Medication
- Traumas
- Surgical procedures
- Sleep patterns
- Back problems
- Physical condition
- Tobacco
- Alcohol
- Drugs.

It is necessary to undergo a general medical and urological health examination to assess the presence of thyroid disorders, hypogonadism, non-insulin dependent diabetes, neurological disorders, urogenital abnormalities and chronic prostatitis. It must also be verified whether or not the patient suffers from back problems to know if there are any contraindications in executing the pelvic movements in the treatment.

General functioning

- Professional functioning
- Psychological functioning
- Relational functioning
- Family functioning.

Are there any professional, psychological, relational or family-related factors that interfere with the management of sexual excitement?

See the sections *Psychological causes* and *Relational causes* in the first part of this book.

Reason for consultation

- What is the patient's complaint?
- What is the main reason for the consultation?
- Is there any hidden agenda?

Identify the patient's problem and assess the reason for the consultation (e.g. for the woman to have more pleasure; for the man not to lose his partner or for him to feel normal . . .).

Clinical impressions

- Non-verbal language (gait, posture, movements, gestures)
- Voice (tone, flow, pitch, speed, volume)
- Clothing
- Speech
- Demeanour
- Interactions between the man and the woman
- Interactions with the therapist.

Confirm the clinical impressions obtained during the first interview with the clinical impressions gleaned during subsequent interviews, with the information provided by the patient on his sexuality and with the manner in which the man executes the exercises during the treatment sessions. Does his manner of moving in everyday life have any connection with his manner of moving when he executes the exercises in the office and when he takes part in sexual activities?

Confirm with the partner the manner in which the man moves during sexual relations.

Sexual functioning

Timing, onset, type and occurrence of ejaculation

Ask the man and woman questions about the following:

- Timing (length of the excitement phase before ejaculation)
    - during foreplay: length of the excitement phase before ejaculation
    - during intercourse: length of the excitement phase before ejaculation (intravaginal ejaculatory latency time (IELT))
    - during masturbation: length of the excitement phase before ejaculation (this question could be changed in the next sessions depending on the patient's sensitivity to this topic and the therapist's judgment)
- Onset: lifelong/primary or acquired/secondary
- Type: absolute/generalized or relative/situational
- Occurrence: chronic or intermittent.

See the section *Symptomatology* in the first part of this book.

Several tools are available for assessing the patient's onset of ejaculation, including the Arabic Index of Premature Ejaculation (Arafa and Shambul, 2007), Premature Ejaculation Profile (Patrick et al., 2009) and the Premature Ejaculation Diagnostic Tool (Symonds et al., 2007).

The European Association of Urology guidelines mention that stopwatch-measured intravaginal ejaculatory latency time is mandatory in research, but the use of self-estimated duration is adequate in the clinical management of premature ejaculation (Althof et al., 2010; Hatzimouratidis et al., 2010).

Sexual history

MAN

- Take his sexual history with his different partners (if he has had more than one) while thoroughly exploring the difficulty with prolonging intercourse and its evolution. Explore any other sexual difficulties he may have had. It may also be necessary to investigate other past sexual events like abuses and traumatisms.
- Take his sexual history with his current partner while thoroughly exploring the difficulty with prolonging intercourse and its evolution. Explore any other sexual difficulties he and his partner may have had.
- Review the last sexual relation he had while thoroughly exploring the difficulty with prolonging intercourse. Explore any other sexual difficulties he and his partner may have had.

WOMAN

- Take her sexual history with her different partners (if she has had more than one) while thoroughly exploring the sexual problems she may have had. It may also be necessary to investigate other past sexual events like abuses and traumatisms.
- Take her sexual history with her current partner while thoroughly exploring the issues of the difficulty with prolonging intercourse. Explore any other sexual difficulties she and her partner may have had.
- Review the last sexual relation she had while thoroughly exploring the issues of the difficulty with prolonging intercourse. Explore any other sexual difficulties she and her partner may have had.

A screening tool, such as the abridged Female Sexual Function Index–6 (Isidori et al., 2007), would be useful in assessing the woman's sexual functioning.

During the assessment of the sexual history, it is also important to uncover the positive aspects of the patients' sexual life. The tendency of most therapists who want to help people is to look for what is going wrong in order to offer solutions. However, it is also essential to bring to light the patients' assets in order for them not to lose these capacities and to include them in their new repertoire of sexual competencies.

Erectile functionality

What are the frequency, rigidity and duration of the patient's erections during the following periods and events:

- Night and morning
- Foreplay
- Intercourse
- Masturbation.

Erectile function can be assessed by the man and the woman during these periods and events using the Erection Hardness Score (EHS) (Mulhall et al., 2007). EHS employs a simple and direct language and rates the hardness of erection on a scale of one to four, with four being the maximal score.

EHS 1 – A score of 1 indicates that the penis is larger than normal, but not hard. It signals a severe dysfunction.

EHS 2 – A score of 2 indicates that the penis is hard, but not hard enough for penetration. It signals a moderate dysfunction.

EHS 3 – A score of 3 indicates that the penis is hard enough for penetration but not completely hard. It signals a mild to moderate dysfunction.

EHS 4 – A score of 4 indicates that the penis is completely hard and fully rigid. It signals a healthy function.

If the patient has fully rigid and durable erections at night, in the morning and during masturbation, but experiences difficulties while engaging in activities with his partner, we could conclude that he has a disorder induced by sexological factors (in many cases due to a lack of perception and erotic enjoyment of sexual stimuli during lovemaking); these sexological factors can be compounded by psychological and relational factors. When erections are incomplete (an EHS score of 3 or less), of short duration (less than 3 minutes[1]) and/or of low frequency (less than once a week[2]), this during various times (masturbation, foreplay, intercourse), we could suspect the presence of organic pathology or the effects of aging (45–50 years and older*). If the cause is organic, there are likely emotional difficulties and, in all cases, changes have occurred within sexual interactions and the couple's relationship.

The following criteria, despite being clinical and not of scientific origin, further help to determine the functionality of the erections and to eliminate the possibility of an organic component.

- Criteria for functional morning/nocturnal erections: an erection with an EHS score of 4 that lasts at least 3 minutes and which occurs at least once a week.
- Criteria for functional erections during foreplay: an erection with an EHS score of 4 that lasts at least 3 minutes.
- Criteria for functional erections during masturbation: an erection with an EHS score of 4 that lasts at least 3 minutes.

The clinician should specifically check if:

- The man rushes foreplay to prevent loss of his erection
- The penis is rigid enough for penetration
- The man is able to sustain his erection during intercourse until ejaculation
- The man precipitates intercourse to avoid loss of his erection.

Is the way in which the patient proceeds to achieve and maintain an erection harmful to the erection? See the section *Sexual information* in the first session in Chapter 3 of this book.

Refer the patient to a urologist specializing in sexology if it appears he has an organic erectile dysfunction.

Sexual positioning

How do the man and the woman position themselves related to sexual identity, sexual orientation and sexual propulsivity/receptivity? These topics need to be explored with tact, without necessarily asking direct questions.

- Sexual identity: sense of belonging to one's biological sex.
- Sexual orientation: capacity to eroticize the other sex.
- Sexual propulsivity (man): assertion of his phallicism/maleness. Capacity to exteriorize his masculinity while becoming erect, while penetrating his partner and while ejaculating inside her vagina.
- Sexual receptivity (woman): assertion of her vaginality/femaleness. Capacity to welcome erotically and lovingly the man inside her internal depths, the intimacy of her womanness.

Examine whether or not sexual positioning influences the manner of managing sexual excitement.

Sexual interaction scripts

- How do the man and woman behave during foreplay, intercourse?
- Does the man try to pleasure the woman? If yes, how does he proceed?
- Does the woman try to give pleasure to the man? If yes, how does she proceed?
- What is the respective importance of the sentimental, sensual and genital exchanges?
- Does the man think about something else? Does he avoid being stimulated?
- Does he stimulate his partner while trying not to get excited?
- Does the woman avoid touching the man, moving, letting herself go?

See the section *Symptomology* in Chapter 1 of this book.

Sexual positions

- Does the couple use positions promoting the management of sexual excitement?
- Does the couple use positions that promote the onset of ejaculation?

See the section *Sexual information* in the ninth session in Chapter 3 of this book.

Bodily movement

- In what manner does the man move during foreplay and intercourse?
- In what manner does the woman move during foreplay and intercourse?

Bodily movement is assessed on an ongoing basis as the exercises are performed during the treatment sessions.

See the section *Global, rapid, hypertonic and low-amplitude bodily movements* in Chapter 1 of this book.

Stimuli

Assess the stimuli stemming from the context, the partner and the individual himself.

- Is there a variety of stimuli (visual, manual, oral, vaginal, phantasmagorical, sentimental, affectionate; man's movements and muscular contractions, woman's movements; man's and woman's actions; stimuli from the man to the woman; stimuli from the woman to the man)?
- Are some stimuli more appreciated than others?
- Is there focalization on particular stimuli?
- Assess on a scale of 1 to 10 the intensity of the diverse stimuli the man perceives during sexual relations.
- What stimuli are associated with the rise of pleasure and excitement?
- What stimuli are associated with the onset of ejaculation?

The patient's personal assessment of the duration of excitement in all of these stimuli conditions should be obtained.

See the sections *The presence of stimuli* and *Focalization on a particular stimulus* in Chapter 1 as well as the section *Sexual information* in the eleventh session in Chapter 3 of this book.

These questions provide more information about the stimuli that are the most appreciated by the man and that are associated with the rapid rise of his sexual excitement and the onset of his ejaculation.

Sexual excitement management strategies and techniques

- Analyse whether the techniques and strategies used to manage sexual excitement by the man and the woman during foreplay and intercourse are effective and pleasurable or not.

See the *Sexual information* sections in the twelve sessions in Chapter 3 of this book.

Capacity to manage sexual excitement

- Evaluate on a scale of 1 to 10 the capacity the man has to manage his sexual excitement during foreplay and intercourse.

Sexual excitement curves

- Ask the man to depict on a graph his curves of sexual excitement during foreplay and intercourse.
- Are they always the same curves?
- According to him, what explains the variations in intensity and duration of his curves of sexual excitement?
- Ask the woman to depict on a graph her curves of sexual excitement during foreplay and intercourse.
- Are they always the same curves?
- According to her, what facilitates and what harms the rise of her sexual excitement?

See the section *The sexual excitement curve* in Chapter 1 and the section *Sexual information* in the first session in Chapter 3 of this book.

Sexual pleasure curve

- Ask the man to depict graphically his sexual pleasure curves during foreplay and intercourse.
- Is it the same pattern as that of his physiological excitement?
- According to him, what explains the variations in intensity and duration of his sexual pleasure curves?
- Ask the woman to draw a graph depicting her sexual pleasure curve during foreplay and intercourse.
- Is it the same curve as that of her physiological excitement?
- According to her, what explains the variations in intensity and duration of her sexual pleasure curves?

Knowledge, beliefs, attitudes and values

- According to what knowledge, beliefs, attitudes and values about male and female sexual functioning do the man and woman guide their sexual conduct?

Thoughts/cognitions

- What are the man and woman's sexual thoughts/cognitions (before sexual relations, during foreplay, during intercourse, after ejaculation)?
- What are the man and woman's non-sexual thoughts/cognitions (before sexual relations, during foreplay, during intercourse, after ejaculation)?

What is the man's inner dialogue? Does what he thinks or says harm the management of his sexual excitement? Does he try not to perceive sexual stimuli in order to avoid becoming too excited?

What is the woman's inner dialogue? Does what she thinks or says harm the rise of her sexual excitement and her sexual pleasure?

Anxiety

Do the man and woman experience any anxiety during sex?

- Man
    - Fear of not satisfying his partner
    - Fear of his partner's reactions
    - Fear of losing his partner
    - Performance anxiety
    - And so on.
- Woman
    - Fear of over-stimulating the man
    - Fear of not being able to achieve orgasm or get enough pleasure
    - Fear of the man's reactions
    - Performance anxiety
    - And so on.

Use a scale of 1 to 10 to measure the man and woman's degree of anxiety.

- Does their anxiety fluctuate during sexual relations?
- Can the man ejaculate while being mildly or moderately excited (and being anxious)?

See the section *Anxiety* in Chapter 1 of this book.

Nature and frequency of sexual activities as a couple

- What is the nature of their sexual activities as a couple?
- What is the frequency of their sexual activities as a couple?

The nature and frequency of sexual activities may provide indications about the man and woman's sexual desires, their interest in having sex together, the number of opportunities the man has to learn to manage his sexual excitement and so on.

Masturbation

What are the ways in which the man and woman masturbate, if they do so?

- What areas are stimulated during masturbation?
- What techniques of stimulation are used (types of touch or movement, pressure, speed, pause)?

- Are any stimuli used (objects, fantasies, photos, movies)?
- What is the length of masturbation?
- What is the man's capacity to manage sexual excitement during masturbation?

Are the techniques used by the man during masturbation compatible with prolonged management of his sexual excitement when with a woman?

See the section *Other sexological factors* in Chapter 1 of this book.

Are the methods used by the woman during masturbation compatible with the conditions that she could encounter during intercourse?

See the section *Suggestions for the woman* in the sixth session in Chapter 3 of this book.

Frequency of ejaculations

- What is the man's monthly ejaculatory frequency with his partner?
- What is the man's monthly ejaculatory frequency alone?

Does the frequency of ejaculations permit the man to regulate his physiological needs for ejaculatory discharge?

Sexual and sentimental fantasies

For the man and woman:

- What is the nature and frequency of their sexual and sentimental fantasies outside of sexual activities?
- What is the nature and frequency of their sexual and sentimental fantasies during masturbation?
- What is the nature and frequency of their sexual and sentimental fantasies during sexual relations?

Is the erotic imagination used by the man during masturbation and intercourse compatible with prolonged management of his sexual excitement with a partner?

See the section *Other sexological factors* in Chapter 1 of this book.

Sexual and sentimental desires

For the man and woman:

- What is the nature and frequency of their sexual and sentimental desires outside of sexual activities?
- What is the nature and frequency of their sexual and sentimental desires during masturbation?
- What is the nature and frequency of their sexual and sentimental desires during sexual relations?

What is the link between the man's frequency of sexual and sentimental desires and the frequency of his ejaculations? Does this indicate whether or not the frequency of his ejaculations corresponds to his physiological needs for ejaculatory discharge?

What is the nature of the man's sexual and sentimental desires? Are they congruent with the desire for prolonged sexual activities?

What is the nature and frequency of the woman's sexual and sentimental desires? Does her motivation to take part in sexual activities stem from sexual desires, desires for reconciliation, closeness, romance, love, emotional needs?

Sensuality

- Are the man and the woman sensual in everyday life?
- Are the man and the woman sensual during masturbation?
- Are the man and the woman sensual during sexual relations?

See the section *Other sexological factors* in Chapter 1 of this book.

Communication

For the man and woman:

- How do they communicate about everyday matters?
- How do they communicate about sexuality?

See the section *Suggestions for the couple* in the second to sixth sessions in Chapter 3 of this book.

Intimacy and emotional closeness

For the man and woman:

- How intimate and emotionally close are they in their everyday life?
- How intimate and emotionally close are they in their sexual life?

See the section *Sexual information* in the sixth session in the third part of this book.

Overall sexual and sentimental satisfaction

Assess on a scale of 1 to 10 the degree of satisfaction that each spouse has towards the context and ambiance of sexual relations, the seduction methods, foreplay, intercourse, the excitement and pleasure obtained, the after-sex phase (postlude), and communication.

- Man
    - Assess the man's degree of sexual satisfaction.
    - Assess the man's degree of sentimental satisfaction.
    - Assess the degree of sexual and sentimental satisfaction the man thinks his partner obtains.
    - Try to confirm these impressions against what the woman actually experiences.
- Woman
    - Assess the woman's degree of sexual satisfaction.
    - Assess the woman's degree of sentimental satisfaction.
    - Assess the degree of sexual and sentimental satisfaction the woman-thinks his partner obtains.
    - Try to confirm these impressions against what the man really experiences.

To counter the tendency towards negativity, ask the man and the woman to talk about the positive aspects of their emotional exchanges and their sexual interactions.

Cognitive, emotional and behavioural reactions to the length of intercourse

- Assess the man and woman's cognitive, emotional and behavioural reactions to the length of intercourse.
- Examine the consequences of the man and woman's cognitive, emotional and behavioural reactions to the length of intercourse on their conjugal relationship.
- Determine if there is any threat of separation on the woman's part.

See the section *Cognitive, emotional, behavioural and relational reactions to the duration of intercourse* in Chapter 1 of this book.

Man's hypotheses regarding his difficulty with prolonging intercourse

- Ask the man what, according to him, is the cause of his difficulty with prolonging the length of intercourse.

The answer to this question is essential to determining the treatment to offer the patient.

Woman's hypotheses regarding her partner's difficulty with prolonging intercourse

- Ask the woman what, according to her, is the cause of her partner's difficulty with prolonging the length of intercourse.

The answer to this question is essential in determining the treatment to offer the patient.

Man's point of view

- Ask the man what he thinks and feels about his difficulty with prolonging the length of intercourse. It's important to dispel any misunderstanding in order to reassure him and ensure the right course of treatment.
- According to him, how does his partner deal with this situation?
- As for himself, how does he cope with this situation?
- Does he have sexual desire?
- Does he get excited and obtain sexual pleasure during sexual activities?
- Can his partner attain orgasm? If yes, in what way?
- Has he lost interest in sexuality?
- What does he think and feel about the overall situation?

Woman's point of view

- Ask the woman what she thinks and feels about the man's difficulty with prolonging the length of intercourse. It's important to dispel any misunderstanding in order to reassure the woman and ensure the right course of treatment.
- According to her, how does her partner deal with this situation?
- As for herself, how does she cope with this situation?
- Does she have sexual desire?
- Does she get excited and obtain sexual pleasure during sexual activities?
- Could she attain orgasm? If yes, in what way?
- Has she lost interest in sexuality?
- What does she think and feel about the overall situation?

Motivation to change

- Use a scale from 0 to 10 to gauge the motivation of both spouses to make changes to their sexual life.
- What are their expectations, what are their hopes?
- Use a scale from 0 to 10 to estimate the importance of sexuality for each spouse.
- Is the man interested in changing his ways?
- Does the woman want to be involved in the treatment process?

Objectives

- What objectives would the man like to achieve for himself and his partner as a result of the treatment?
- What objectives would the woman like to achieve for herself and her partner as a result of the treatment?

Outcome

At the end of the interview, the therapist is in a position to state whether the man's difficulty with prolonging intercourse is primary (lifelong), secondary (acquired), global or situational, chronic or intermittent. He knows whether the man's erections are sufficiently rigid for intercourse and if he possesses the knowledge, skills and strategies to manage his sexual excitement. He has verified whether there are any professional, psychological, conjugal or family-related factors that interfere with his ability to prolong the length of intercourse. He has identified the reactions of both partners and probed their motivation to make changes to their sexual life. He has determined whether the situation is urgent and requires immediate intervention. It only remains for him to prescribe the medical examinations (it is imperative, as mentioned before, that these examinations are performed by a physician specializing in sexology).

After receiving the results of the medical examinations and compiling the information from the clinical interview, the therapist will review the outcome with the patient. He will explain the cause or causes of his difficulty with prolonging intercourse and present the treatment options available to him. If the cause is organic, the therapist will refer the patient to an appropriate physician because this type of disorders should be treated first (Hatzimouratidis et al., 2010). If no pathology is detected, the therapist will move on to the next step. He will describe the treatment modalities chosen by the patient and, in the case where the patient opts for the sexual excitement management programme for difficulty with prolonging intercourse, he will establish with him the meeting schedule.

In conclusion, the clinical interview is particularly useful in assessing all the sexological as well as professional, psychological, conjugal or family-related variables likely to lead to a difficulty with prolonging intercourse. It allows, in conjunction with the medical examinations, to pinpoint the factors that influence the man's ability to manage his sexual excitement. It also provides information about the reactions of both partners and on the consequences that these reactions have had on their sexual life and their conjugal relationship. With knowledge of these factors and reactions, the therapist may design a treatment adapted to the entirety of the problem confronting the man and his partner.

Notes

1 This is an arbitrary figure derived from clinical experience.
2 This is an arbitrary figure derived from clinical experience.

3 The sexual excitement management programme for difficulty with prolonging intercourse

Introduction

The third part of this book is devoted to presenting the sexual excitement management programme (or functional sex therapy treatment) for difficulty with prolonging intercourse, also referred to as premature ejaculation. The therapist will find a complete and structured sexological programme that in many cases can be used on patients as written. He will also have the flexibility to adapt this programme whenever the need arises. He may at that point modify the programme, add psychological or relational interventions to it or insert it into a more comprehensive therapeutic approach.

Unlike traditional sex therapy that requires the participation of both spouses, the sexual excitement management programme is as effective for men who consult alone as it is for couples. There are a large number of men who do not want to or cannot seek therapy accompanied by their partner. Among these men, some do not wish to divulge to their wife that they are seeing a sex therapist. Others are with a woman who is not interested in taking part in such a process. A number are beginning a new relationship and feel it is inappropriate to ask their new companion to participate in a sexological treatment. There are also men who do not have a partner and who have no desire to get involved in a romantic relationship until they have found a solution to their sexual difficulty. Many among these men do not want to take antidepressants or have tried them without success. Fortunately for them, the clinical experience of therapists who have been trained in the functional sex therapy has repeatedly demonstrated that committing oneself alone to this programme does not constitute a handicap. And even when their difficulty with prolonging intercourse draws its origins from marital difficulties, men are able to learn to prolong the length of intercourse despite the absence of their companion in therapy.

The presentation format chosen here for the sexual excitement management programme for the difficulty with prolonging intercourse is a self-help book. This format reproduces in its entirety the instruction provided to patients during clinical sessions. It obviously does not include the observations, discussions or the reactions that complete the therapeutic process. The self-help format offers the clearest and most explicit way to present the information and exercises in the programme. In addition, it equips the therapist with a tested intervention model that he could adopt as a whole, conform to his personal style or, when necessary, tailor to his patient's specific needs.

The self-help book format gives individuals who prefer to proceed autonomously the opportunity to find a solution for their problem on their own. It should be mentioned that self-help manuals do not come into conflict with the sex therapist's practice. In fact, there are various ways of learning that suit different types of learners. Take for example learning how to play golf. Some people read a book with the goal of improving their game, others take a lesson, many turn to the services of a personal golf coach and quite a few people use all of these methods. The same applies to people who want to improve their sexual functioning. For those who prefer to consult a therapist, the self-help manual could be used as a complement to the therapy or simply as an aide-mémoire. For those who choose to go ahead on their own, it becomes a reference work permitting to introduce new ways of behaving.

In this book I have structured the sexual excitement management programme for the difficulty with prolonging intercourse as I usually do when I see people in consultation, that is to say in twelve sessions spread over twelve weeks. Each session is divided into six sections. The first section consists of information about sexuality. The second covers technical exercises. The third, entitled *Exercises for the week* includes two sub-sections. The sub-section *Exercises without sexual excitement* is dedicated to technical exercises to repeat during the week. The sub-section *Exercises with sexual excitement* outlines how to put into practice during sexual activities the strategies and techniques dealt with in the session. The fourth section provides complementary information for men who do not have a partner or who do not have regular sexual relations with their partner. For the sake of convenience and for lack of a more appropriate term, this section has been entitled *Suggestions for the single man.* The fifth section offers advice to women whose partner has difficulty with prolonging intercourse. These women may therefore better understand this difficulty and more easily help their partner to manage the course of their sexual excitement. Lastly, the sixth section contains specific suggestions for people who are following the programme as a couple. It focuses on communication and team spirit to promote collaboration and spousal satisfaction.

The pages that follow include the presentation of the programme to the patients, the twelve therapy sessions as well as the recommendations to give to men and women at the end of the treatment.

Presentation of the programme to patients

The presentation of the sexual excitement management programme for the difficulty with prolonging intercourse (or premature ejaculation) serves to inform the patient about the content that will be covered, the methods that will be used, the goals he will aim to achieve, the work he will need to do and the stages he will go through. There are many ways to present a treatment such as the one below. It is to be noted that this approach is regularly modified in order to take into account the patient's intellectual level and sexual knowledge.

Guidelines for presenting the programme to the patient

The programme you will follow is based on the learning of techniques and strategies. These will help you manage your sexual excitement and prolong the duration of your sexual relations. It is important to know that when your excitement increases, your body becomes tenser. This is a normal phenomenon. Excitement causes the contraction of certain muscles. In return, the contraction of these muscles supports the rise of excitement. The instant excitement becomes sufficiently intense, it triggers ejaculation. When your muscles are relaxed, it is virtually impossible to ejaculate. In order to be able to extend the length of intercourse, you must become aware of the contraction of these muscles and relax them before excitement reaches levels that are too high.

The sexual excitement management programme for the difficulty with prolonging intercourse consists of twelve sessions. It is best to complete one session per week or at least one session every two weeks. Beyond this period, the acquisition of skills proves more difficult and you risk becoming unmotivated. To maximize your chances of success, it would be preferable that you complete the twelve sessions in less than 18 weeks.

This programme includes information about sexuality and exercises. These exercises are progressive. It is necessary to master the first to move on to the following and so on until the end. The ability to delay the arrival of ejaculation is achieved only at the end of the programme! You will not improve, for example, by 30 seconds every session. It is only once all the techniques are incorporated that you will be able to manage your excitement. We can compare learning this programme to a swimming lesson. Within the latter, you learn to breathe first, then to kick your legs, and then to move your arms. You're only able to swim when all these actions are synchronized into a unified movement. The same holds true for this programme. You must complete it entirely in order to incorporate the diverse techniques. Otherwise, you will not achieve your objectives. If, however, you are able to manage your excitement before the end of the programme, it is strongly recommended to finish it anyway. Such control is usually fragile. You must learn all of the information and techniques to maintain a solid and lasting command.

It is advised to practise the exercises in each session at least three times before moving ahead to the next session. This is absolutely essential because even though your mind could understand very quickly, your body needs to repeat the movements several times to succeed in integrating them.

You can continue to have sexual relations according to your usual frequency. All the sex you have will allow you to experiment and make progress. It is the totality of these various acquisitions that will equip you with the ability to well-manage your sexual excitement and to prolong the length of intercourse. On the other hand, you should expect, at the start, to experience the same frustrations as before. Indeed, it will take you some time before you get a good grasp of the techniques and feel perfectly at ease. In the beginning, you will need to concentrate on what you do. It may make you feel awkward or uncomfortable. You will go through a period of trial and error. The best way to set about this period is to consider it an exploratory period within which you will experiment with new behaviours and choose those that suit you most. It is clear that if you tackle these new situations with a bit of humour, this learning phase will be a lot more pleasant.

Over time, the techniques will integrate into your way of making love and you will no longer have to pay much attention to them. They will not hinder your lovemaking and will not be detectable. It is a little bit like when you learnt how to drive a car. The first few times you were behind the wheel, you were probably very concentrated on what you had to do. Now, you could do several things at a time and you no longer think about, for example, how to shift gears. This is the case in the sphere of sexuality. You will discover new ways of doing things that will require concentration initially, but which will become quite natural afterwards. With practice and perseverance, you will make remarkable progress and your sex life will be much more satisfying.

FIRST SESSION

Sexual information

The zones of the male sexual excitement curve

This programme will provide you with the information you need to increase your lovemaking without ejaculating too early. It is based on understanding the reactions that take place inside the zones of the male sexual excitement curve.[1] If a man wants to prolong the length of intercourse, he must manage his sexual excitement. To do so, he has to identify the bodily reactions that occur within each zone and apply the appropriate management techniques.

The male sexual excitement curve is divided into four zones (Figure 3.1).[2] Zone 1 is that of the appearance and disappearance of the erection. A man obtains an erection when he perceives and takes pleasure in different sexual stimuli. This can be the scent of his partner, the shape of her body, her facial expressions, the warmth of her vagina, the movement of her hips, etc.

Erection occurs naturally when a man lets himself go to perceive and enjoy sexual sensations. It is useless to squeeze the buttocks or voluntarily contract the perineal muscles (those that enable small movements with the penis or stop the flow of urine during miction) to attain or maintain an erection. But many men, believing that they will lose their erection if they do not do this, contract these muscles intentionally. However, it was mentioned earlier that sexual excitement naturally produces muscular tension. It was also noted that if an individual tenses his muscles when he is excited, he increases his sexual excitement. If by fear of not being able to have a sufficiently rigid erection, a man contracts his buttock muscles and those of his perineum, he creates a surplus of muscular tension. This surplus of tension adds to the muscular tension already

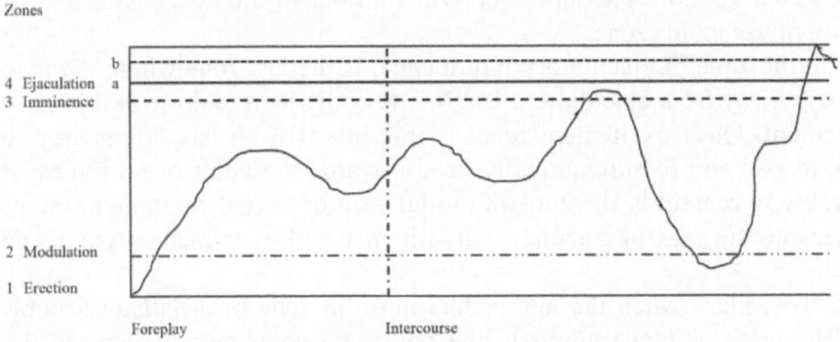

Figure 3.1 The zones of the male sexual excitement curve

Zone 1: The appearance and disappearance of the erection zone. Zone 2: The modulation of sexual excitement zone. Zone 3: The ejaculatory imminence zone. Zone 4: The ejaculation zone (a: the emission reflex or point of no return; b: the expulsion reflex).

generated by sexual excitement and causes him to progress rapidly towards the ejaculatory reflex.

Certain men, because they do not know that the penis undergoes normal highs and lows of rigidity during sexual activities, worry and attempt to artificially maintain a constant maximal firmness. To do this, they over-stimulate themselves or tense their muscles without realizing that these efforts contribute to the rise of their excitement. It is better to accept these normal erectile variations. They are an indication of healthy physiological, psychological and sexological processes. During prolonged sexual activity, the stiffness of the penis varies a lot. For example, when the atmosphere of the encounter changes and becomes less erotic and more affectionate, the erection diminishes. If the man desires to regain a firmer erection, all he needs to do is shift his attention back to sexual stimuli and take pleasure in them. The same phenomenon occurs when applying the techniques of this programme. The man can distance his excitement so far from the zone of ejaculation that it falls back down . . . into the zone of the appearance and disappearance of the erection! What he needs to do at that moment, if he wants to have another erection, is to perceive some sexual stimuli and delight in them (by making a few thrusting movements with his pelvis, for example). Wanting to continually maintain the hardness of the penis at 100 per cent is to head automatically towards failure.

Zone 2, the zone of modulation of sexual excitement, is where the man prolongs the duration of sexual activities. He is excited enough to have an erection, but not enough to reach ejaculation. It is in this zone that he applies most of the techniques taught here; while experiencing pleasure he observes from time to time his body's reactions to stimulation and acts accordingly.

The bodily reactions and behaviours in a man that indicate his sexual excitement is growing in intensity in the zone of modulation are numerous. He tends to move more quickly, make shorter thrusting movements of the pelvis, tense his muscles more, breathe from the rib cage, focus his attention on specific sexual stimuli and derive more pleasure. You will find out in the next sessions what techniques to use in this zone.

Zone 3, the zone of ejaculatory imminence, is the last zone where the man could move away from ejaculation. But it is very difficult to do so at this level of excitement. Once excitement reaches this intensity, it has a tendency to continue to rise and to automatically head towards the point of no return. It is preferable to remain in the zone of modulation of sexual excitement rather than enter into the zone of ejaculatory imminence and try to manoeuvre inside of it.

What takes place when the man enters into the zone of ejaculatory imminence? The testicles move closer to the body, the penis gets harder and the perineum muscles contract stronger. Some men experience quivers along the shaft of the penis or tingling at the tip of the urethra; others have the impression that their glans will explode. These signals indicate that excitement is very high and that a slight surplus of stimulation will be enough to reach the ejaculatory reflex threshold.

Important note

Danger zone

We can compare the zone of ejaculatory imminence to ground on which it is dangerous to venture. It's a bit like the red zone on the rev counter of a sports car. The speed is intoxicating, but when the rev counter needle goes into the red zone and the engine overheats, the risk of failure is imminent. Or also like the sirens' song. It seduces the sailor . . . and leads him onto the reefs where his ship will run aground. The same holds true for the peaks of sexual pleasure the man experiences in the zone of ejaculatory imminence. They are exquisite . . . and make him ejaculate the very next instant.

Zone 4, the zone of ejaculation, consists of two phases: the emission phase and the expulsion phase. These two phases are reflex and take place successively. When sexual excitement becomes sufficiently intense, it triggers the emission reflex. This reflex manifests itself through involuntary spasms in the accessory reproductive organs. To begin with, the afferent vessels of the testicles contract. These contractions then spread out to the epididymis, the vas deferens, the seminal vesicles and the prostate. The different components secreted by these organs form the seminal fluid that accumulates in the prostatic urethra. At that very moment, the urethral bulb expands to double or triple in size.

On a subjective level, men perceive a rush of sensations during the emission reflex, which they describe in this way in popular speech: "I'm about to come", "I feel it", "I'm coming". There is not anything apparent (the semen has not yet been expelled from the penis), but they know that ejaculation has been triggered. They experience what is called the feeling of ejaculatory inevitability. This feeling is justified because, once provoked, the contractions of these ducts and glands cannot be stopped. They are reflexes and consequently independent of the will.

Sexologists call the moment when the man attains the level of excitement (threshold) that triggers the emission reflex "the point of no return". This very eloquent expression signifies that the man can no longer return to lower excitement levels, neither avoid ejaculation nor continue intercourse. Excitement is too high, the reflex threshold of emission has been reached, ejaculation begins to take place and its unfolding continues until the end, no matter what the man attempts to do.

Once the prostatic urethra is distended enough by the accumulation of seminal fluid, the expulsion phase begins. A series of spasmodic contractions occur involving the urethral bulb and the pelvic floor muscles. The seminal fluid is then propelled from the prostatic urethra into the penile urethra and then outside of the urinary meatus. Just like the contractions of the emission phase, those of the expulsion phase are reflex and cannot be governed by will. These contractions allow for the discharge of physiological and sexual emotional tensions and constitute an immense source of pleasure for the majority of men.

We find in most articles published in sexological and medical reviews the affirmation that premature ejaculation (the difficulty with prolonging intercourse) is caused by a lack of control over the ejaculatory reflex. This conception is contradictory because a reflex, by definition, cannot be the object of voluntary control. Moreover, the anatomical structures that contract during the first reflex (emission reflex) are tubes (epididymis . . .) and glands (prostate . . .) over which the man cannot under any circumstance exercise voluntary control. And once the emission reflex occurs, the expulsion reflex is programmed to unfold and, consequently, the erection will disappear and intercourse will be impossible to continue. Irrespective of the means used, ejaculation cannot be stopped once it is released.

In fact, the difficulty with prolonging the length of intercourse is not due to an ejaculation problem. It is engendered by poor management of sexual excitement. Ejaculation is not at fault; rather it is excitement or, more precisely, its regulation. Ejaculation is absolutely normal; its physiology is healthy and its processes occur naturally. The problem is caused by the excitement that – when ill-managed – reaches the release threshold of the emission reflex and leads to ejaculation earlier than the individuals involved desire. This reality applies to all men, whether they are said to be "normal" or "premature ejaculators". No person has control over their ejaculation, only over their excitement. If a man wishes to prolong the length of intercourse, he must keep his excitement under the degree of excitement that triggers the emission reflex. And this remains the case, during his entire lifetime, in all circumstances and with all partners.

Because it is impossible to put a stop to either one of these two reflexes, it is pointless for a man to try to suppress ejaculation by squeezing his thighs, contracting his buttocks, sucking in his stomach, pinching his penis or pulling on his testicles. The strategy to apply when he reaches the point of no return and his ejaculation is triggered thus becomes very simple: to just let go and enjoy the moment to its fullest, even if it occurs much sooner than desired. He will act differently the next time. But for now, it is best that he enjoys it rather than get angry and end up ruining the mood he created with his partner. Besides, many women report that they deplore their spouse's unpleasant attitude towards the brevity of intercourse far more than the brevity of intercourse itself.

The only strategy a man has to delay the moment of arrival of ejaculation is to proceed at a level of sexual excitement inferior to that which activates the ejaculatory reflex. In other words, he just has to remain below the point of no return, preferably in the zone of modulation of sexual excitement, in order to prolong the length of intercourse.

In summary, the programme you are following is based on the following premises:

1 Ejaculation is a reflex which, as such, cannot be voluntarily controlled.
2 The reflex of ejaculation is triggered by sexual excitement when it reaches a sufficient intensity.
3 The reflex of ejaculation cannot occur when excitement is kept at a level of excitement below that which triggers the ejaculatory reflex.

4 The course of excitement can be managed.
5 As ejaculation cannot be controlled, but its cause – sexual excitement – can be, it is essential to manage the course of excitement to prolong the length of intercourse.
6 To properly manage excitement, it is in the first place important to recognize the bodily reactions that take place inside each zone of the sexual excitement curve.
7 Secondly – according to the bodily reactions observed – techniques and strategies that have the power to modulate sexual excitement must be applied.

Exercises

Exercise 1. Identifying the breathing process in a state of relaxation with the help of hands

Objective: to identify how you breathe when you are relaxed in order to be able to use this type of breathing during sexual relations.

We have seen that sexual excitement causes muscular tension. This muscular tension supports the rise of sexual excitement and the arrival of ejaculation. The abdominals and the intercostals are among the muscles that tighten up when a person becomes excited. In a state of relaxation, the abdominal muscles are relaxed and inhalation swells the stomach outward, on the sides and very slightly towards the back. When a person becomes excited, the abdominal muscles contract and the stomach moves a lot less under the effect of inhalation. The intercostal muscles work harder and breathing becomes more thoracic. This is a normal reaction within the excitatory process leading to ejaculation.

In order for a man to better manage the course of his sexual excitement, he must reverse these reactions and return to abdominal breathing. To achieve this objective, you must identify what is taking place in the area of your rib cage and abdomen when you are relaxed. The following exercise will help you to do this.

Sit comfortably in a chair or an armchair. Place your back right up against the back of the chair. Place your feet flat on the floor and spread shoulder width apart. If you are wearing tight pants, loosen them. It is important that the stomach is completely unrestricted to do this exercise. Place one hand on your chest and the other one on your stomach. In this position, you will be able to identify how you breathe when you're relaxed.

a Become relaxed.
b While you breathe calmly, try to feel where your breathing is located. (10 respirations)

(continued)

(continued)

c Notice the movement of your chest when you inhale. (10 respirations)

d Observe what is taking place in your chest area when you exhale. (10 respirations)

**

e Now move on to your stomach.

f Does it move when you breathe? (10 respirations)

g Try to feel what is taking place when you inhale. Does your stomach push your hand outward? (10 respirations)

h When you exhale, what happens? Do your stomach and hand come back down? (10 respirations)

Where was your breathing located during the exercise you just completed? Some of you might have noted that it took place mainly in the chest. Others probably observed that it happened equally in the chest and in the stomach. Finally, several of you would have remarked that it principally occurred into the stomach. Breathing changes locations and speed depending on the activity you do, the emotions you feel or the degree of sexual excitement you experience. However, when you are well relaxed, it is located a little in the chest and a lot in the stomach (Figures 3.2 and 3.3).

If you did not breathe from your abdomen (that is to say if you did not inflate your stomach like a balloon upon inhalation), try the following approach. Relax your abdominal muscles and concentrate on the border between your lungs and stomach, there where your diaphragm is located. Relax this region, from front to rear. Next, sense the movement of your breathing in this location. Little by little, let your breath descend into your stomach, right to your pubic bone. Feel your stomach inflate a little more each time you inhale and deflate each time you exhale. One trick is to imagine that the air enters through the mouth and descends deep down to the bottom of your stomach, right until your pelvic floor (or perineum or crotch area). Of course, this is only an image. The air does not descend beyond the lungs. It is only a matter of the diaphragm contracting and pressing down on the internal organs, which causes the stomach to expend. You will notice that as you progress, the upper part of your chest will get less involved and the lower part of your stomach will move more.

Exercise 2. Identifying the breathing process in a state of relaxation without the help of hands

Objective: to enhance your awareness of what is taking place at the level of your chest and stomach during relaxed breathing.

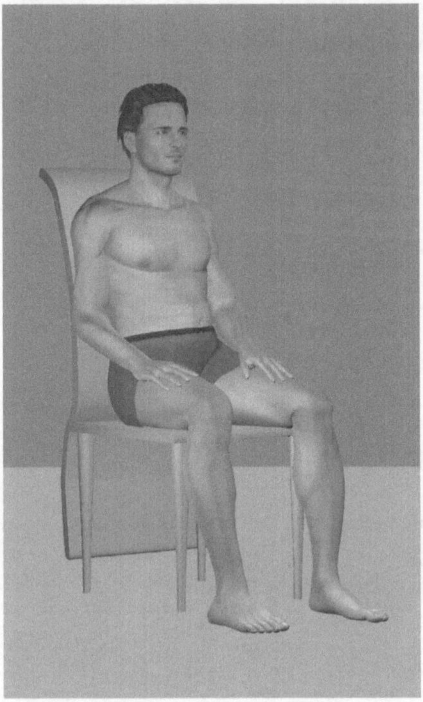

Figure 3.2 Abdominal breathing (inhalation)

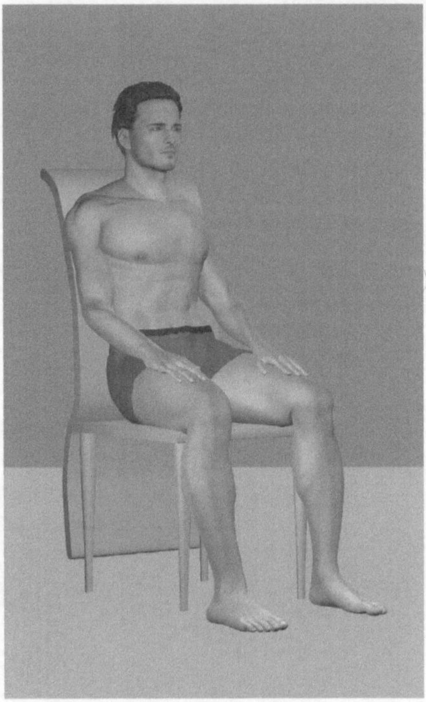

Figure 3.3 Abdominal breathing (exhalation)

The next exercise is the same as the previous one except that you place your hands on your thighs or on the arms of the chair instead of your stomach. It is a bit more difficult to feel your stomach without the help of your hands. This explains why you began with the previous exercise. You will now receive additional information about breathing. Your programme, as you can see yourself, is progressive.

Sit comfortably in a chair. Place your feet flat on the floor shoulder width apart. Rest your hands on your thighs or the arms of the chair.

a Inhale. Observe the movement of your chest. (Figure 3.2)
  Does it rise slightly upward and towards the back?
b Exhale. Pay attention to your chest. (Figure 3.3)
  Does it incline gently downward and towards the front?
  Let the air flow out by itself, without forcing your exhalation.

(continued)

(continued)

The exhalation will stop itself and will produce a short pause before the next inhalation.
Take advantage of this short pause to become even more relaxed.

(15 repetitions)

**

a Inhale. Observe the movement of your stomach. (Figure 3.2)
Does it expand outward?
Does it expand to the sides?
Does the air fill up the entire pelvic cavity?
Does the air go right to your pelvic floor?

b Exhale. Pay attention to your stomach. (Figure 3.3)
Does it deflate and move downward?
Let the air flow out on its own, without forcing your exhalation.
Exhalation stops by itself and produces a short pause before the next inhalation.
Take advantage of this short pause to make yourself more relaxed.

(15 repetitions)

**

a Inhale.
b Exhale and your stomach relaxes.
c Inhale.
d Exhale and your chest relaxes.
e Inhale.
f Exhale and your shoulders relax.
g Inhale.
h Exhale and your neck relaxes.
i Inhale.
j Exhale and your lips relax.
k Inhale.
l Exhale and your tongue relaxes.
m Inhale.
n Exhale and your entire body relaxes.

(5 repetitions)

After these two exercises, you should be well relaxed. You might be asking yourself therefore what the difference is between this programme and a relaxation course. The answer is very simple. A relaxation course shows you how to relax in a stationary position. This programme teaches you to manage your tension when you're moving sexually. This training is done in two steps. First, you learn how to relax while motionless – like in a relaxation course – because it is easier. Next, you grasp how to move sexually without generating unnecessary tension. This distinction is of fundamental importance because during sexual relations you are not immobile but active. You move and this is when you have to be able to control the degree of tension in your muscles. It is a very different approach to traditional relaxation even if the first two exercises you just did are identical. Consider this example. If a person wants to learn how to swim, sculpt or drive a car, he/she does not enrol in a relaxation course. That person takes a swimming, sculpting or driving course. The same goes for sexuality. There are specific skills to acquire and this programme is designed to teach you them. In sports an eloquent expression is used: "You get what you train for". If you ride a bike and accumulate miles, you will become a better cyclist. But you will not turn into a better gymnast or a better archer. The same principle applies to the sexual sphere. At the present time, you want to learn how to make love better, not how to relax better. And that's why this programme was developed.

Exercise 3. Reversal of the breathing process when in a state of excitement (slow speed)

Objective: to perceive the phenomena which take place in your breathing when you are sexually excited.

First part: Technique

This technique is associated with others that you will come across throughout the programme. It will help you to decrease your muscular tension, modulate your sexual excitement and delay the arrival of your ejaculation.

Sitting comfortably in a chair, place your hands on the armrest or on your thighs. Place your feet flat on the floor spread shoulder distance apart.

- a Pull in your stomach, that is to say, contract your abdominal muscles, and keep them pulled in.
- b Breathe from the rib cage. (Figure 3.4)
- c While continuing to breathe in this way, feel the tension in your abdominal muscles.
  Become fully aware that your stomach is pulled in.
  Realize that your breathing is occurring at the level of the chest.
  (three respirations)
- d Now, relax your abdominal muscles and return to abdominal breathing.
- e When you inhale, let your stomach inflate like a balloon. (Figure 3.2)
- f When the air comes out, let your stomach relax. (Figure 3.3)
- g During the pause between inhalation and exhalation, you let your stomach and chest relax even more.
  (three respirations)

Repeat this exercise three times.

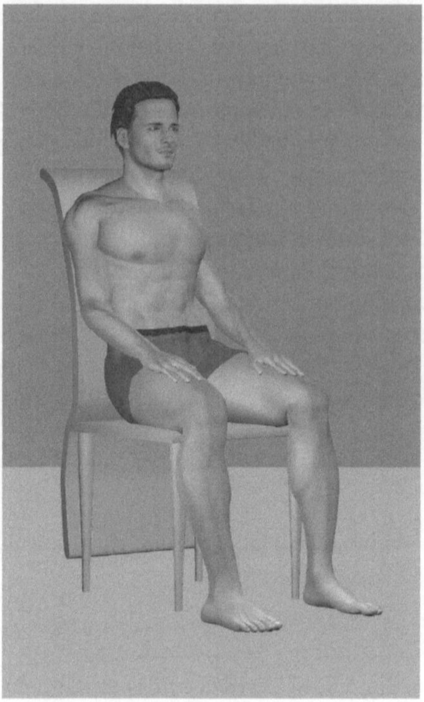

Figure 3.4 Thoracic breathing

Second part: Simulation exercise

Repeat the previous exercise, but this time imagine that you are involved in a sexual relationship.

> Sit comfortably in a chair. Place your feet flat on the floor shoulder width apart. Rest your hands on the armrests or on your thighs.
>
> a Pull in your stomach.
> b Breathe only from your chest.
> c Now, imagine that you are engaged in a sexual encounter and that you are at the foreplay stage.
> In this situation it would be important to make the following verification:
> You would ask yourself these questions: "Is my stomach pulled in? Am I only breathing from my chest?
> Yes, this is normal. This reaction is caused by sexual excitement.

Can I reverse this process?
Can I breathe again from the stomach in order to reduce my sexual excitement and stay away from ejaculation?"
(three respirations)

d You would relax your stomach and chest muscles.
Relax them now.
e Allow your stomach to expand when you inhale.
f Relax your stomach and chest when you exhale.
g During the pause between exhalation and inhalation, further relax your stomach and chest.
(three respirations)

**

a Pull in your stomach a second time.
b Breathe only from the chest.
c Imagine that you are beginning intercourse.
You would therefore tell yourself: "I'm going to verify the following:
Is my stomach pulled in?
Am I only breathing from my chest?
Yes, this is normal. This reaction is caused by sexual excitement.
Could I reverse this process?
Could I begin to breathe from the stomach in order to decrease my excitement and stay away from ejaculation?"
(three respirations)

d You would relax the muscles in your stomach and chest.
Relax them now.
e Allow your stomach to inflate when you breathe in.
f Relax your stomach and chest when you breathe out.
g During the pause between expiration and inspiration, further relax your stomach and chest.
(three respirations)

**

a For the last time, pull in your stomach.
b Breathe only from the chest.
c Imagine that you are having intercourse.
You would therefore ask yourself: "Is my stomach pulled in?
Am I breathing only from my chest?
Yes, this is normal. This reaction is caused by sexual excitement.

(continued)

(continued)

Could I reverse this process?
Could I begin to breathe abdominally in order to decrease my excitement and stay away from ejaculation?"
(three respirations)

d You would relax the muscles in your stomach and chest.
You relax them now.
e You let your stomach expand when you inhale.
f You relax your stomach and chest when you exhale.
g During the pause between expiration and inspiration, you further relax your stomach and chest.
(three respirations)

The exercise you have just completed simulates the bodily reactions that take place during sexual activities. As previously seen, when a man becomes sexually excited, his abdominal muscles contract and his breathing becomes more thoracic. You have learnt how to reverse, by mimicking, the breathing process that occurs naturally when you are sexually excited. Within the realm of sexuality, you do not have to voluntarily contract these muscles. These contractions will occur by themselves under the influence of excitement. You only need to relax them. This training, combined with the integration of specific movements which you will come across over the course of the next sessions, will give you better control over the rise of your excitement. It will allow you to prolong the length of intercourse and to enjoy a more gratifying sexual experience.

Exercises for the week

a) Exercises without sexual excitement

The following exercises must be done three times during the week. The number of repetitions is indicated in the description of each exercise. All of the exercises should be performed slowly in a calm atmosphere conducive to concentration.

Exercise 1. Identifying the breathing process in a state of relaxation with the help of hands.
This exercise is described in this session.

Exercise 2. Identifying the breathing process in a state of relaxation without the help of hands.
This exercise is described in this session.

Exercise 3. Reversal of the respiratory process when in a state of excitement (slow speed).
First part: Technique
Second part: Simulation exercise
These exercises are described in this session.

b) Exercises with sexual excitement

This week, your training will be to identify the reactions that occur in your body when you enter the zone of ejaculatory imminence and that of the emission reflex (point of no return). It is the perception of these sensations that will enable you to adequately manage your excitement. It is better at the start to do this exploration on your own. Set aside a tranquil half-hour and find yourself a quiet place where you can experiment without being disturbed. Stimulate yourself slowly until ejaculation and observe what happens in your body.

The first times, as the rhythm is likely to be fast, you will only be able to identify these sensations in retrospect. The zone of ejaculatory imminence begins with sensations that develop primarily in the genitals and perineum. These may be quivers along the shaft of the penis, a tightening in the perineum region, the feeling that the penis is reaching its maximum size, tickling sensations at the tip of the urethra or even the impression that the glans will explode. This zone ends a few moments later as the first contractions occur in the emission phase. The emission phase is characterized by the involuntary contraction of ducts and glands (epididymis, vas deferens, prostate, seminal vesicles). Men describe the subjective impressions they experience during this phase in the following manner: "I'm coming!", "I'm about to come!" In fact, these contractions are reflexes. The ejaculatory process has started and nothing can stop it.

Next time, stimulate yourself more slowly so that you become aware of the different phases one after the other. As soon as you perceive the sensations that indicate that you have reached the zone of ejaculatory imminence, cease all stimulation. Do not move and let your sexual excitement descend right down to the zone of the appearance and disappearance of the erection. In other words, let your erection subside a little bit. At that moment, you would have succeeded in modulating your sexual excitement and avoiding the point of no return. Congratulations! This is only the beginning, this is true, but you did it! Practise this exercise three times. The last time, continue until ejaculation. On each occasion, pay attention to all the sensations of your body in order to get to know yourself better. You can see in Figure 3.5 the course your excitement will take during this exercise.

There are two reasons why it is better for you to let your excitement drop to zone 1. First of all, it is very important that you diminish it sufficiently. Many men only make a brief stop. Their excitement has barely descended when they resume the movements of penetration with great intensity. Under these conditions, it is futile to hope to prolong the sexual act. In fact, you should know that it is very difficult to perform at high levels of excitement without quickly reaching ejaculation. Secondly, it is essential for you to realize that a decrease in erection is not so dramatic and that your penis will become hard again naturally when you pay attention to sexual stimuli that you like. Once you get used to managing an unexpected entry into zone 3, you will be able to make shorter stops and you will not have to let your excitement drop as low. But still here, after crossing into the zone of ejaculatory imminence, it will always be necessary for you to give yourself some respite.

As for masturbation, the best way to proceed is to hold unto the penis with one hand and to carry out back-and-forth movements along it, in the same manner as what takes place during intercourse. Do not try to achieve ejaculation by applying pressure to the penis, whether it is by hand or by use of an object (cushion, pillow, mattress), or by strongly contracting the buttock muscles. Stimulating yourself with the help of gentle friction (rubbing, stroking, fondling) will place you in conditions similar to those of intercourse. This way of acting ensures the best transition between self-stimulation and coitus.

Make sure you practise the exercise just described above two or three times alone, and then execute it with your partner. The stimulation could be given manually or orally. You follow the same procedure. She stimulates you and you pay attention to your bodily reactions. The first time, you let yourself go until ejaculation. The following times, you stop all stimulation as soon as you perceive the sensations that indicate you're entering the zone of ejaculatory imminence. You tell your partner that she's exciting you a lot and that you must stop in order to make the pleasure last longer. You allow your excitement to decrease until the zone of the appearance and disappearance of the erection. If your erection fades away this is a good sign. It means that you're applying this strategy correctly. You have succeeded in lowering your excitement.

The following information on the physiology of the erection will help you feel more confident. The erection of the penis consists of two phenomena: an increase in size (length and volume) and an increase in rigidity. The increase in size is caused by an influx of blood into the penis (vasocongestion). As for rigidity, it is ensured by the

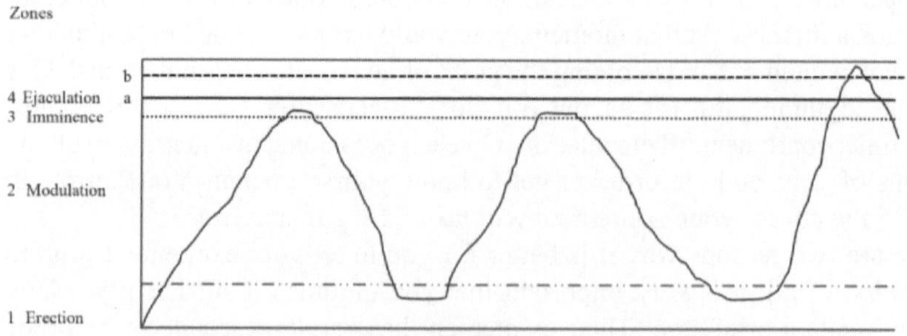

Figure 3.5 An example of the sexual excitement curve that may result from the exercise of identifying bodily sensations in zones 3 and 4

Zone 1: The appearance and disappearance of the erection zone. Zone 2: The modulation of sexual excitement zone. Zone 3: The ejaculatory imminence zone. Zone 4: The ejaculation zone (a: the emission reflex or point of no return; b: the expulsion reflex).

contraction of the muscles of the perineum. When you stop and relax, it is very likely that you will feel as if your erection has diminished by half. In fact, it only decreases by about five per cent. But since you also relax the muscles of the perineum, the firmness lessens a little. This slight reduction in rigidity curiously enough gives the impression that it produces a significant loss of erection. In reality, this is not the case. You can see this yourself by looking at your penis at this moment. You will realize then that this small diminution of rigidity is not great enough to affect your partner.

The next step consists of perceiving the sensations indicative of ejaculatory imminence and the point of no return during intercourse. Things will still unfold too quickly, but what's important at this stage is to observe and learn. It is preferable to assume the position where then man is lying down on his back and to let your partner carry out the back-and-forth movements. Do just one thing: observe the sensations of your body and particularly those of your penis and your perineum.

Becoming aware of your bodily reactions is essential. Knowledge of what is happening inside you will dictate how to behave and will allow you to manage your excitement well.

Suggestions for the single man

During the exercises with sexual excitement, you apply exactly the same techniques and the same strategies as the men who have a spouse, except that you resort to masturbation and use sexual fantasies. You will obtain the same results by using autoeroticism and by imagining the stimulation that a partner would provide. You invent sex scenarios in which you interact with a woman and at the same time follow these programme instructions.

Suggestions for the woman

The woman can help the man manage his sexual excitement. She can apply very simple strategies that will contribute to maintaining his excitement below the point of no return. Over the course of the next sessions, you will receive a wealth of information to help you achieve this objective. These are proven strategies and have been successfully taught to a large number of women.

This programme is built around the fact that the man cannot stop ejaculation from occurring once it is triggered. It is a reflex process and as such cannot be subject to voluntary control. This reality – which imposes a limitation on the couple's sexual expression – can however be circumvented insofar as the man and woman take this into account during their lovemaking. By making compromises in relation to their own sexual aspirations and engaging in sexual activity in a sensual manner, they could journey together longer.

Suggestions for the couple

You've decided to team up and take part in this programme together. Congratulations, it is a laudable undertaking! By defining common goals and working together to achieve them, you will strengthen the ties that bind you.

Addressing the subject of sexuality with one's spouse is not always easy. This often requires courage and humility. Sexuality has been and always will be an intimate subject. Talking about it means opening yourself up and exposing your vulnerabilities. But at the same time, it is about growing and evolving both on a personal and relationship level.

Working as a team is about sharing a state of mind and a way of behaving. It is thinking as "one" while taking into consideration each other's characteristics. This requires putting aside your frustrations, which is not necessarily easy, and looking ahead.

Working together avoids isolation and generates a creative energy. The participation of each of you will prove an asset for increasing the length of intercourse. You could apply by common consent new strategies and reflect together on the effects that they produce. On the other hand it is important that neither of you takes on a superior or dominant position, by becoming the other's therapist, for example.

It will be beneficial therefore that at each session the two of you discuss the contents of the sections *Sexual information* and *Suggestions for the couple*.

This week, you could discuss the nature of your involvement as an individual and as a couple in this programme. Obviously you will not be doing everything together. There are sections – such as the technical exercises – which do not require the collaboration of both spouses. However, everything related to communications, the development of sensuality and the application of new ways of making love, is facilitated by the participation of both partners.

Application of the instructions in this book will bring about profound changes in your sex life and your conjugal relationship. It is a step in your life as a couple and dealing with it together will only enrich your relationship.

SECOND SESSION

Sexual information

Sexual acclimatization

We can consider foreplay as the base of lovemaking. In the same way as the foundation supports the structure of a building, foreplay provides the framework for sexual relations and helps to lengthen the duration of intercourse. A lot of men imagine that by cutting short foreplay, they will be able to last longer inside the vagina. In reality, the exact opposite can occur. If you shorten sex play, you risk reducing your chances of prolonging sexual intercourse. Why? Because your body has not acclimatized to sexual excitement.

Sexual acclimatization is a concept developed by De Sutter (2001). According to this researcher, human beings possess a prodigious capacity for adaptation. They adjust to great polar cold as well as extreme desert heat. Humans can survive with practically no food, hardly any water and with little sleep. They even end up withstanding pain. Conversely, they quickly get used to comfort and end up losing a big part of their endurance if their living conditions become too easy. This incredible capability for acclimatization also enables a man to become accustomed to sexual excitement.

This is in fact something that can be observed by any man watching a film with sexual content. During the first few minutes, an ordinary undressing scene excites him enormously. After an hour of watching, even the most sexually explicit scenes barely have any effect on him. The man has become habituated to, acclimatized to sexual stimuli. The same is true during sexual activity with his partner. The more he receives stimuli (if this is done in a progressive manner) during foreplay, the more he increases his capacity for acclimatization.

The majority of men who ejaculate quickly avoid being touched by their partner during foreplay. They fear becoming too excited and ejaculating prematurely. Erotic games are one-sided. They stimulate their partner and when she is ready, they proceed to intercourse. They shun all stimulation, be it caresses, bodily contact or fondling of the penis. To become even less excited, they try to think about something else or look elsewhere. They hope that by doing this they will last longer. Unfortunately, this behaviour produces the very opposite outcome. When it is time for intercourse, they are not sufficiently acclimatized to sexual excitement. The sensations related to intercourse are so intense that they are quickly overwhelmed. Furthermore, not having experimented with high levels of excitement, they do not know how to handle this situation. So they ejaculate rapidly.

From now on, it is suggested that you spend 20 to 30 minutes on foreplay. This will allow you to acclimatize physically and emotionally to sexual stimuli. You will have time to observe the effects sexual excitement have on your body. You will be able to test, at your own pace, the effect the techniques have on the rise of your sexual excitement. Finally, you will obtain sufficient stimulation and practice time to familiarize yourself with managing high levels of sexual excitement in conditions less difficult than those of intercourse.

Important note

The woman's pleasure

Among the reasons cited by women to explain their difficulty in reaching orgasm during intercourse, there are fatigue, the preoccupations of everyday life, marital conflict, lack of affection, alcohol abuse, disinterest towards their partner, the desire to perform well, lack of vaginal lubrication, rapid ejaculation and . . . inadequate foreplay (Darling et al., 1991).

Figure 3.6 illustrates foreplay where the man acclimatized to sexual stimulation and has managed high levels of excitement.

It can be seen that the man experienced various degrees of excitement. He even verged on the zone of ejaculatory imminence. But, and this is a key point, he succeeded in diminishing his excitement level during foreplay. And how did he do it? It is quite simple. All it took was for him to cease direct stimulation to the penis, relax his muscles (you will see more precisely which ones in the coming sessions) and breathe from the stomach.

You will not always want to extend foreplay. Sometimes, you will move ahead with great impatience. And, true, it is pleasurable to make love passionately and in the heat of the moment. However, this manner of proceeding will not help you acquire the means for prolonging intercourse. It would be beneficial in the beginning to follow the instructions to the letter and take the time to engage in foreplay for more than 20 minutes. This will allow you to verify the effects of sexual acclimatization. These effects occur, among other things, through an increase in tolerance to stimulation. In other words, after a while, your body adjusts to excitement

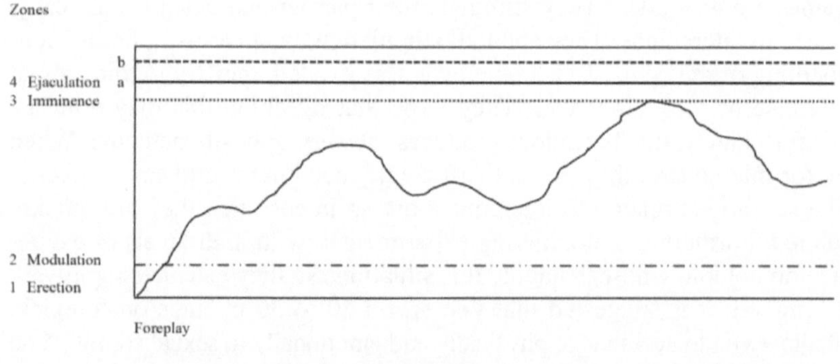

Figure 3.6 An example of a sexual excitement curve where the man acclimatized to sexual stimulation during foreplay

Zone 1: The appearance and disappearance of the erection zone. Zone 2: The modulation of sexual excitement zone. Zone 3: The ejaculatory imminence zone. Zone 4: The ejaculation zone (a: the emission reflex or point of no return; b: the expulsion reflex).

and you need more stimulation for the ejaculation reflex to be triggered. Some men report that, beyond 15 minutes of intercourse, they experience difficulty ejaculating! Does this mean that a temporary rise in the point of no return occurs (ejaculatory reflex threshold)? This hypothesis is plausible, but research in neurobiology has not yet answered this question. However, from a subjective standpoint, that is the impression given.

Moreover, it is possible that you already practise lengthy foreplay but still have not been able to prolong the length of intercourse. It is normal for this to happen if it is the only strategy you have applied. As a matter of fact, you must become proficient at several methods in order to be able to last longer. In addition, the acclimatization process is neither mechanical nor automatic. Some days, no matter what you do, you will feel that your threshold is low and that just about anything could trigger your ejaculation. Other days, on the contrary, everything will seem easy for you. The idea is to stack the odds in your favour and have a varied repertoire of techniques and strategies.

A pause at the beginning of intercourse

The intromission of the penis into the vagina is an intense moment of the sexual act. Just as you did during foreplay, you must acclimatize to the sensations it brings about and the symbolism that accompanies it. Unfortunately, a large number of men have developed the habit of executing in-and-out movements from the start of intercourse. This practice, although it is extremely enjoyable, is risky. Intromission is in itself already a particularly exciting activity for the man and woman. Adding another source of excitement by moving right from the start quickly causes ejaculation in many men.

As indicated in the graph below, the man's excitement heightens at the moment of intromission of the penis in the vagina. If there's additional stimulation caused by the pelvic thrusts of either the man or woman, the point of no return is quickly reached (Figure 3.7). On the other hand, if the couple makes a pause at the beginning of intercourse, it provides an additional means to prevent the man's excitement from getting too high. The man can expect to see his excitement increase even if he makes a pause (because of the vaginal stimulation) and then decrease (because both the man and woman are not moving) rather than progress towards the ejaculatory reflex (Figure 3.8).

To avoid losing control over the rise of your excitement, it is wiser for you to make a pause at the start of coitus. You do not even have to insert your penis completely inside the woman's vagina. You can proceed in stages and acclimatize to each of them, a bit like a mountain climber who ascends in increments to get used to the rarefaction of oxygen. You place your penis at the opening of the vagina and you stop. You breathe and relax your muscles. You perceive the sensations and savour this new intimacy with your partner. Is she yearning for more? So much the better! She will fully appreciate what she has desired so much. You penetrate her half an inch and once again stop. It becomes an erotic game.

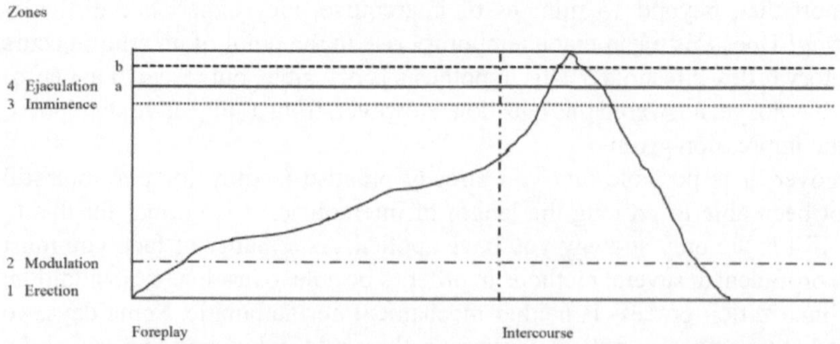

Figure 3.7 An example of a sexual excitement curve where the man progresses towards the zone of ejaculation due to continuous pelvic thrusts at the beginning of intercourse

Zone 1: The appearance and disappearance of the erection zone. Zone 2: The modulation of sexual excitement zone. Zone 3: The ejaculatory imminence zone. Zone 4: The ejaculation zone (a: the emission reflex or point of no return; b: the expulsion reflex).

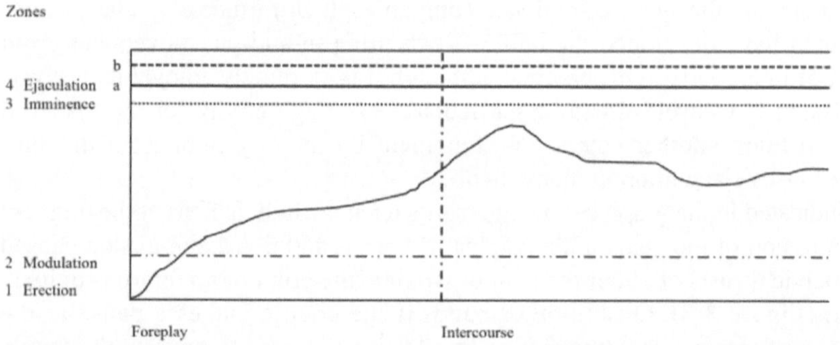

Figure 3.8 An example of a sexual excitement curve diminishing in intensity following a pause immediately after the intromission of the penis in the vagina

Zone 1: The appearance and disappearance of the erection zone. Zone 2: The modulation of sexual excitement zone. Zone 3: The ejaculatory imminence zone. Zone 4: The ejaculation zone (a: the emission reflex or point of no return; b: the expulsion reflex).

How long should your partner and you stay motionless? The time needed for your excitement to drop close to the zone of the appearance and disappearance of the erection. It may take more than a minute at first. When you feel your excitement stabilize, you begin to move slowly. If your excitement climbs too quickly, make another pause. You will be able to see in detail, in the fifth session, what can be done during these breaks.

When you master all of the techniques and have more experience, you can play around a bit more with the length of the pause. But the beginning of intercourse will always remain a particularly rich moment full of sensations and symbols to which you will have to acclimatize in order to prolong sexual intercourse.

Important note

Love is an art

Just like music or painting, love is an art that requires the fusion of three elements: talent, technique and experience. This programme contains the most advanced and most refined techniques that exist at the present time. However, talent and simply reading this manual are not enough to improve your sex life and make it more interesting. It is essential that you practise the exercises and apply the suggestions proposed in this programme. After much trial and error, sometimes comical, sometimes pathetic, but never dramatic, you will discover a whole new world of sensuality and pleasure. You will learn to put your new know-how to work with your talent and you will succeed in becoming the wonderful lover you always dreamed of being.

Exercises

The same exercises must be performed over several sessions to ensure their integration. Their repetition is part of the learning process; they help to acquire ease and to establish the necessary bases for the acquisition of more complex skills. You will therefore practice the exercises from the first session again. Afterwards, you will be able to learn new techniques that will interconnect with one another right up until the end of the programme.

Exercise 2. Identification of the breathing process in a state of relaxation without the help of hands

This exercise is described in the first session.

Exercise 3. Reversal of the breathing process when in a state of excitement (slow speed)

First part: Technique

This exercise is described in the first session.

Second part: Simulation exercise

This exercise is described in the first session.

Exercise 4. Reversal of the breathing process when in a state of excitement (fast speed)

Objective: to move quickly from thoracic breathing to abdominal breathing

The exercise of the reversal of the breathing process when in a state of excitement was performed at slow speed to make it easier for you to learn. However, during sexual relations, a man must react faster; if not ejaculation will occur long before he has had the time to apply the entire technique. Exercise 4 is, therefore, the same as exercise 3, except that you reverse your breathing more quickly.

Sit comfortably in a chair. Place your feet flat on the floor and spread shoulder width apart. Place your hands on the arms of the chair or on your thighs.

a Pull in your stomach and keep it pulled in.
b Breathe from the rib cage. (three respirations)
c Feel the tension in your stomach and your rib cage.
d Relax your stomach and your rib cage.
e With the next inhalation, let your stomach swell like a balloon.
f When the air comes out, relax your stomach, your rib cage and your whole body.
g During the interval between exhalation and inhalation, let your stomach and rib cage relax even more. (three respirations).

Repeat this exercise four times.

Exercise 5. Movement of the pelvis with support

Objective: to learn how to dissociate the movement of the pelvis

Most men who ejaculate rapidly move the trunk as a single unit. They do not dissociate the pelvis from the torso and make short and quick movements. This way of moving creates a great deal of muscle tension and promotes the arrival of ejaculation. To reduce the amount of muscle tension and delay ejaculation, it is important to move the pelvis in isolation, separately from the back. Moving the pelvis in such a way also gives the man the opportunity to harmonize with the woman's movements. This leaves her with greater freedom of movement, enabling her to further express herself with her pelvis and have more pleasure.

The following exercise is the best there is to learn how to mobilize the pelvis in isolation, which is to say independently of the back and thighs. This exercise is also called the cat exercise because it is reminiscent of a cat stretching and arching its back.

First part: Technique

For educational purposes aimed at facilitating learning, these exercises are called "movement of the pelvis forward" and "movement of the pelvis backward", but the correct anatomical terms are retroversion and anteversion of the pelvis.

Position yourself on the floor, resting on your hands and knees. Your arms and your thighs are perpendicular to the floor.

a Like a cat stretching, round out your back. (Figure 3.9)
b Like a cat hollowing its back, hollow your back while pushing out your buttocks. (Figure 3.10)

Repeat this exercise 30 times.

Figure 3.9 Movement of the pelvis forward with support

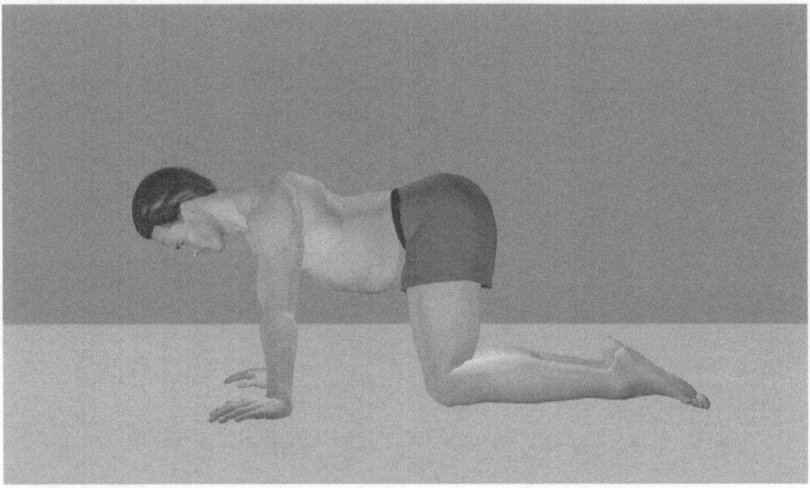

Figure 3.10 Movement of the pelvis backward with support

Ideally, it is best to do this exercise in front of a mirror aligning your body sideways. Be careful not to move forward (Figure 3.11, error 1) or move backward (Figure 3.12, error 2) when going up or down. The lower back and stomach are working, not the arms or legs. The arms do not bend at the elbows (Figure 3.13, error 3). Observe that the pelvis pivots as if carrying out a movement of penetration.

Second part: Breathing

This exercise is the same as the previous one except that another element has been added. This time, you will synchronize the movement of the pelvis with your

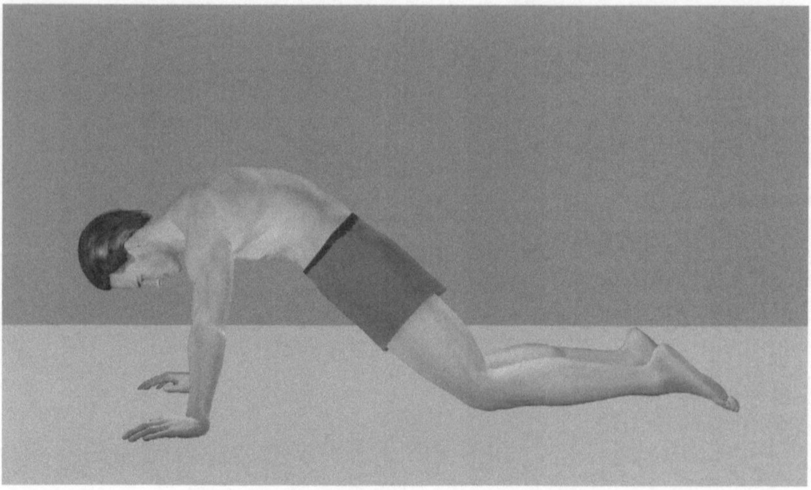

Figure 3.11 Movement of the pelvis with support (error 1)

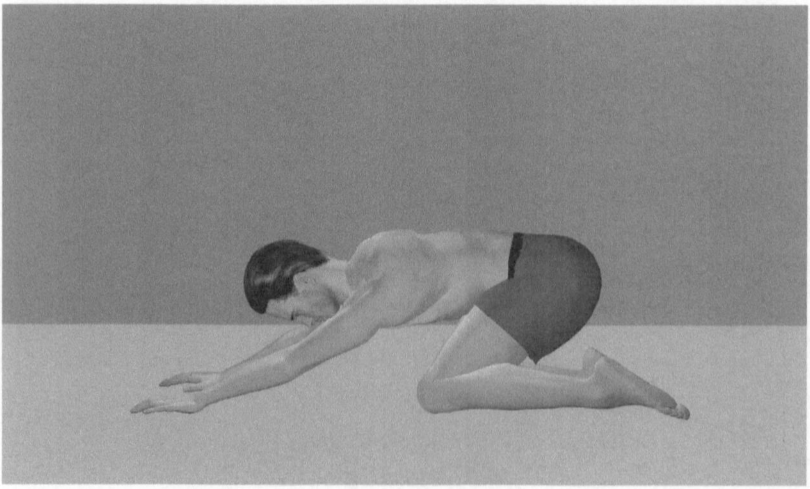

Figure 3.12 Movement of the pelvis with support (error 2)

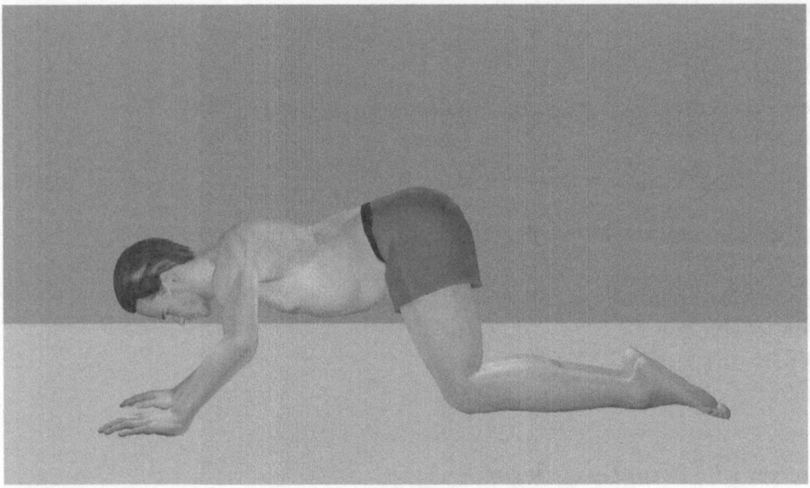

Figure 3.13 Movement of the pelvis with support (error 3)

breathing. To make it easier, imagine that you are blowing out a candle when you push your back up high. You can breathe audibly in order to be fully aware of what you are doing. During sexual relations, it is preferable however to be more discreet so as not to give the impression that you are practising an exercise.

Position yourself on the floor, resting on your hands and knees.

a When you exhale, round out your back. (Figure 3.9)
b When you inhale, lower your back. (Figure 3.10)

Repeat this exercise 30 times.

Exercises for the week

a) Exercises without sexual excitement

Practise the following exercises three times during the week. The number of repetitions for each exercise is indicated with the description of the exercise. To derive the maximum benefit from these exercises, you must do them slowly, in a calm and relaxing atmosphere.

Exercise 2. Identifying the breathing process in a state of relaxation without the help of hands
This exercise is described in the first session.

Exercise 3. Reversal of the breathing process when in a state of excitement (slow speed)
First part: Technique
Second part: Simulation exercise
These exercises are described in the first session.

Exercise 4. Reversal of the breathing process when in a state of excitement (fast speed)
This exercise is described in this session.

Exercise 5. Movement of the pelvis with support
First part: Technique
Second part: Breathing
These exercises are described in this session.

b) Exercises with sexual excitement

For your programme to be effective, you must apply the techniques you learn in the sessions during your sexual activities. What you could do this week, and which would be very beneficial to you, would be to observe what is taking place in your breathing during masturbatory activities or foreplay. Examine, when you are sexually excited, if your stomach is pulled in and if your breathing is thoracic. If this is the case, then try to reverse this process and return to abdominal breathing (at least five respirations). Take note of the effects this technique has on your excitement. It is not necessary to breathe continuously from the stomach during sexual relations. That being said, abdominal breathing will remain one of the best tools for managing your sexual excitement.

With regards to the pelvis, verify the way you move it during intercourse. It is, however, too soon to attempt to modify your current way of moving.

If you engage in lengthy foreplay, you have the opportunity to analyse your body's reactions and apply your techniques. You also benefit from the effect of acclimatization. You can start with a sensual massage which takes place alternately. One of you gives the caresses while the other receives them; then, you switch roles. This obviously does not take the form of a deep massage. This would be too relaxing and would put you to sleep. It is preferable to use massage oil when doing this exploration to avoid unpleasant friction to the skin. Begin with the non-sexual areas of the body (shoulders, nape of the neck, back) in order to end with the most erogenous zones. Take time to discover and enjoy all the sensations that can be prompted by caresses and an inviting atmosphere (candles, music, etc.). Intercourse is not necessary. If it occurs, however, you should expect ejaculation to come as quickly as usual. At this point, you do not have sufficient techniques to fully manage the course of your excitement. You're still at the observation and learning stage.

Suggestions for the single man

During the exercises with sexual excitement, stimulate yourself while paying close attention to the changes in your breathing. Next, promote sexual acclimatization by extending the duration of stimulation. You can use sexual fantasies during these activities.

Suggestions for the woman

Quite a few men avoid being touched during foreplay out of fear of becoming too excited. When intercourse begins, they are disconcerted by the large influx of stimuli and do not know how to manage the situation. Many women refrain from touching their partner for fear of exciting them too much. This is a good intention, but you must proceed differently. The woman has to caress the man on his body and sex organs in order for him to become accustomed to experiencing high levels of excitement and so that he learns to apply the techniques to manage his excitement.

Suggestions for the couple

It would be beneficial for the two of you to talk about the way you reacted to the difficulty with prolonging intercourse. Now that you know solutions exist and your sex life can be improved, you can envisage the future more serenely and take stock of what you've been through so far. This will make you feel better and help you break free from the isolation into which you are both locked, if this is the case.

The emotions felt by a man who is unable to prolong the length of intercourse for as long as desired range from slight frustration to total discouragement. He may be ashamed of himself, question his masculinity or be afraid to engage in sexual activities. As for the woman, if at the start she's understanding and even flattered at provoking such an intense reaction, she may, following multiple rapid performances by her partner, become irritated, feel like she is not being respected and lose interest in sex. If then she tends to avoid sexual intimacy, she runs the risk of feeling unloved, neglected or abandoned. It is possible that you became involved into acerbic discussions because of your sexual limitations; these conflicts may have extended to other areas of coupledom and the marital relationship as a whole could have deteriorated.

Responding to the following questions will help you to more easily identify the way you have reacted to your sexual difficulties. To the man: when you think of your own experience, do you feel anxious, incompetent, disappointed? Do you avoid participating in sexual activities in order not to endure "failure"? Do you act as if there is not a problem? Do you do all you can to ensure your partner has an orgasm to compensate for your sexual shortcomings? Do you cut short foreplay to prevent your ejaculation from occurring too quickly? Have you lost confidence in yourself?

And you, the woman, do you spurn the advances of your partner? Do you make derogatory remarks about him? Do you shorten sexual activities to avoid reliving a frustrating situation? Do you think your spouse is selfish and only thinks about his own pleasure? Do you feel like you do not mean a lot to him? Are you disappointed that he did not seek help to solve his problem?

Do you both argue all the time? Has your communication deteriorated? Do you still share moments of intimacy and tenderness? Do you feel uncomfortable in each other's presence? Has doubt come between you? Have you lost confidence in your spouse? Do you feel like your partner is rejecting you? Are you worried your relationship might be coming to an end?

When this sexual dissatisfaction is not addressed, it often results in negative consequences. You have reached the point where you must set aside all of the frustrations and avoidances and begin the healing process together. It is important that the woman expresses her dissatisfaction to her partner without blaming, insulting, ridiculing or threatening to leave him. It is essential that the man does not isolate himself and that he talks about his concerns and fears.

The objective of this session was to foster communication and reconciliation between the two of you with the intention of eliminating misunderstanding and negative feelings. In the third session, you will work on becoming more assertive so that you can share with your spouse your desires and aspirations for this programme.

THIRD SESSION

Sexual information

The frequency of ejaculatory discharges

We can compare a man's sexual appetite to his appetite for food. We know that in terms of the alimentary appetite, hunger grows as the hours pass. After a man has eaten enough, this appetite is curbed. This is also the case for the sexual appetite. With the passage of time, the sexual appetite increases. When ejaculatory discharge occurs, this appetite dissipates.

What happens if an individual does not consume food for a long period of time? In general, his appetite will increase. And when he sits down at the table, there's a good chance he will eat what's on his plate very quickly. We witness an identical phenomenon in terms of the sexual appetite. If a man remains abstinent for too long in relation to his need, it is likely that his sexual tension will amplify and that he will ejaculate prematurely the next time he has sexual intercourse. Whether with respect to his sexual or alimentary needs, his physiology – when it is deprived – has a forceful effect and propels him towards rapidity.

Although reality is more complex, this comparison is used to highlight the necessity for a man to maintain an ejaculatory frequency corresponding to the frequency of his sexual needs. It is essential that he respects this physiological fact. When his sexual appetite is regularized, it is easier for him to take his time, interact with his spouse, apply his techniques and manage his excitement.

What if the frequency of sexual desire is not the same for both spouses? Some suggest meeting halfway. For example, if the woman wants to make love twice a week and the man four times, each makes a compromise and the couple engages in sexual activity three times a week. The idea is interesting and, indeed, compromise fosters harmony within most areas of the couple's life. However, this approach finds its place with difficulty in the regulation of physiological needs in human beings. Let's return to the comparison with food. Imagine a couple where a man likes to have four meals a day and the woman two. Since they enjoy eating together and they want to please each other, they reach a compromise of three meals a day. Under these conditions, there's a high probability that the man remains hungry and the woman becomes turned off by food. The same reactions occur in the domain of sexuality. A man who does not respond to his sexual needs risks experiencing frustration and a woman who forces herself to make love more often than she desires has good chances of being unhappy. Some will suggest that eating whets the appetite. They will add that many women never initiate sex, but they get pleasure when their partner begins caressing them. This is true . . . up to a certain point. We must keep in mind that physiological needs only have limited extensibility.

To summarize, a man cannot continually deprive himself and be satisfied; a woman cannot force herself to make love over the long haul more often than she desires and feel good. The best solution therefore is for the couple to adjust to the sexual rhythm of the spouse who has less desire. If it is twice a week for one and four times for the other, the ideal frequency for the couple is twice a week. This way, the one who has the lesser need will actually desire to participate in sexual relations. In turn, the individual with the greater sexual appetite may resort to autoeroticism to satisfy his/her needs. This simple solution, however, does not appeal to everyone. Some men question, for example, the point of being married if they have to stimulate themselves. Many women assume that their husband either does not love them or no longer finds them desirable if he engages in a sexual activity alone. There is not an ideal response to these reactions. However, it is much easier for men to accept this option if they establish a clear distinction between their sexual needs (for example, their need to ejaculate) and their desire to participate in a romantic encounter (where they seduce their partner, attend to their needs and make sure to give them pleasure). In fact, it is like the appetite towards food. Appeasing one's hunger does not rank on the same level as a gastronomic feast where one prepares a nice meal with a fancy tablecloth, candles, cutlery and ambient music. As for the woman, if she has lesser needs, she will feel a lot better if she steps back and realizes that her partner's sexuality possesses a physiological constraint dissociable in large part from the feeling of love. Self-stimulation is a perfectly sound and universally widespread practice. In addition, resorting to masturbation allows a man to refine his techniques and, accordingly, better manage his excitement.

Important note

Love is also a sport!

We can compare love to art but also to gastronomy and sports. Indeed, love possesses likenesses to art in that it requires imagination and mastery. It leans towards gastronomy because it appeals to sensibility and sensuality. It is similar to sports because of the demands it imposes in terms of learning and practice.

Regarding the analogy to sports, it is natural to draw a parallel between the training of an athlete and that of a man who desires to improve the duration of his sexual relations. Before the competition period, an athlete spends time training alone to refine his moves and acquire top physical form. The same goes for a man who has difficulty managing his sexual excitement. He also derives benefits from training alone. Autoeroticism becomes at that point an excellent school where it is possible for him to experiment, learn and integrate new skills without the fear of not satisfying his partner.

Just like for a seasoned athlete, training will equip a man with winning skills and strategies. It will make him a competent lover, capable of managing his excitement, meeting the needs of his partner and being happier himself.

Exercises

Practise once again the breathing exercises seen in previous sessions. Breathing forms the basis of the management techniques. Moreover, innumerable therapeutic methods – western and eastern – use breathing as a privileged tool for personal development. This programme does this as well, but from a sexological perspective. Abdominal breathing brings about greater mastery over sexual excitement. In addition, it contributes to the emergence of sensuality and the obtainment of more pleasure during sexual relations. We will look at the role and benefits of sensuality in the eighth session.

Exercise 2. Identifying the breathing process in a state of relaxation without the help of hands

This exercise is described in the first session.

Exercise 3. Reversal of the breathing process when in a state of excitement (slow speed)

First part: Technique

This exercise is described in the first session.

Second part: Simulation exercise

This exercise is described in the first session.

Exercise 6. Reversal of the breathing process when in a state of excitement in the zone of ejaculatory imminence

Objective: it is important for you to be able to reverse your breathing quickly once you enter into the zone of ejaculatory imminence and as you get closer to the point of no return. In fact, the situation has become urgent and you must act promptly and effectively.

Sit comfortably in a chair. Place your feet flat on the floor spread shoulder width apart. Rest your hands on the armrests or on your thighs.

- a Pull in your stomach and keep it pulled in.
- b Breathe from your rib cage and accelerate the rhythm of your breathing as if you were approaching and then entering into the zone of ejaculatory imminence. (8 to 10 respirations)
- c Swiftly, relax your stomach.

(continued)

(continued)

d With the next inhalation, let your stomach inflate like a balloon and allow the air to descend right to the bottom your abdomen.
e When you exhale, relax your stomach and rib cage. (5 respirations)

Repeat this exercise three times.

***

a Pull in your stomach again and keep it pulled in.
b Breathe from your rib cage and accelerate the rhythm of your breathing.
c Now, imagine you are engaging in sexual relations. You would approach the zone of ejaculatory imminence and then you would enter into that zone. (8 to 10 respirations)
d You would perceive sensations in your penis and perineal area.
You would notice that your stomach is contracted and your breathing is rapid and thoracic.
You would approach the point of no return!
So you would quickly reverse your breathing.
Do so now.
Let your stomach swell like a balloon as you inhale.
e As the air flows out, relax your stomach and rib cage. (5 respirations)

Repeat this exercise five times.

Exercise 5. The movement of the pelvis with support

First part: Technique

This exercise is described in the second session.

Second part: Breathing

This exercise is described in the second session.

You will now hone your skills by working on the intensity and speed of the movement of your pelvis. These two characteristics exert a major influence on the progression of your sexual excitement. It is essential for you to master these.

Third part: Intensity

Objective: To execute the movement of the pelvis with minimum muscular tension.

You have seen that the contraction of muscles in the body favours ejaculation. Today, you will learn how to execute the movement of the pelvis using minimum muscular tension. After this, you can vary the level of muscular tension during your sexual activities and move in a voluptuous way, which is much more pleasurable. It is not necessary to move forcefully when you make love. You can do so with suppleness.

You will be using the technique of contrast. It is very important that you feel the difference between a tense movement and a relaxed movement. If you recognize this distinction now, it will be easier for you to identify the muscular tensions that manifest during sexual relations and to vary their intensity when this will be necessary.

Position yourself on the floor, resting on your hands and knees.

a Lift your back while exhaling and imagining that you are pushing a very heavy load – a 100 pound bag of cement, for example – upwards and that this requires considerable effort on your part.
b Lower your back while inhaling and resisting against this same weight. Do one lift and one descent while remaining very tense.
c Lift your back while exhaling and imagining this time that a feather is placed on your back. You thus lift while as relaxed as possible.
d Lower your back while inhaling and remaining as relaxed as possible. Do three lifts and three descents while remaining very relaxed.

Repeat this exercise four times.

Fourth part: Speed

Objective: To execute the movement of the pelvis very slowly.

As mentioned several times before, muscular contractions encourage ejaculation. However, they are not alone in contributing to its arrival. The speed of the in-and-out movements of the penis inside the vagina also plays an important role. In fact, the more intercourse proceeds at a fast-paced rhythm, the more stimulation increases and the more sexual excitement builds. And when excitement reaches a sufficiently high level, it automatically triggers ejaculation. Consequently, a man who desires to influence the moment of his ejaculation must learn to move his pelvis slowly in order to avoid his excitement from rising too high too fast.

The exercise you will be doing will help you develop the ability to move slowly. Just like the exercise on intensity, you will use the method of contrast: you will perform the movement as quickly as possible, and then as slowly as possible.

Position yourself on the floor, resting on your hands and knees.

a Lift your back while exhaling.
b Lower your back while inhaling.
c Calmly, accelerate the speed of your movement.
d Go as fast as you can.
e Reduce the speed of your movement.
f Move as slowly as possible.
g Count up to five (about 5 seconds) to lift upwards.
h Count up to five (about 5 seconds) to descend.
Do three lifts and three descents extremely slowly.

Repeat this exercise four times.

It is very important to be able to move slowly during sexual intercourse. This allows a man to not get too excited and to stay away from the point of no return. In addition, moving slowly is much more seductive and increases loving and sensual communication between a man and a woman.

Exercises for the week

a) Exercises without sexual excitement

You will perform the following exercises three times during the week. The number of repetitions is indicated at the end of each exercise. You must do them slowly in a calm and pleasant atmosphere.

Exercise 2. Identification of the breathing process in a state of relaxation without the help of hands
This exercise is described in the first session.

Exercise 3. Reversal of the breathing process when in a state of excitement (slow speed)
First part: Technique
Second part: Simulation exercise
These exercises are described in the first session.

Exercise 6. Reversal of the breathing process when in a state of excitement in the zone of ejaculatory imminence.
This exercise is described in this session.

Exercise 5. Movement of the pelvis with support
First part: Technique

Second part: Breathing
These exercises are described in the second session.

Exercise 5. Movement of the pelvis with support
Third part: Intensity
Fourth part: Speed
These exercises are described in this session.

b) Exercises with sexual excitement

Over the course of the first week, you identified the sensations indicating entry into the zone of ejaculatory imminence and also entry into the zone of ejaculation (emission phase). In the second week, you focused attention on the changes that occur in your breathing when you get excited. The next step is to perceive the sensations in your whole body associated with the progression of your sexual excitement. When you start getting excited, does your stomach contract? Does your breathing become thoracic? Does the rhythm of your breathing accelerate? Are the muscles of your face, jaw, neck, hands, arms, legs tenser? When your sexual excitement rises, are your movements faster? Are you more concentrated on sexual stimuli? Do you feel more pleasure? If you answer yes to these questions, it means that you perceive well the signs indicating your different sexual excitement levels. You now have concrete benchmarks for applying the techniques at the appropriate time. Gaining awareness of your bodily reactions and becoming familiar with these is certainly a stimulating exploration that will help you establish the bases to manage your sexual excitement well.

Beginning this week, try to establish the natural frequency of your physiological needs of ejaculatory discharges and conform to them. In other words, when you feel the urge to satisfy yourself sexually, do not hesitate to do so in order not to accumulate tensions.

Suggestions for the single man

This week, during the exercises with sexual excitement, you will concentrate on all the bodily reactions you feel as your sexual excitement increases. You will use masturbation and visualization of sexual scenarios to sustain your excitement.

Suggestions for the woman

You can read the body signs indicating the rise of your partner's sexual excitement. The more skilful you become at detecting what is happening inside of him, the easier you will adopt a course of action adapted to the situation. This applies just the same to the women whose spouse reads this book as to those whose husband has no knowledge of any of these techniques. If your partner becomes tenser, if he moves faster, if he breathes harder and higher in his chest, if his attention seems more focused, he is approaching ejaculation. You must therefore stop the stimulation (later you will only be able to decrease it) until he relaxes and sees his excitement level drop back down.

The woman can also help her partner manage his excitement by modulating the stimulation she gives him. She will vary the quantity, speed and force of her touches. She will make stops. She will touch other places. She will talk. These alternations between light and firm caresses, touches on the lower and upper body, slow and fast movements of the pelvis, will modulate the stimulation that she brings to the man and as a result will help him modulate his excitement. The woman could also use imagination and fantasy. For example, why not come up with some form of foreplay where you combine drink, food and sensuality? This variety of games and interactions will also have a modulating effect.

Suggestions for the couple

This week, you could discuss the expectations you hold pertaining to the length of intercourse.

The following questions will help you broach this subject:

- What would be the duration of satisfactory intercourse?
- What are your reasons for wanting to prolong the time of intercourse?
- Does the achievement of orgasm by your partner during intercourse happen to be one of your objectives?
- What would you do during intercourse that goes on for a long time? Be more intimate, more loving, more affectionate, more vigorous?
- Can prolonged intercourse include pauses and reductions in speed or should it continue without interruption?
- In what positions would you like to make love longer?

Expressing your desires and clarifying your expectations constitute the first step towards success. The next step will consist of verifying their feasibility in light of the information you receive in this programme. There are certain things you could do easily. There are others that will turn out to be unrealizable due to the constraints the male physiology imposes on a couple's sexual expression. You could equally come across in either one of you quite normal limitations that will curb your sexual impulses, such as fluctuating sexual desire, little interest in sex, sexual aversion, reduced sensitivity, lack of body skill, presence of pain, difficulty concentrating on sexual stimuli, etc. Acceptance may therefore be the most reasonable option to consider.

This programme will allow you to increase the length of intercourse and improve the quality of your intimate interactions. It can also be used to take stock of your sexuality. In the following sessions you will deal with other aspects of your emotional and love life. This will give you the opportunity to continue and deepen your reflection.

Important note

The first quarter!

You have already completed the first quarter of your programme. Congratulations! You now know that there are concrete ways to delay the arrival of your ejaculation. You know that men who are able to satisfy their partner during intercourse are not sorcerers. They just have a bag of tricks. You are starting to get the gist of what you too should do to manage your sexual excitement correctly. Now, you must continue! Being able to maintain your motivation at this stage of the programme is crucial. Here are three good ways to succeed in doing this:

1. Concentrate on the guidelines suggested in each session rather than on the programme in its entirety. The tasks at hand will appear accomplishable and you will stay motivated.
2. Focus on what you have already achieved and congratulate yourself rather than become discouraged because you still do not manage your excitement as well as you would like.
3. Compare yourself to yourself instead of to others. You will thus observe your progress and this will incite you to carry on.

FOURTH SESSION

Sexual information

Letting go and holding back as management techniques

When getting close to the point of no return, a lot of men make colossal efforts to prevent ejaculation from taking place. They arch their back, squeeze their buttocks, pull in their stomach, hold their breath, clench their fists, bite their lips, etc. This practice is based on a certain logic. In fact, when a person desires to prevent a physiological function from occurring (for example, when they wish to control the need to urinate or defecate), they make efforts, they restrain themselves. However, if this behaviour is effective in controlling certain bodily functions, it is not at all for holding back ejaculation. On the contrary, it hastens its occurrence.

The reason this way of doing things does not yield the expected results is easy to understand. By restraining themselves, these men contract different muscles in their body. Yet we have already seen that the contraction of muscles, when in a state of excitement, favours ejaculation. Consequently, the processes employed, although they are appropriate to govern certain functions, are of little use when it comes to delaying ejaculation.

What you need to do, when approaching the point of no return, is let yourself go, relax all of your muscles. Do not attempt to restrain yourself. Get rid of all the muscular tension in your body. Relax your stomach, buttocks, hands, jaw, etc. Your muscular tension, by decreasing, will bring your sexual excitement back down. You will return to the zone of modulation and avoid ejaculation.

Important note

Sexual competence versus sexual performance

There's a difference between wishing to become a better lover and demanding it of oneself. It's quite normal to want to improve yourself and to hope to experience a more pleasurable sex life. However, if you force yourself to perform at all costs and consider the fact of not prolonging the duration of your lovemaking a catastrophe, you will create conditions conducive to . . . non-performance. You will lose your spontaneity and the pleasure of making love. It is likely that you will experience performance anxiety, which we find at the source of many sexual dysfunctions. Performance anxiety rests on the obligation, accompanied by self-intransigence, to conduct oneself according to elitist criteria, criteria which one invents or borrows from society. This obligation to perform, which aims more to achieve results than to obtain pleasure, differs from the desire to become more sexually competent, that is to say from the desire to expand one's repertoire of knowledge and skills for a better erotic life.

On the contrary, some sexologists who are proponents of a naturalist view of sexuality oppose all forms of learning. They assert that if the barriers to individuals' freedom of expression were removed, these individuals would be freed from their sexual difficulties. They would regain their spontaneity and their sexuality would flourish on its own. To this I reply with an old maxim: "Sex is perfectly natural, but not naturally perfect." All activities carried out by adults are strongly influenced by learning and are perfectible. Take for example the manner in which you speak, cook or drive your car. Your ways of doing things have evolved over the years. The same applies to sexuality. Just think back to the first time you made love. Certainly today you no longer comport yourself in the same manner. You have acquired new knowledge, reflected on your experience and adapted in many ways to your partner.

Limiting yourself to the naturalist way and to spontaneity is restrictive. On the other hand, obligating yourself to perform is hardly more appropriate. In between the two, there is a vast universe where freedom of self-expression and learning unite to create enjoyable sexual interactions for both partners.

Opening up the body

To better manage your sexual excitement, it is preferable to keep your eyes open, mouth half-open and legs apart during sexual relations. When a man has his eyes closed, he has a tendency to concentrate more on the sensations of his penis and curl up his body. By no longer moving his body and in particular his pelvis, he tenses up a lot more and advances towards ejaculation more easily.

Regarding your mouth, it is preferable to keep it half-open so that air can enter and exits through it. When your mouth is slightly open, air exits more quickly from the lungs than when you breathe through your nose. Consequently, the pressure inside the rib cage decreases more rapidly. When there is less pressure inside the rib cage, it is easier to relax your muscles. In addition, when your mouth is partially open, the muscles in your jaw and lips are not contracted and relaxation of your whole body is facilitated.

As for your legs, they naturally come closer together when you become excited. The muscles that contract therefore are the thigh adductors. Keeping your legs apart goes against this natural tendency and thus increases the ability to delay ejaculation.

Exercises

This is the last week in which you have to perform the breathing exercises in a specific manner. In the weeks that follow, your breathing will be completely integrated into the different movements. Do not deny yourself, however, from practising a few breathing exercises when you feel the need.

Exercise 2. Identification of the breathing process in a state of relaxation without the help of hands

This exercise is described in the first session.

Exercise 3. Reversal of the breathing process when in a state of excitement (slow speed)

First part: Technique

This exercise is described in the first session.

Second part: Simulation exercise

This exercise is described in the first session.

Exercise 7. Reversal of the breathing process when in a state of excitement in the zone of ejaculatory imminence in relation to the principle of letting go

Objective: to be able to quickly return to abdominal breathing and reverse all of the muscular contractions caused by sexual excitement at the moment of arrival in the zone of ejaculatory imminence.

Sit comfortably in a chair. Place your feet flat on the floor and spread shoulder width apart. Rest your hands on the arms of the chair or on your thighs.

- a Pull in your stomach and keep it pulled in.
- b Breathe from your rib cage and accelerate the rhythm of your breathing as if you are approaching and then entering into the zone of ejaculatory imminence. (8 to 10 respirations)
- c Promptly, relax your stomach and your whole body.
- d With the next inhalation, let your stomach swell like a balloon and allow the air to descend right to the bottom of your abdomen.
- e When you exhale, relax your stomach, rib cage, shoulders, neck, jaw, arms and legs. (5 respirations)

Repeat this exercise three times.

(continued)

(continued)

**

a Pull in your stomach again and keep it pulled in.
b Breathe from your rib cage and accelerate the rhythm of your breathing.
c Imagine that you are engaging in sexual relations. Approach and then enter into the zone of ejaculatory imminence. (8 to 10 respirations)
d Perceive sensations in your penis and perineal area. Notice that your stomach is contracted and that your breathing is thoracic and rapid. You are approaching the point of no return.
e Quickly relax your stomach and your whole body.
f Let your stomach inflate like a balloon as you inhale.
g When the air flows out, relax your stomach, rib cage, shoulders, neck, jaw, arms and legs. (5 respirations)

Repeat this exercise three times.

Exercise 5. The movement of the pelvis with support

First part: Technique

This exercise is described in the second session.

Second part: Breathing

This exercise is described in the second session.

The series of pelvis movement exercises with support have enabled you to become aware of your pelvis and increase your repertoire of movements. With the exercise that follows, you will cross a stage in your learning by integrating real-life experience with technique.

Exercise 5. The movement of the pelvis with support

Fifth part: Sensuality

Objective: To progressively integrate technique into sexuality.

The techniques you are learning are not an end in themselves. Their aim is to help you enjoy more pleasurable and satisfying sexual activities. From now on, you will progressively go beyond technique and begin to appreciate the diverse elements of sexuality. The first step in this progression consists of perceiving the sensations that emanate from the movements and to savour them. You will therefore think less and less about technique and become more and more sensual. While managing your sexual excitement, you will get more pleasure. You will perceive and enjoy sexual stimuli at the same time as you maintain your excitement a good distance from the point of no return.

You will begin this new learning by executing the movement of the pelvis in the position where you are resting on your hands and knees. You will move slowly and savour the bodily sensations that come from your back, rib cage, stomach and pelvis.

Position yourself on the floor, resting on your hands and knees.

a As you lift your back and exhale, feel your upper back.
b As you lower your back and inhale, feel your chest.
c As you lift your back and exhale, feel your lower back.
d As you lower your back and inhale, feel your stomach.
e As you lift your back and exhale, feel your pelvis.
f As you lower your back and inhale, feel your pelvis.

Repeat this exercise three times.

Now you improvise. Do the back movements upwards and downwards very slowly. Accelerate. Pause. Feel your body. Start again. Make very large movements, then very small ones, etc. Relish the different sensations the movements give you. These sensations are neither very strong nor very particular, but you can still derive pleasure from them. The goal of the exercise is to refine your ability to perceive a range of sensations and to develop sensual bodily movement.

Do this improvisation for 3 minutes. Take a break for 3 minutes and then repeat this improvisation for another 3 minutes.

Exercise 8. The movement of the pelvis in a standing position

Objective: To execute the movement of the pelvis while dissociating it from the back.

The next exercise consists of moving your pelvis without mobilizing your entire back. It is more difficult to execute than the pelvis movement while resting on your hands and knees. This is why you learn it second. Just like the exercise of the pelvis movement on your hands and knees, the pelvis exercise while standing aims to bring you to modulate your excitement during sexual relations. In fact, by moving your pelvis independently, you use fewer muscles.

Additionally, the alternation of movements will create tension and then relaxation of the muscles. You will have pleasure and at the same time you will manage the progression of your excitement. You will modulate it by making it rise and fall as desired.

First part: technique

Stand upright, legs spread shoulder distance apart, feet parallel and knees bent.

a Rotate your pelvis forward. (Figure 3.14)
b Rotate your pelvis backward. (Figure 3.15)

Repeat this exercise 30 times.

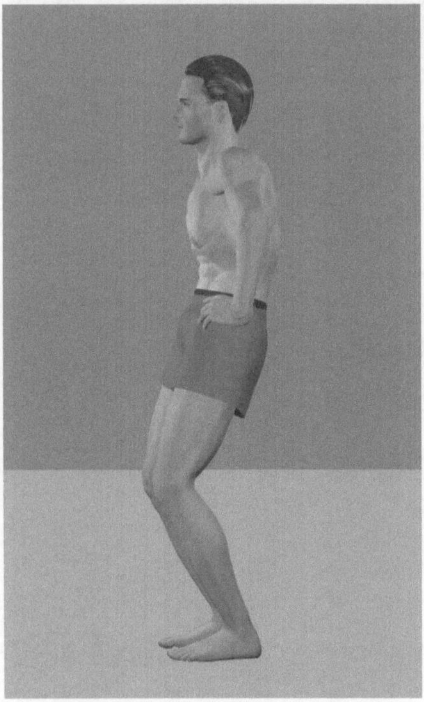

Figure 3.14 Movement of the pelvis forward in a standing position

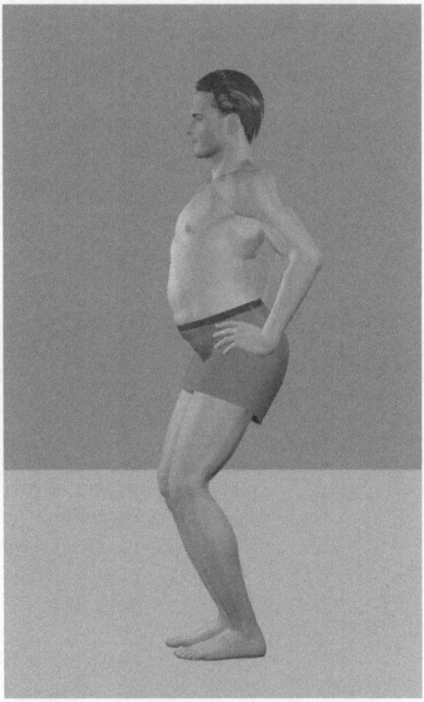

Figure 3.15 Movement of the pelvis backward in a standing position

You can place your hands on your hips to better rotate your pelvis. The use of a mirror will facilitate your learning. It is a matter of well isolating the movement of the pelvis. Note that when you rotate your pelvis forward, it will go not only forward but also upward. The same applies when moving your pelvis backward: it goes not only backward but also upward. You must not move your whole body, nor lean backward (Figure 3.16, error 1) nor lean forward (Figure 3.17, error 2). Keep your knees well bent throughout the exercise. Do not stretch out your legs when you rotate your pelvis forward and upwards (Figure 3.18, error 3).

Second part: Breathing

You will now synchronize the movement of your pelvis with your breathing. A mnemonic trick is to remember that you breathe out when the penis goes forward (penetration inside the woman's vagina) and that you breathe in when the penis withdraws (exiting the vagina).

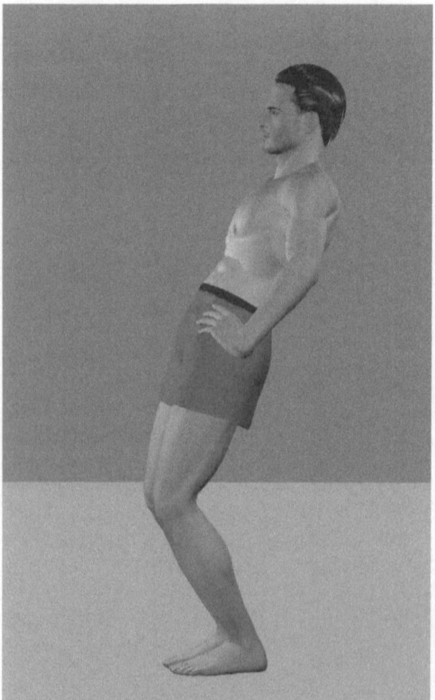

Figure 3.16 Common error encountered during the execution of the movement of the pelvis in a standing position (error 1)

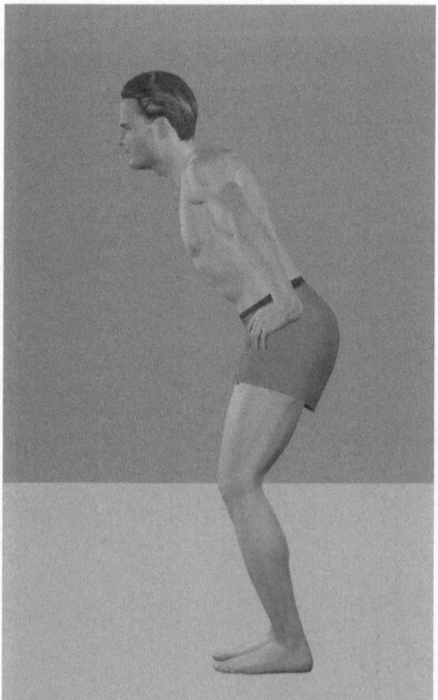

Figure 3.17 Common error encountered during the execution of the movement of the pelvis in a standing position (error 2)

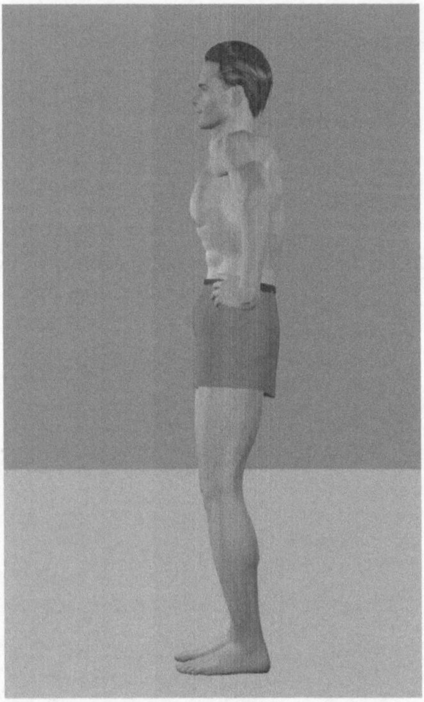

Figure 3.18 Common error encountered during the execution of the movement of the pelvis in a standing position (error 3)

You stand up, legs shoulder width apart, feet parallel and knees bent.

a Exhale while rotating your pelvis forward. (Figure 3.14)
b Inhale while rotating your pelvis backward. (Figure 3.15)

Repeat this exercise 30 times.

**

Repeat the exercise making sure to inhale fully into your stomach and to make a broad movement with your pelvis. This will give you the impression of diffusing sexual excitement in the genital organs throughout the entire body and thus decrease its intensity.

(continued)

(continued)

a Exhale while rotating your pelvis forward in a broad movement.
b Inhale while rotating your pelvis backward in a broad movement.

Repeat this exercise 30 times.

**

Do the exercise again letting your rib cage sink down when you exhale and as you rotate your pelvis forward. This will enable you to reduce your muscular tension considerably.

a Exhale while rotating the pelvis forward and letting your chest collapse. (Figure 3.19)
b Inhale while rotating the pelvis backward. (Figure 3.20)

Repeat this exercise 30 times.

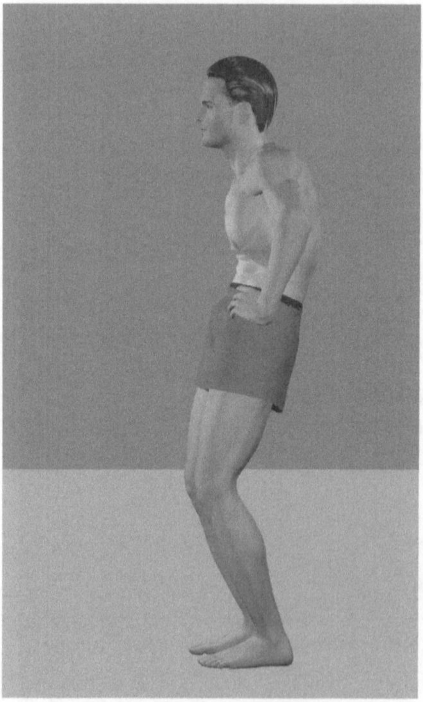

Figure 3.19 Movement of the pelvis forward in a standing position with exhalation and collapsing of the chest

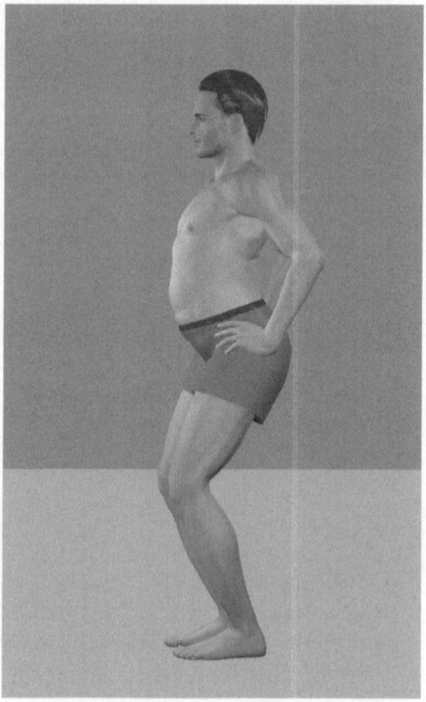

Figure 3.20 Movement of the pelvis backward in a standing position with inhalation

Exercises for the week

a) Exercises without sexual excitement

You will perform the following exercises three times during the week. The number of repetitions is indicated after each exercise. In order for them to be the most beneficial to you, you must set aside time and do them slowly while perceiving the sensations that accompany them.

Exercise 2. Identification of the breathing process in a state of relaxation without the help of hands
This exercise is described in the first session.

Exercise 3. Reversal of the breathing process when in a state of excitement (slow speed)
First part: Technique
Second part: Simulation exercise
These exercises are described in the first session.

Exercise 7. Reversal of the breathing process when in a state of excitement in the zone of ejaculatory imminence in relation to the principle of letting go
This exercise is described in this session.

Exercise 5. The movement of the pelvis with support
First part: Technique
Second part: Breathing
These exercises are described in the second session.

Exercise 5. The movement of the pelvis with support
Fifth part: Sensuality
This exercise is described in this session.

Exercise 8. The movement of the pelvis in a standing position
First part: Technique
Second part: Breathing
These exercises are described in this session.

b) Exercises with sexual excitement

Starting today, try to adopt an open body attitude during sexual activities. Keep your eyes open, mouth half-open and legs apart, whether it being during foreplay or intercourse.

Also incorporate the principle of letting go during sexual relations. When you enter the zone of ejaculatory imminence and approach the point of no return, do not hold yourself back to control ejaculation but let yourself go. Relax every muscle in your body and breathe with your stomach. As for your pelvis, it can now be used in the way described in this session while you are making love.

Suggestions for the single man

During masturbatory activities, take an open position and apply the principle of letting go as you bring your sexual excitement down. Do not hesitate to use foreplay and intercourse scenarios to mentally immerse yourself in conditions similar to those of your future sexual relations.

Suggestions for the woman

The woman can help the man manage his sexual excitement during intercourse by varying the stimulation she gives him. This will be easier to do if she adopts the Andromache position (man lying on his back, woman sitting on him) or one of its variants. She then moves her pelvis forward and backward rather than up and down. This pendulum movement has two advantages. First, it decreases friction on the penis from the vagina (we know that the penis is more sensitive to friction than it is to pressure). Second, it increases pressure of the penis against the vagina (we also know that the vagina responds more to pressure than to friction). While the man is less stimulated, the woman is more so. The rocking motion of the woman's pelvis is therefore advantageous for both spouses. In addition, it is easier for the man to begin penetration while lying on his back. In this position, he is not obliged to support himself or move his pelvis, that which greatly reduces his muscular tension. He can also breathe more easily from the stomach and release the muscular tensions caused by sexual excitement.

The woman also varies the speed of the movement of her pelvis. She accelerates, slows down and makes preventive stops. In the fifth session, we shall see the benefits of pauses for both the man and woman. When the man moves too much and becomes hyper-excited, the woman can immobilize him by lowering herself onto him. This creates a pause and enables the man to temper his enthusiasm. The combination of the woman's interventions with the man's application of his techniques will increase the couple's chances of prolonging the duration of their sexual activities.

Suggestions for the couple

All sexologists mention that communication is essential for healthy couple sexual functioning. This is even truer when people are struggling with a chronic dissatisfaction. In order to structure your discussions, the various components of communication have been grouped into three categories, specifically: its content, form and timing.

Communication content refers to information, messages that you transmit to your partner. These messages not only include what you think, but also what you feel. Here's a short list of things you can convey to your spouse within the domain of sexuality:

- Thoughts: Preferences, fantasies, dreams, goals, aversions, satisfactions, frustrations, etc.
- Emotions and feelings: Affection, love, attraction, admiration, urges, passion, impulses, desires, pleasures, excitement, feelings of power and strength, receptivity, etc.

It is important to establish a distinction between expressing an emotion at a given moment and talking about this same emotion after the fact. These two types of communication are very different. For example, one evening a man demonstrates his tenderness for his wife by gently caressing her on the forearm. The next day, during a discussion about their love life and sexual relationship, he speaks of the tenderness he felt for her the evening before. In the first case, the tenderness is given. In the second, it becomes the subject of a conversation. These two forms of communication each require particular skills. Discussing a feeling is not the same thing as expressing it directly. It would be captivating to take stock of the subjects you talk about together and the emotions you demonstrate, verbally and physically, in your sex and love life.

You may also address the way you feel when you bring up the subject of your sexuality with your partner. This will help you feel more at ease and communicate more easily.

FIFTH SESSION

Sexual information

The intensity of foreplay

Many men ejaculating shortly after the beginning of intercourse try to bring their spouse to orgasm during foreplay as a preventive measure. They want to make certain she has the opportunity to climax knowing that she will not have time during intercourse. This is a sensible practice, but it needs to be nuanced. Women actually differ as regards to the frequency and intensity of the orgasms they can obtain during a sexual encounter. Some have only one and are completely satisfied. Others have several, with the first being the most fulfilling. For these two types of women, it is not recommended that their husband give them an orgasm before intercourse. They will be sated and will neither have enough energy nor the necessary interest to engage in long-lasting intercourse. Despite all of the techniques the man will have learnt, he will not realize his stated objective, namely to give his companion pleasure through intercourse. Yet, for women who have multiple orgasms and in which the last one brings them the most pleasure, there is no contraindication to whether or not their partner gratifies them with one or several orgasms before intercourse.

However, in all cases, it is extremely important that neither the woman nor the man approaches coitus in a hyper-excited state. In fact, it is very common to meet, among the men who ejaculate rapidly, individuals who stimulate their partner intensely during foreplay so that they are able to reach orgasm during the short length of time intercourse lasts. In general, they concentrate their efforts on their spouse's clitoris and stimulate it until she is highly excited. At the same time, the woman avoids stimulating the man in order for him not to become too excited. When she reaches a very high level of excitement, the man proceeds to intercourse and they both move very quickly in hopes that the woman will achieve orgasm before the man ejaculates. Unfortunately, they rarely attain this goal (Figure 3.21).

The reasons why these couples do not achieve the desired results are numerous. First, even though the woman avoids touching the man, he still experiences considerable stimulation watching his partner become more and more excited and, in general, he gets excited as well. He therefore embarks on intercourse at hardly-manageable levels of excitement. And if the couple moves frenziedly so that the woman can orgasm before the man, it causes so much stimulation for the man that he is led ineluctably toward the ejaculatory reflex before his companion tastes ecstasy.

Second, when the woman is very excited, she has a tendency to move her pelvis very fast from the beginning of intercourse, even if her goal is not to move immediately toward orgasm. This increases the amount of stimulation on the man's penis and contributes to the arrival of ejaculation.

Third, the start of coitus is a critical moment for the man. In the first place, the symbolism associated with that of penetrating a woman is in itself very exhilarating. Then, the vaginal heat and lubrication as well as the rubbing sensations inside the woman's sexual organ are very stimulating. In addition, if the entrance to the woman's vagina is somewhat tight, the pressure it exerts on the glans provokes a reflex contraction of the muscles at the base of the penis and this contraction promotes ejaculation. Finally, if the man is in the superior position, he must make some effort to support the weight of his body when he introduces his penis into the vagina. This effort necessitates the contraction of different muscles, which has the effect of increasing the overall level of muscular tension and putting in place the conditions that lead to ejaculation.

Fourth, the man is not acclimatized to the new sensations. This means that he less easily endures intense stimulation at the beginning of intercourse than later on. It is important therefore that he is not too stimulated immediately after introducing his penis inside the vagina. If his partner is extremely excited at that moment, she will tend to move quickly and will become a contributing factor to his quick ejaculation.

Fifth, if the woman was very excited during foreplay and she has to refrain from moving at the start of intercourse so as not to provoke the man's ejaculation, it is likely that she will experience frustration suppressing her sexual impulses in this way. In addition, she may later have difficulty obtaining orgasm. To rise to high levels of excitement may require some effort on her part and it is possible that she then finds it difficult to become excited again if she expended a large amount of energy. As the man requires slowness at the beginning of intercourse, it is not a good idea that he stimulates the woman intensely right before intercourse

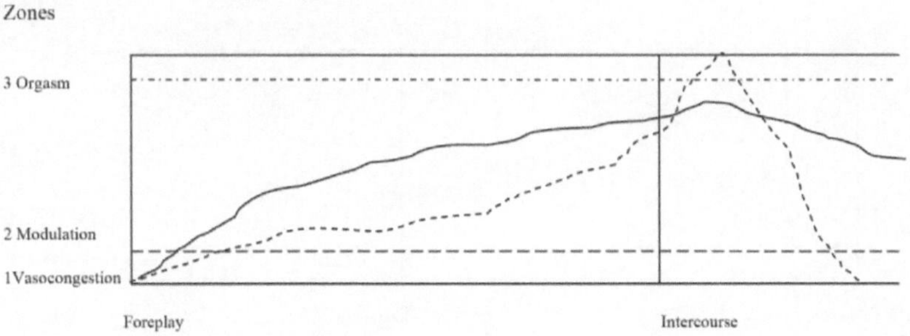

Figure 3.21 An example of sexual activity where the man tries to bring the woman to orgasm before he ejaculates

The female sexual excitement curve: ——. The male excitement curve: ------. Zone 1: The zone of the appearance and disappearance of vasocongestion (vaginal lubrication in the woman, erection in the man). Zone 2: The zone of the modulation of sexual excitement (for the man and woman). Zone 3: The zone of the orgasm (for the man and woman). N.B.: In this example not all zones of the female and male sexual excitement curves are presented.

since she will have to contain herself during the first minutes of intercourse in order not to make him ejaculate.

Sixth, having the woman focus on her clitoris just before coitus has major drawbacks. First and foremost, a woman who polarizes her attention on her clitoris during foreplay will have a tendency to do the same during intercourse. When she is fixated on her clitoris, she generally executes short and rapid pelvis movements (friction or rubbing) during intercourse to stimulate this sexual organ and reach orgasm. This obviously tends to precipitate the man's ejaculation.

It is therefore more advantageous for the man and woman to approach intercourse at moderate levels of excitement. The woman can be stimulated on her clitoris during foreplay and achieve high degrees of excitement or orgasm. However, when the couple moves toward intercourse, it is preferable that the woman makes the transition from her clitoris to her vagina. She can breathe from her stomach, decrease tension in her muscles, move her pelvis and become aware of the sensations coming from her internal genital organs. The man can stimulate his spouse's internal genital organs, either by means of pressure on the anterior and posterior walls of her vagina, or by pressure on her lower abdomen. This will lead her to prefer slow and deep movements of penetration, which will have a positive influence on both the development of her inner sexuality and on the modulation of the man's sexual excitement.

As for the man, he can also experiment with high levels of sexual excitement during foreplay. However, it is in his interest to bring down his excitement and to keep a certain distance from the point of no return when it is time for intercourse. He will in this way have a margin of manoeuvre to familiarize himself with the sensations, symbolism and physical demands of the intromission of the penis into the woman's vagina (Figure 3.22).

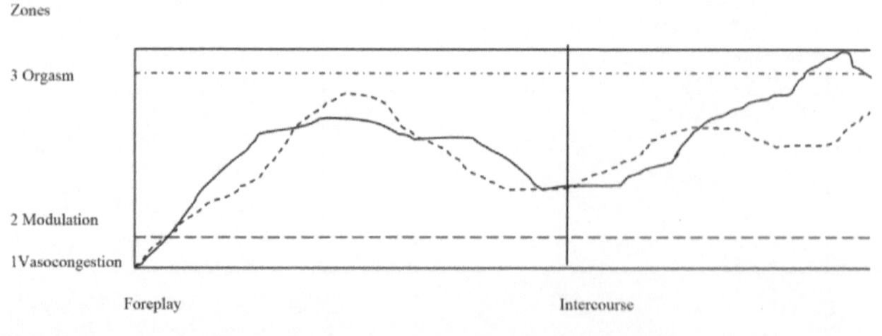

Figure 3.22 An example of sexual activity where the man and the woman initiate intercourse at moderate levels of excitement

The female sexual excitement curve: ——. The male excitement curve: -------. Zone 1: The zone of the appearance and disappearance of vasocongestion (vaginal lubrication in the woman, erection in the man). Zone 2: The zone of the modulation of sexual excitement (for the man and woman). Zone 3: The zone of the orgasm (for the man and woman).

A successful attitude is to regard intercourse as the continuation of foreplay rather than as the beginning of a race to orgasm. This provides the opportunity for the man to acclimatize, the woman to perceive her inner sensations and for the couple to calmly begin their erotic journey. Many have cultivated the habit of moving on to intercourse when the excitement of both partners is at its peak. This habit, despite its noble intentions, has the downsides mentioned above. It is more beneficial to consider intromission of the penis inside of the vagina as a simple transitional event, a pleasant moment that is but the prelude to other enjoyable episodes. It is advisable therefore to begin this new stage in a moderately excited state. If the couple has already reached a heightened level of excitement they will not be able to carry on with their lovemaking for very long.

Exercises

Exercise 8. The movement of the pelvis in a standing position

First part: Technique

Second part: Breathing

These exercises are described in the fourth session.

Exercise 9. The gluteal muscles

Objective: To perceive, tense and relax the gluteal muscles.

Many men use, consciously or unconsciously, their gluteal muscles to perform the movement of the pelvis during intercourse. But be aware that these muscles are the second largest muscles in the human body after those of the thigh (quadriceps). When they contract, they generate a considerable amount of muscular tension. Consequently, it is important not to contract them during sexual relations in order not to trigger early ejaculation.

Moreover, unlike many other muscles, the contraction of the gluteals produces sexual excitement. When you squeeze your buttocks by propelling your pelvis forward, it is a bit like if you're self-stimulating. This really is not needed when one is prone to ejaculate prematurely.

What you will learn today is to execute the movement of the pelvis without using these muscles. To begin with, you will identify the difference between the contraction and relaxation of the gluteal muscles. You will position yourself in the same way as you did for the pelvis exercise in a standing position. This time, however, you keep your legs stretched out. You can help yourself by placing your hands on your buttocks to check if the muscles are contracted or relaxed.

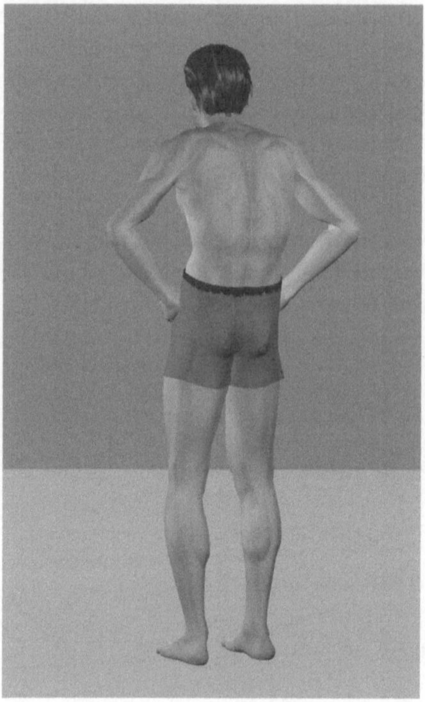

Figure 3.23 Contraction of the gluteal muscles

Stand upright, legs stretched out (without bending your knees), feet parallel and spaced shoulder width apart.

- a Contract your gluteals. (Figure 3.23)
- b Feel the contraction of these muscles.
- c Slowly relax them.
- d Feel that they are relaxed.
- e Notice the difference between the state of tension and the state of relaxation of your gluteals.

Repeat this exercise 30 times.

Exercise 8. The movement of the pelvis in a standing position

Just as you did for the pelvis movement exercise on the floor resting on your hands and knees, you will fine-tune your skills by working on the intensity, as well as the speed of the movement of your pelvis. It is essential that you pay very close attention to these two elements when you execute your in-and-out movements because they have a decisive influence on the build-up of your sexual excitement.

Third part: Intensity

Objective: To execute the movement of the pelvis with minimum muscular tension.

You have learnt to recognize when the gluteal muscles are contracted and when they are relaxed. The subsequent step consists in performing the movement of the pelvis without employing the gluteal muscles. Note that we tend to contract these muscles when we move forward. They automatically relax when we move backward. To have good success in this programme, it is really very important to perform the pelvis movement using the least amount of muscular tension. You must therefore apply yourself to be as relaxed as possible when you move.

In order to distinguish the movement of the pelvis executed with the gluteals from the one done without their help, you will perform the two alternately. You can place your hands on your buttocks in order to feel the contraction and relaxation of the gluteal muscles.

You stand upright, legs spaced shoulder-width apart, feet parallel and knees bent.

a Exhale while rotating your pelvis forward and contracting your gluteals (during sexual intercourse, you must avoid contracting your gluteals). (Figure 3.24)
b Feel the contraction of your gluteals (in order to know what not to do during sexual relations).
c Inhale while rotating the pelvis backward (your gluteals automatically relax). (Figure 3.25)

Repeat this exercise 10 times.

**

Stand upright, legs spaced shoulder width apart, feet parallel and knees bent.

a Exhale while rotating your pelvis forward without contracting your gluteals (you will get the impression of advancing much less, but this is only a feeling; look at yourself in a mirror and you will see that the difference is only about half an inch; however, in terms of the amount of muscular tension the gap is huge!) (Figure 3.26)

(continued)

(continued)

b Feel the relaxation of your gluteals (during sexual relations, that is the way it will have to be done).
c Inhale while rotating your pelvis backward. (Figure 3.27)

Repeat this exercise 10 times.

**

Repeat the first part of this exercise 10 times (movement of the pelvis forward and backward contracting the gluteals).

**

Repeat the second part of this exercise 10 times (movement of the pelvis forward and backward without contracting the gluteals).

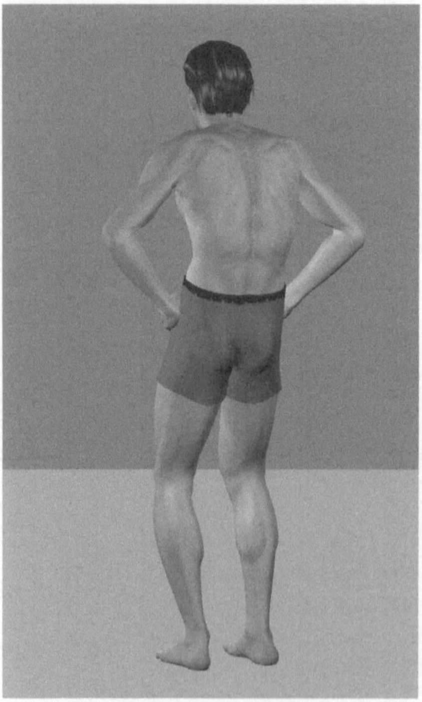

Figure 3.24 Movement of the pelvis forward contracting the gluteal muscles

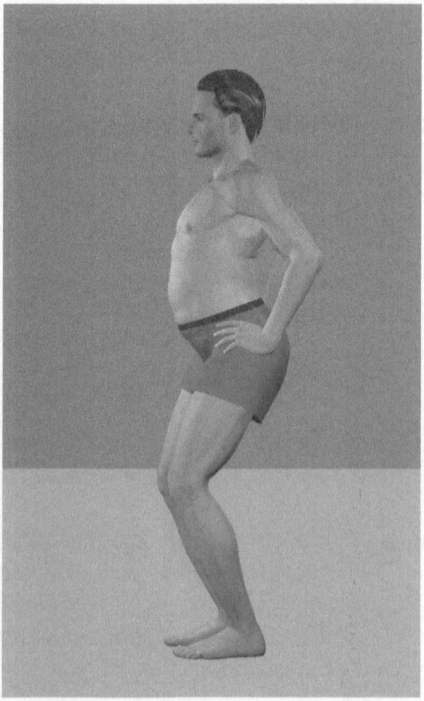

Figure 3.25 Movement of the pelvis backward

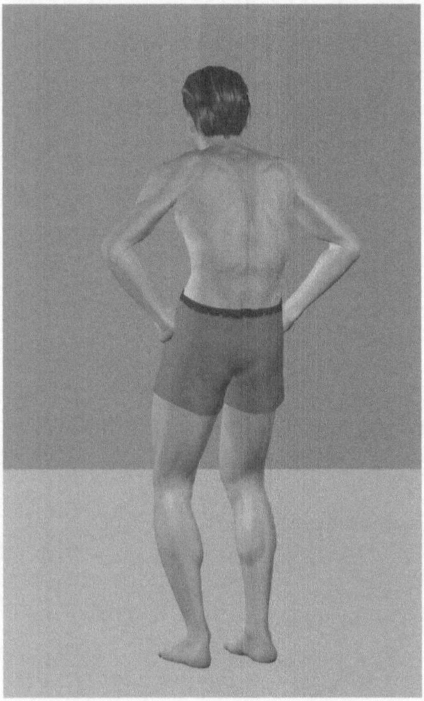

Figure 3.26 Movement of the pelvis forward without contracting the gluteal muscles

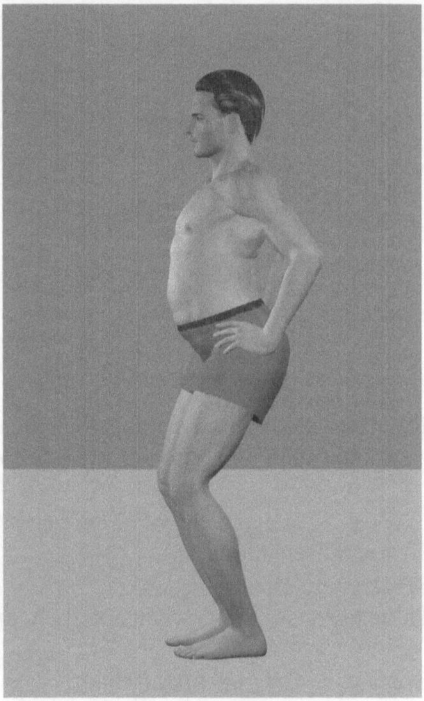

Figure 3.27 Movement of the pelvis backward

Fourth part: Speed

Objective: To execute the movement of the pelvis very slowly.

I cannot stress this enough: move slowly. When I see men in therapy, I ask them to move slowly and without even realizing it, they move their pelvis quickly. It is not easy. You must concentrate on what you are doing. Counting to five to rotate forward and counting to five to go back will help you move more slowly.

Stand upright, legs spaced shoulder width apart, feet parallel and knees bent.

a Exhale while rotating your pelvis forward.
b Inhale while rotating your pelvis backward.
c Calmly, accelerate the speed of your movement.
d Go as fast as you can.

(continued)

(continued)

e Very quickly, slow down.

f Do three forward-backward movements extremely slowly; count to five (about 5 seconds) to rotate your pelvis forward; count to five (about 5 seconds) to rotate your pelvis backward.

Repeat this exercise three times.

Exercises for the week

a) Exercises without sexual excitement

The exercises without sexual excitement will be repeated three times during the week, in a calm and relaxing atmosphere.

Exercise 8. The movement of the pelvis in a standing position
First part: Technique
Second part: Breathing
These exercises are described in the fourth session.

Exercise 9. The gluteal muscles
This exercise is described in this session.

Exercise 8. The movement of the pelvis in a standing position
Third part: Intensity
Fourth part: Speed
These exercises are described in this session.

b) Exercises with sexual excitement

You and your spouse will avoid engaging in intercourse when you are at high levels of sexual excitement. This way, she will not move too quickly at the beginning of intercourse and will not get frustrated having to suppress her sexual impulses thereafter. You will both wait for your excitement to drop to a moderate level before initiating intercourse.

With regard to your gluteal muscles, check to see if you contract them when you rotate your pelvis. If that is the case, try to relax them while executing your movements.

Suggestions for the single man

Try to contract and relax your gluteal muscles during masturbation. Stimulate yourself as well by moving your pelvis forward and backward as you contract and relax your gluteals. You will immediately see the effects.

During the pauses you make while masturbating, imagine everything you could do with your new partner to enrich your sexual interactions.

Suggestions for the woman

It is better to refrain from making negative comments about your companion's erection. If his penis loses some of its rigidity, this does not mean that he is no longer excited by you. On the contrary, it is possible that he had to lower his sexual excitement because you were exciting him too much! He wants to prolong the length of intercourse and needs to keep his distance from the point of no return, like any other man. That being said, your frustration is understandable. But negative comments are not a sexual turn-on and will not help get his erection back! In addition, they can easily set the stage for erectile dysfunction! It is not appropriate either to say things like "Do not worry, it's okay" or "Next time it will be better" because you are removing yourself from the erotic ambience and you stop releasing sexual stimuli. Since there's nothing left to support his excitement, he will lose what remains of his erection. The next time, he risks worrying, not focusing on sexual stimuli and not having . . . an erection. The best thing to do when a man loses his erection is to remain sensual and continue to take pleasure in his presence. The sexual atmosphere will be maintained and his erection will return.

Do not forget to praise your partner when he demonstrates better management. Encouraging the slightest progress contributes to help him reduce his stress and build his confidence. Male sexuality is fragile.

Suggestions for the couple

In the previous session, we dealt with the content of communication. In this session, we will study its form.

The form of communication relates to the manner in which you transmit your messages (ideas and feelings) to your partner. In general, interpersonal communication is distinguished between verbal and non-verbal forms. Speech is an excellent vehicle to convey what you think and feel about your sex life. Some people are more at ease than others expressing themselves in this way. This is often the case for women. For many men, conversing is a real challenge. To make it easier, I suggest that you address specific topics and avoid vague questions such as: "Tell me what you're feeling?", "What do you think about our sex life?", "Where do we stand in our relationship?", "What's your problem?" The following ways are preferable: "I'd like to talk about the frequency of our sexual relations", "What would you say to a nice romantic evening?", "I often get the feeling you want to give me pleasure at all costs. You know, for me what really counts is . . .", "I just read a fascinating article on seduction. If you'd like to read it, we could discuss it together. It has already given me a few ideas . . .".

Here's another proven tip. It is preferable to begin your sentences with "I" rather than "you". This approach encourages communication while lessening the probability of blaming each other. “I’d like us to have longer foreplay” will be better received than “You never caress me”.

Even more eloquent than words is non-verbal language. Looks, gestures, facial expressions, body movement, actions, moans, head nods, smiles, caresses and hugs are the mirrors of the soul. Their use, even if clumsy, is the best expression of your feelings and emotions. Try to discover what means of communication you each use most often. Then, ask your partner in what manner you’d like him or her to express their emotions and feelings if your preferences differ. You can also try to appreciate the way your loved one is communicating to you.

SIXTH SESSION

Sexual information

Stimulating the woman during foreplay

One of your goals, if not the first and foremost as you follow this programme, is to sustain intercourse sufficiently long to please your spouse. You need to note, however, that most of the time, prolonged intercourse is not in itself enough to realize this objective. If a man desires to satisfy his partner, he must lead into intercourse in a manner suitable to the particularities of female eroticism.

In general, a woman likes to experience her sexuality in a romantic framework and a loving ambiance marked by an exchange of tenderness and affection. To create a romantic context, it is not necessary to always watch a sunset in Maui, visit the castles of the Loire Valley or ski in Whistler. In other words, it is not essential to spend a fortune or invest a considerable amount of time whenever you want to create a romantic atmosphere. Going to the movies, walking leisurely in the countryside, eating at a restaurant, taking an evening stroll around your neighbourhood, dining by candlelight, talking about everything and nothing, and watching TV cuddled up next to each other are also activities that allow for closeness and give rise to the emergence of feelings. Such a framework is beneficial because removing a woman from her daily routine and inviting her to share in intimacy creates fertile ground for the awakening of her sensuality. It must be remembered that a woman has less testosterone (sex hormone) than a man and that her sexual desire is increased by the nature of the context and the quality of loving exchanges. This intimate, romantic and loving ambiance is reserved for the couple and evidently excludes the presence of children, relatives or friends.

We just noted above that love and affection constitute essential elements of a woman's sexual life. In fact, they are so important that we can regard them as the gateway to her sexuality. Now, in what parts of the body are love and affection experienced? It is not in the feet, legs, knees, thighs, genital organs, stomach nor breasts. Women, like men, experience love and affection in the upper part of the body. This region includes the top of the hands, forearms, arms and shoulders; the upper back; the back of the neck, head, forehead and cheeks. This excludes the sides and front of the neck, ears and lips. In fact, this is the same area we focus on when comforting a person. So when you caress your spouse it is best to begin with the upper part of the body. There are few women who like to begin sexual relations regularly by having their breasts or genitals fondled.

In concrete terms, this means it is better for the woman that the man conducts foreplay by caressing her on the hands, forearms, arms, shoulders, upper back, back of the neck, head and forehead and by wrapping her in his arms. This part of foreplay can easily last 5, 10 or 15 minutes. This approach is very emotionally stimulating for the woman, and, progressively, it can also become very sexually exciting.

You can then expand your caresses to the entire body: the sides, stomach, breasts, hips, legs, buttocks and finally the genitals. One way to fondle a woman's genitals is to start with the mount of Venus. You then move on to the labia majora, labia minora and finally the clitoris. The clitoris could be approached in a thousand ways. Back-and-forth movements along the shaft of the clitoris, traction on the pubis, pinching or caressing constitute entirely suitable methods of stimulating this organ. However, it is best to avoid direct contact with the glans because it is usually a hypersensitive region.

Finally, you can prepare the vagina for approaching intercourse. The vagina, contrary to the penis, is more responsive to pressure than to light touch. For this reason, it is preferable to press your fingers against the wall of the vagina rather than apply back-and-forth movements along it.

The procedure which was just suggested to you is not immutable. It is but an indication of what in general is well-suited to the psychology and physiology of a woman. We recommend that you add variety to your approach. It is in fact good to change your ways of caressing, kissing or embracing. If you always follow the same procedure, it is likely to result in boredom and reduce interest. On the other hand, the method of progression we just taught you (the upper body before the breasts and the genital organs) is most valuable. We suggest you try it several times before making a decision about it.

This approach, based on the creation of a romantic mood and loving atmosphere, sparks the woman's excitement during foreplay and intercourse. It suits the characteristics of female sexuality. It also has the huge advantage, contrary to popular male belief, of not relying exclusively on a continuous and intense genital stimulation. This saves the man from having to perform non-stop penis movements in the vagina and allows him to prolong intercourse while satisfying his partner a lot more.

Behaving in a romantic and loving way also works wonders during intercourse. Sharing, exchanges and complicity are worth a thousand pelvic thrusts from an individual withdrawn into his own world. In terms of female eroticism, the other's presence and communication surpass – and by a long way – athletic performance.

Exercises

Exercise 10. The movement of the pelvis while lying on the back

Objective: To execute the movement of the pelvis while lying on your back.

From this point on, you will perform the exercises lying down in order to put yourself in the conditions most similar to those encountered during sexual intercourse. In this session, you repeat on your back the exercises that you did standing. You will follow a pedagogical progression that goes from easier to more difficult. It is more arduous to do these exercises lying down than standing up and more complex to execute them lying on your stomach than on your back. Moreover, the execution of the movement of the pelvis requires proper technique in each position and it is important not to leave the learning of this technique to chance. That's why you will learn how to rotate your pelvis in the positions most commonly used.

First part: Technique

Lying on your back, legs bent and feet flat on the mattress, rotate your pelvis forward and backward. You can place your hands on your hips and rotate your pelvis with their help in order to perform your movement better. The use of a mirror will also facilitate your learning. It is a matter of isolating the movement of the pelvis well. Remember that the pelvis cannot go very far forward because of the way the hip joint is constructed. Therefore do not force unnecessarily, this will increase your muscular tension.

Lie on your back. Your legs should be bent and spread out at least shoulder width apart, your feet flat on the mattress, your lips slightly parted and your eyes open.

a Rotate your pelvis forward. (Figure 3.28)
b Rotate your pelvis backward. (Figure 3.29)

Repeat this exercise 30 times.

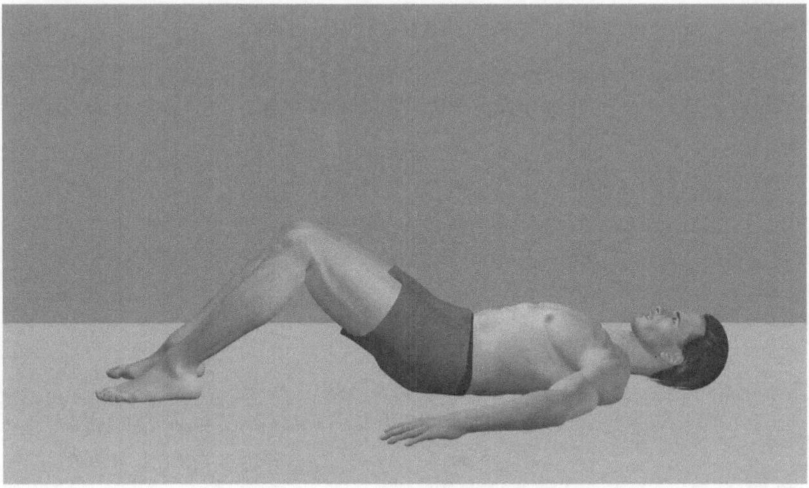

Figure 3.28 Movement of the pelvis forward while lying on the back

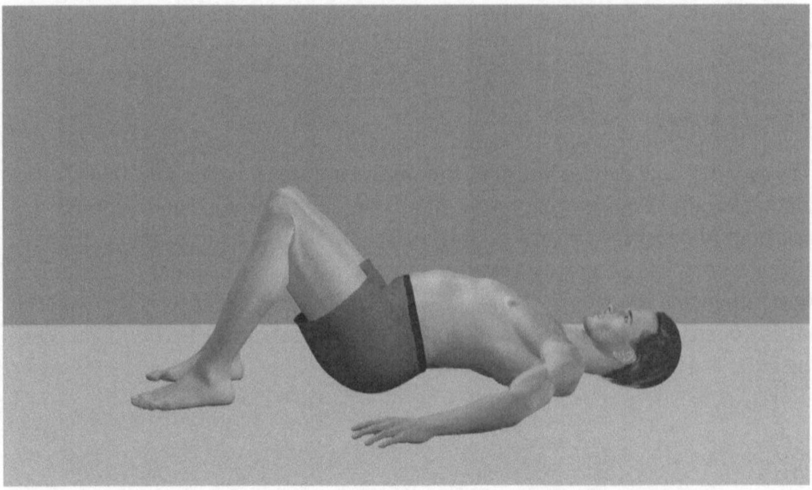

Figure 3.29 Movement of the pelvis backward while lying on the back

This movement is difficult because the forward range of motion of the pelvis is very limited, given the way in which the thigh articulates with the pelvis (coxo-femoral articulation). Most men compensate for this anatomical limitation by placing weight on their heels, lifting up the pelvis and pushing with their buttocks. You should avoid compensating in this way. Figure 3.30 indicates what not to do.

Second part: Breathing

You will now match your breathing to the movement of your pelvis. Make sure your inhalation descends very deep into your abdomen, right to your genital organs, right to your crotch area.

Lie on your back. Your legs should be bent and spread at least shoulder width apart, your feet flat on the mattress, your lips slightly parted and your eyes open.

a Exhale and rotate your pelvis forward. (Figure 3.28)
b Inhale from the stomach and rotate your pelvis backward. (Figure 3.29)

Repeat this exercise 30 times.

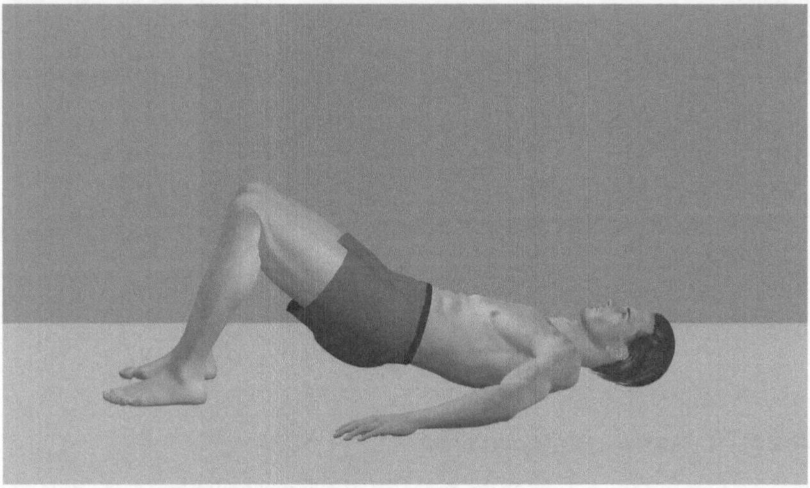

Figure 3.30 An example of a man making the error of putting weight on the heels and lifting the pelvis while contracting his buttocks during the execution of the movement of the pelvis while lying on the back

Exercise 11. The contraction and relaxation of the gluteal muscles while lying on the back

Objective: To perceive the tension and relaxation of the gluteal muscles while lying on your back.

Lie on your back, legs stretched out and spread at least shoulder width apart, lips slightly parted and eyes open. Place your hands flat on the bed underneath your buttocks. This will enable you to better feel the contraction and relaxation of your gluteals.

a Slowly contract your gluteal muscles.
b Feel the contraction of these muscles.
c Slowly relax them.
d Feel that they are relaxed.
e Perceive the difference between the state of tension and the state of relaxation of your gluteals.

Repeat this exercise 30 times.

(continued)

(continued)

**

- a Exhale and slowly contract your gluteal muscles.
- b Feel the contraction of these muscles.
- c Inhale and slowly relax them.
- d Feel that they are relaxed.
- e You perceive the difference between the state of tension and the state of relaxation of your gluteals.

Repeat this exercise 30 times.

Exercise 12. The muscles of the perineum

Objective: To identify the action of the muscles of the perineum and to be able to relax them in order to manage the course of your sexual excitement.

There is a set of small muscles that plays a predominant role in the management of the rise of sexual excitement. These muscles are located in the area between the legs and form the pelvic floor. Some of them are attached to the penis and contribute to the rigidity of the erection. When you use them, the muscles of the perineum contract in unison and give the impression that there is only one muscle working.

The muscles of the perineum contract reflexively as soon as sexual excitement begins. These contractions are barely perceptible during the excitement state and a certain amount of training is required to become aware of them during sexual intercourse. When you are able to easily identify the contraction of the muscles in your perineum and can relax them on command, you will then be in a position to manage your excitement correctly and delay the moment of your ejaculation.

The following information will help you discover exactly where the muscles of the perineum are located. These are the muscles that you contract when you are erect and which enable you to make small movements with your penis. They are also the ones that you contract when you voluntarily stop the flow of urine during urination. Finally, if you have a hard time finding them, you will notice that when the anus is contracted, they are also contracted. You therefore just have to contract the anus and you will immediately perceive the muscles of the perineum.

Lying on your back, you will try to pinpoint where the muscles in your perineum are located. If you have difficulty finding them, contract your anus and you will feel something moving in your crotch area, just under your testicles. The thing that is moving is precisely the muscles in your perineum. You must not contract your buttocks. These two muscles groups are completely independent. It is therefore essential to isolate them and to be able to contract them separately.

Lie on your back, legs stretched out and spread at least shoulder width apart, lips slightly parted and eyes open.

a Slowly contract the muscles in your perineum.
b Feel the contraction of these muscles.
c Slowly relax them.
d Feel that they are relaxed.
e Perceive the difference between the state of tension and the state of relaxation of the muscles in your perineum.

Repeat this exercise 30 times.

**

a Exhale and slowly contract the muscles in your perineum.
b Feel the contraction of these muscles.
c Inhale and slowly relax them.
d Feel that they are relaxed.
e You perceive the difference between the state of tension and the state of relaxation of the muscles in your perineum.

Repeat this exercise 30 times.

The perineal muscles are more difficult to feel during sexual intercourse than during the exercises you just did. A little trick consists of gently contracting them voluntarily (to slightly move your erect penis) and then immediately relaxing them. This voluntary contraction will help you better feel them and consequently better relax them.

Contrary to what is written in certain books and magazines, you should definitely not try to hold back your ejaculation by contracting the muscles of the perineum. If you do that, you increase both your muscular tension and your sexual excitement and we know this greatly risks triggering ejaculation.

There are some people on the Internet who offer a programme to strengthen the muscles of the perineum in order to "control" ejaculation. They say that if you ejaculate before you want to, it is because these muscles are not strong enough to hold back ejaculation. According to them, you must first train your perineal muscles and then use them in the following manner during sexual relations: you completely contract the muscles of the perineum when the emission phase (first phase of ejaculation) begins in order to prevent ejaculation from occurring. This approach is erroneous. Essentially, it must be understood that contracting the perineal muscles in no way halts the emission phase because these muscles are not linked in any way to the ducts and glands (efferent vessels of the testicles, epididymis, vas deferens, seminal vesicles, prostate) that are activated during this phase. And if a man wanted to change strategy and contract these ducts and glands instead of the muscles of the perineum, he could not. In fact, they are made of smooth muscles (such as the stomach and intestines) and human beings have no power over these kinds of muscles.

The only effect the muscles of the perineum exert is to counteract the normal process of the expulsion phase (second phase of ejaculation) by preventing the sperm from exiting outside of the penis. However, since the first phase of ejaculation has already taken place, you lose your erection all the same and can no longer continue intercourse. In fact, as we have already explained, when ejaculation is triggered, it is simply impossible to stop. It is a reflex. And when it is about to occur, that is to say when you enter into the zone of ejaculatory imminence, you definitely should not try to withhold your ejaculation by contracting the muscles of the perineum. On the contrary, it is necessary at this point to stop all stimulation and bring down your excitement by breathing from the abdomen, relaxing the muscles of the perineum and releasing all other muscles.

In order to completely master the technique of slightly contracting your perineal muscles (to better perceive them) and then relaxing them during intercourse, you will do the following exercise. This exercise is somewhat difficult to accomplish because the muscles of the perineum have a tendency to relax rapidly when the penis is not erect.

Lie on your back, legs stretched out and spread at least shoulder width apart, lips slightly parted and eyes open.

a Contract the muscles in your perineum.
b Feel the contraction of these muscles.
c Contract them a bit more.
d Relax them.
e Feel that they are relaxed.
f Perceive the difference between the state of tension and the state of relaxation of the muscles in your perineum.

Repeat this exercise 30 times.

Important note

Emergency strategy

When you enter into the zone of ejaculatory imminence and you sense that ejaculation will occur very shortly and you'd like to prolong the length of intercourse, apply the following emergency strategy:

- Make a pause (neither the man nor the woman moves their pelvis).
- Relax all of your muscles.
- Relax the muscles in your perineum.
- Breathe from your abdomen.

Exercises for the week

The exercises without sexual excitement should be practiced three times during the week in an atmosphere of serenity and well-being.

a) Exercises without sexual excitement

Exercise 10. Movement of the pelvis while lying on the back
First part: Technique
Second part: Breathing
These exercises are described in this session.

Exercise 11. The contraction and relaxation of the gluteal muscles while lying on the back
This exercise is described in this session.

Exercise 12. The muscles of the perineum
This exercise is described in this session.

b) Exercises with sexual excitement

This week is devoted to the muscles of the perineum. You will try to establish the distinction between the states of contraction and relaxation of these muscles when you are excited, observing what takes place in both cases. In the beginning, this research is best done alone, that is to say by means of masturbation, as it requires a lot of concentration. Thereafter, you will incorporate this exploration into your sexual relations, either during foreplay or intercourse.

Suggestions for the single man

You too will pay attention to the muscles in your perineum during masturbation. You will relax them and observe the effect this has on your sexual excitement.

Then, lying on your back, rock your pelvis forward and backward while breathing from your abdomen and stimulating yourself. You will become aware of your perineal muscles and you will relax them, several times if necessary. When you come to be with a woman, you will do exactly the same thing.

On two separate occasions, you will create two different sexual scenarios each time: one for foreplay and one for sexual intercourse. While visualizing these scenarios and stimulating yourself, you will apply the instructions described earlier. Through the application of these scenarios, your masturbatory practices will be more adapted to future sexual relations with your new partner.

Suggestions for the woman

During sexual relations, it would also be good for you to breathe from your stomach and move your pelvis forward and backward, but for reasons totally different from those of the man. Abdominal breathing helps you to better perceive your internal genital sensations. It gives you access to your inner universe and your femininity. The movement of your pelvis, in turn, allows the penis to exert pressure on the vaginal walls and as a result you get more sensations and pleasure during sexual intercourse. In addition, when you move your pelvis, you encourage the awakening and heightening of your sexual receptivity, that is to say, of your ability to welcome inside of you the man who you love and find exciting.

Exhale when your pelvis goes forward. Inhale as it heads backward and as you hollow your back and push out your buttocks. When you go forward, unlike the man, you can contract your gluteal muscles. This will increase your sexual excitement without bringing your partner additional stimulation.

Suggestions for the couple

In this session, we will be examining the third and final component of communication, namely the moment to which communication relates.

By compartmentalizing the moments of your sexual and love life into past, present and future, you can focus more attention on precise topics and find solutions faster.

The past

Talking about past sexual satisfactions and frustrations allows you to celebrate ancient pleasures, discharge old tensions and make some changes by keeping what you like and eliminating what you least like. Take time to review what you've been through together. Now you have some perspective and you can relativize past events. A good way to play down the difficult moments of the past is to express to your spouse all the emotions you experienced at that time. Another way, one that is more personal, is to imagine them in a transparent bubble. Then you observe them, enclosed in this bubble, varying the size of the bubble and moving it in space: higher, lower, farther, closer, to the right, to the left . . . This very effective technique stemming from neuro-linguistic programming has a tremendous liberating effect.

The present

What is happening now? What would you like to remain the same? What would you like to change? In order to avoid chronic frustration and disappointment, it is better to be straightforward with your partner about what you do not appreciate. On the other hand, when you like his/her attitude and behaviour, do not hesitate to let him/her know. An expression of gratitude, a compliment or a thank you is always welcome.

The present time is also the moment of truth, the moment you live in and can express your feelings and emotions to the person you love. Do not hesitate to declare your commitment, demonstrate your affection, expose your passion, divulge your sexual desires or express your sexual excitement to your partner.

The future

This is the time for wishes and plans, hopes and dreams, fantasies and the wildest ideas. What do you both expect for the future? What would you like to do, give, receive in 5 seconds? In 5 minutes? In 5 days? In 5 years? Do not limit your imagination. Let yourself dream. However, no one is a mind reader and the way to satisfy your most cherished desires is to communicating them to your companion.

Communication is a source of great pleasure and great satisfaction. It will be a good idea for you to take the time to reflect on the substance and style of your exchanges. This will give you the opportunity to enrich your communication repertoire, reduce your disappointments and increase your marital happiness.

Important note

The halfway mark!

You have completed the first half of your programme. Congratulations!

However, it is possible that your initial enthusiasm has been tempered and that a certain weariness has set in. You have understood several principles but have not yet obtained any results. This is normal. You must possess all of the knowledge and techniques included in this programme for it to work. And this takes 12 sessions. To encourage you, it is helpful to remember that these 12 sessions will not only enable you to manage your sexual excitement better, but also give you greater competence to interact with the opposite sex. You must not get demotivated!

SEVENTH SESSION

Sexual information

Determining the amount, speed and intensity of stimuli

The amount, speed and intensity of stimuli a man can receive must be determined by . . . the man himself! Only he knows exactly what level of sexual excitement he is experiencing at any such moment during the sexual relation. He alone knows how excited he is feeling on that given day. If he would like to give his spouse pleasure through lengthy intercourse, he must evaluate the amount, speed and intensity of stimulation that he can endure without reaching the level of excitement that triggers ejaculation.

This observation implies that sometimes the man will have to slow down or stop the movements of penetration in order to reduce the stimulation applied to his penis, with the consequences that this could entail for the woman's sexual excitement and pleasure.

It also means the woman must adapt to the limitations imposed by the man's ejaculatory reflex on the couple's sexuality. If, in order not to ejaculate too soon, her spouse needs her to interrupt the movement of her pelvis, it is preferable for her to act accordingly. And if she experiences a decline in her own sexual excitement, it is in her best interest to accept it. This decrease is not dramatic! The woman can also learn to modulate her excitement. She does not have to fear not being able to become excited again if her sexual excitement diminishes. The fact that her excitement fluctuates is perfectly normal. On the other hand, if the woman is demanding and requires her partner to perform quickly every minute of the sexual encounter, there is a great risk that this overly energetic activity will lead to a rapid arrival of his ejaculation.

This way of managing the man's excitement causes interruptions in the movements of penetration. But these stops do not necessarily signify discontinuation of sexual interaction or cessation of stimulation provided to the woman. On the contrary, these pauses can be an occasion for emotional and sensual enrichment conducive to the woman's excitement and pleasure.

This leads us to reflect on the elements that feed sexual tension during intercourse. The key ones are variety of rhythms, diversity of activities and the interaction between desire and pleasure.

The variety of sexual rhythms compares to the diversity of rhythms in music and dance. It adds interest by enriching the emotional and excitatory responses arising from the multiplication of sensations. Accelerations, decelerations, breaks, the back and forth between gentleness and vigour: all these ingredients help nourish the sexual relationship and give it character. By contrast, intercourse carried out with a continuous tempo comes across as quite unexciting.

The diversity of activities relates to all of the actions of the partners. This includes kissing, hugging, fondling, pressure of the penis in the vagina, pauses at the entrance, penetration movements, passionate looks, sharing of feelings, verbal exchanges, humour, etc. As you can see, not performing in-and-out movements in the vagina does not mean doing nothing at all! You can still provide your partner with many pleasant sensations. Moreover, the man can very well justify this stop in movement by explaining very frankly: "I'm really turned on by you. But if I continue moving, I am going to come too quickly." This is courteous and pays tribute to the partner.

All men who last long make pauses. And if you need to make pauses, it is not because you're a "premature ejaculator", it is because you're a normal man! Male physiology has this limitation that requires all men to stop every so often in order to lower their sexual excitement and distance themselves from the point of no return.

If you stimulate your partner intensely and then pause just as she is about to orgasm, the chances are she will become frustrated. Conversely, she will also be disappointed if you ejaculate too quickly. As we have already noted, you and your companion should approach intercourse at moderate levels of sexual excitement, so that the pauses integrate into your sexual activities. Under these circumstances, the pauses will be experienced favourably by your spouse. She will appreciate a lover who knows how to take his time and savour the romantic encounter.

Preventive pauses – less abrupt than the pauses executed in the zone of ejaculatory imminence – are experienced in a different frame of mind. "Let's not move, just enjoy this moment …" could be one way of introducing them. Initiated in this way, they take on an undeniably romantic and erotic character.

This brings us to another action that a man can do during pauses: talk. Some couples talk while making love. However, there are fewer who communicate during intercourse. This is unfortunate because talking during sexual activities nurtures communication and allows for greater mutual understanding. In addition, when a man speaks, he breathes and his sexual excitement decreases. It is not necessary to make big, long speeches. You can simply share your sensations, emotions, desires and feelings.

Important note

A pause inside, a pause outside

Should you make a pause inside or outside the vagina? The choice is yours. If you make it inside, you maintain the atmosphere of intimacy that has developed between you and your partner. If you make it outside, it takes the form of a halt or becomes part of a change in position. An external pause is easier to manage than an internal pause. Nevertheless, you should know that when you withdraw, a surplus of stimulation is produced by rubbing the penis on the vaginal wall which may be sufficient to trigger ejaculation. It is therefore safer, when you remove your penis from the woman, to do so slowly and, above all, before you are too excited.

The third element that nourishes sexual tension during intercourse is the interaction between desire and pleasure. This interaction is based on the alternation between stopping and resuming an activity considered to be pleasant, be it kissing, caressing or penetrating. Cessation causes desire by creating a lack; resumption, because it is desired, produces even more pleasure. This alternation amplifies emotional activation and heightens the sexual experience. Applied to intercourse, it has the dual benefit of stimulating the woman at the same time as giving respite to the man in the genital area, just where he is the most sensitive and the most vulnerable.

Male sexuality includes an element that imposes a significant limitation on the couple, namely, the ejaculatory reflex. When this reflex occurs, it causes a loss of erection and puts an end to intercourse. This obviously prevents continuing to bring pleasure to the woman by way of the in-and-out movements of the penis inside the vagina. The man, since he possesses within him the indicator signals of the arrival of the ejaculatory reflex, holds the responsibility for establishing the amount and intensity of stimuli that he can accept at any time during the sexual relation. If the couple wishes to prolong the length of intercourse and the man's excitement soars too high, he must act suitably and slow down the pace of their lovemaking or ask his spouse to do so. Dealt with creatively, these slowdowns, including a variety of rhythms and activities, nourish the couple's erotic experience. In addition, they decrease the intense stimulation stemming from the fast movements of the penis inside the vagina that are often the source of rapid ejaculation.

The length of the pause depends on the objective you set for yourself. If it is to indulge in an exquisite moment of your love life, make it last as long as you desire. If it is solely to decrease your sexual excitement, the duration of the stop will be relative to your ability to bring it down. Generally, a man who is able to quickly return to abdominal breathing and relax his muscles will be able to allow himself pauses of around 15 seconds. A very excited man who has ejaculated fast for years will need pauses of 1 minute.

At first, especially if you ejaculate shortly after intromission of the penis into the vagina, you will have to make numerous pauses. You will stop after only three or four thrusting movements inside the vagina and the pauses will last from 30 to 60 seconds. But as you get used to the sexual sensations of the vagina, you will be able to make more movements and fewer pauses. The phenomenon of sexual acclimatization will come into play. After a few months of using the techniques proposed in this book, the number and duration of the pauses will be reduced. An experienced man who has gained confidence in himself will allow for briefer pauses. But for the rest of his life, if he wants intercourse to last a certain length of time, he will have to rely on these pauses.

Exercises

Exercise 13. Relaxing different parts of the body

Objective: To engage in sexual activities while having low muscle tone.

In everyday life, we use different muscles in our body to accomplish various actions. The use of these muscles entails their contraction. When you get into bed, these muscles could still be tense. If you immediately begin foreplay, these tensions will add to those caused by sexual excitement. It is therefore important for you to get yourself relaxed before starting to caress or kiss your partner in an effort to reduce your muscle tone. An excellent way to relax consists of simply perceiving the different parts of your body one after the other and relaxing them progressively.

Lie on your back, legs spread at least a shoulder width apart, lips slightly parted and eyes open.

a Feel your feet . . .
b Your calves . . .
c Your thighs . . .
d Your back . . .
e Your shoulders . . .
f Your arms . . .
g Your forearms . . .
h Your hands . . .
i Your fingers . . .
j Your neck . . .
k Your forehead . . .
l Your face . . .
m Your lips . . .
n Your tongue . . .
o Feel your stomach expand like a balloon when the air enters . . .
p Feel it relax when the air leaves . . .
q Once again, feel your stomach expand when you inhale . . .
r Feel it relax when you exhale . . .
s Feel the air move right to your genital organs when you inhale . . .
t Feel your stomach relax when you exhale, your rib cage relax, your shoulders relax, your face relax . . .

Do this exercise only once.

Exercise 12. The muscles of the perineum

This exercise is described in the sixth session.

Exercise 10. The movement of the pelvis while lying on the back

First part: Technique

Second part: Breathing

These exercises are described in the sixth session.

Third part: Intensity

Objective: To execute the movement of the pelvis with a minimum amount of muscular tension while lying on your back.

You already know how to identify when your gluteal muscles are contracted and when they are relaxed. The next step is to perform the movement of the pelvis while lying on your back, without employing the gluteal muscles. This exercise is done with legs stretched out and not bent as in the previous exercises. The pelvis cannot go as far forward. There is no need therefore to apply force to have the same range of motion as before.

Lie on your back, legs stretched out and spread at least shoulder width apart, lips slightly parted and eyes open. Slide your hands flat on the bed underneath your buttocks.

a Exhale while rotating your pelvis forward and contracting your gluteals (during sexual relations, you must avoid contracting your gluteals).
b Feel the contraction of your gluteals (in order to know what not to do during sexual relations).
c Inhale while rotating the pelvis backward (your gluteals release automatically).

Repeat this exercise 10 times.

**

a Exhale while rotating your pelvis forward without contracting your gluteals (during intercourse, this is the way it must be done).
b Feel the relaxation of your gluteals.
c Inhale while rotating your pelvis backward.

Repeat this exercise 10 times.

**

Lie on your back, legs stretched out and spread at least shoulder width apart, lips slightly parted and eyes open. Remove your hands from underneath your buttocks and place your arms on the bed alongside your body.

a Exhale while rotating your pelvis forward and contracting your gluteals.
b Feel the contraction of your gluteals (during sexual relations, you must avoid contracting your gluteals).
c Inhale while rotating your pelvis backward (your gluteals relax automatically).

Repeat this exercise 10 times.

**

a Exhale while rotating your pelvis forward without contracting your gluteals.
b Feel the relaxation of your gluteals (during sexual relations, this is the way it must be done).
c Inhale while rotating your pelvis backward.

Repeat this exercise 10 times.

Fourth part: Speed

Objective: To execute the movement of the pelvis very slowly while lying on your back.

In order to reduce the speed of the movement of the pelvis and the intensity of muscular contractions, it is important that the movement of the pelvis follows the rhythm of your breathing. Natural breathing has its own rhythm. It produces a slowdown and relaxation phase at the end of inhalation as well as a pause and relaxation phase at the end of exhalation. When the pelvis follows the natural breathing rhythm, it too slows down and relaxes at the end of inhalation and stops and relaxes at the end of exhalation.

This makes it possible to modulate sexual excitement and delay the moment when ejaculation happens. Even when you are very active and excited, it is preferable to synchronize the movement of your pelvis with the rhythm of your breathing.

It is essential not to do the opposite. If your breathing is following the rhythm of your pelvis, the movement will get out of control and drive you quickly to ejaculation. So listen well to your breathing and harmonize the rhythm of your pelvis with its rhythm. Take extreme care not to accelerate your movement when you go forward. For this reason, it is better that you count to five for each movement you do.

Lie on your back, legs stretched out and spread at least shoulder width apart, lips slightly parted and eyes open.

a Inhale and rotate your pelvis backward while counting up to five (about 5 seconds).
b At the end of the inhalation, there is a suspension; make a micropause with your pelvis during this suspension in inhalation and relax yourself before moving forward.

(continued)

(continued)

c Exhale and rotate your pelvis forward, counting up to five (about 5 seconds).

d At the end of the exhalation, there is a stop of about 1 second; make a micropause with your pelvis during this stop and relax yourself before going back.

Repeat this exercise 30 times.

When placed at the end of the movements these micropauses have helped more than one person solve their difficulty with prolonging intercourse. Why? It is because they prevent the movement from becoming continuous. Even slow, continuous movement causes a rapid increase in sexual excitement. When you stop this movement – even for a second – sexual excitement fades and drops.

Exercises for the week

a) Exercises without sexual excitement

The exercises without sexual excitement should be practised three times during the week in a calm and relaxing setting.

Exercise 13. Relaxing different parts of the body
This exercise is described in this session.

Exercise 12. The muscles of the perineum
This exercise is described in the sixth session.

Exercise 10. The movement of the pelvis while lying on the back
First part: Technique
Second part: Breathing
These exercises are described in the sixth session.

Exercise 10. The movement of the pelvis while lying on the back
Third part: Intensity
Fourth part: Speed
These exercises are described in this session.

b) Exercises with sexual excitement

Before starting any sexual stimulation, you will perceive and relax every part of your body in order to reduce your overall muscle tone.

During sexual relations, ensure that you adopt a rhythm that suits you. If you must moderate the speed of the movement of your pelvis in order to prevent your sexual excitement from reaching levels that are too high, you will do so. If you also need your partner to slow down her movement, you will let her know. If you have to make pauses, you will make them for as long as it takes to lower your sexual excitement close to the zone of the appearance and disappearance of the erection. It is important for you to determine the amount of stimuli you could receive and act accordingly, even if this sometimes means a dip in your partner's excitement.

Sexual intercourse for 10 minutes!

This week, you will have intercourse that will last 10 minutes. For many of you, this will be a considerable challenge. But you can do it. The objective of this exercise is to develop your ability to remain a long time inside your partner's vagina.

No matter if you must make 15 or 20 pauses. No matter if you lose your erection. No matter if your partner's sexual excitement decreases. Your goal is to maintain intercourse for 10 minutes. You now have sufficient technique to remain inside your partner's vagina for this period of time. Remember that, like all men, you will always need to resort to pauses.

To accomplish this objective, we suggest you adopt the position where the man is lying on his back and the woman is on top of him. In this position, you will not move your pelvis and you will avoid contracting your gluteal muscles.

If you are able to stay several minutes inside your partner's vagina, acclimatizing to this sensation, your mission will be accomplished. In fact, you will break out of the vicious cycle where intercourse equals ejaculation. You will be on the right track to appropriate management and mutual pleasure.

When you have succeeded in staying like this for 10 minutes over ten sexual encounters, you should increase the speed of your pelvic movements. Later, when you have become comfortable moving quickly, you should make more vigorous movements (but only after 10 minutes of intercourse). The suggested progression is as follows:

Step one: Make sure that you can remain inside your partner for 10 minutes.

Step two: Increase the speed of your movements.

Step three: Amplify the intensity of your movements.

Do not attempt to reverse this order. Do not try, for example, to move quickly and progressively increase the duration. Clinical experience has shown that this does not work. Focus first and foremost on the duration. This will build a base. Only afterwards concern yourself with moving faster and stronger. Wanting to do everything at the same time complicates things, generates anxiety and leads to failure. You will get better results if you proceed in stages and start off with lower expectations.

Suggestions for the single man

You should also focus on the duration. You should masturbate for 10 minutes. This is how you will establish your base. You should do this using all the techniques you know, including pauses. If you can already easily achieve 10 minutes, do the exercise regardless but while increasing the level of difficulty (for example by stimulating yourself more quickly) and applying many management techniques. In this way, you will boost your ability to receive more and more intense stimuli and to better manage your excitement. The transfer of these skills into a couple relationship will require a few adjustments, but you will have acquired the foundation that will allow you to prolong the length of intercourse.

Once again this time, you should imagine on two separate occasions two different sexual scenarios: one, involving foreplay and the other, intercourse. While visualizing these scenarios, you will follow the guidelines prescribed until now. You will integrate the observation of your bodily reactions and the application of your techniques into your sexual practice.

Suggestions for the woman

Even when you are sufficiently excited and feel ready, leave the timing of intercourse up to the man. In fact, if you ask him to penetrate you when he's on the verge of ejaculating, he will not be able to last very long. It would be ideal if both of you approached intercourse at moderate levels of excitement.

You can encourage your partner not to immediately begin the in-and-out motions of intercourse as soon as he penetrates you. Suggest that he remain a long time without moving. Then, when you feel his erection diminishing, you can gently stimulate him. You can start with small vaginal contractions on his penis or with slow and sensual movements of your pelvis.

You can also set yourself as an objective intercourse lasting 10 minutes. If your spouse seems overwhelmed, you can take charge of the unfolding activities. Lead him to lie on his back and place yourself in the female-superior position. Make multiple and long pauses. Turn the fact of being motionless into a pleasant game and not a chore. After achieving intercourse for 10 minutes, continue to remain in control of the activities. Tone down your partner's impulses if he appears to want to pleasure you at all costs. In a tranquil manner, begin to move your pelvis forward and backward (and not up and down). Make additional pauses and take pleasure in the fact that you are on good terms with your lover. Your goal is uniquely to increase the length of intercourse, without striving for performance or orgasm. The most unbridled sexual escapades will come later.

Suggestions for the couple

Many couples contain their sexual impulses in order to keep the man's excitement at low levels and delay the onset of ejaculation. The woman avoids moving and touching the man for fear of arousing him too much. The man thinks about something else and stimulates the woman in every way imaginable so as to bring her to orgasm before he ejaculates. These manoeuvres are restrictive and frustrating. Now that you have new and effective management methods at your disposal, it would be good, for your pleasure and satisfaction, to begin to expand your sexual behaviour repertoire. There is an exercise for this purpose – "sensate focus" or awareness of touch – with a proven track record spanning decades. Developed by Masters and Johnson (1970), this technique consists of exploring sensations through various forms of touch. Here's how it works.

The man and woman retire to a calm and comfortable location. Taking turns, they share the roles of giver and receiver. For 10 minutes, the receiver lies on his/her stomach and the giver caresses him/her all over the body, except on the breasts and genitals. This is not a massage with pressure intended to relax tense muscles, but sensual touching aiming to provide pleasant sensations. The receiver must only focus his/her attention on the touches and identify the sensations he/she likes the most and those he/she likes the least. There's no obligation to perform, react in a particular way or to reciprocate what is being done to the giver. If the receiver has any sort of preference, he/she could make this known to the giver, either verbally, with his/her hand, or by moving his/her body. The same exercise is then repeated with the receiver this time lying on his/her back. When the exploration is completed, the partners switch roles.

The sensate focus exercise seeks to help you pay attention to sensations and to appreciate them fully without any stress or any type of obligation. Sensuality is at the basis of sexuality and your male partner's difficulty of management has perhaps led you both to unknowingly become diverted away from this. The objective of this exercise is to get you to once again savour the simple sensations derived from touch without your mind being burdened by any worries. Subsequently, you will explore a diversity of rhythms, locations, speeds, caresses, kisses and embraces, always maintaining this open and welcoming attitude. When you will be comfortable receiving fully, you will move on to a more reciprocal approach where you will give and receive at the same time, spontaneously and freely, fully enjoying the fact of giving and receiving, without demand of performance or success.

After each sensate focus session, it would be good for you to talk about what you liked and appreciated the least, what you experienced and what you thought. This will allow you to get to know each other better and to respond more appropriately to each other's desires. And since it is easier for men to communicate based upon a concrete and recent experience rather than talk about their sexual life in general, you will benefit as well from more interesting discussions.

EIGHTH SESSION

Sexual information

The perception of stimuli

A significant number of men who ejaculate rapidly avoid being caressed by their partner during foreplay. They're afraid of getting too excited and ejaculating too soon. Erotic games are therefore one-sided. They stimulate their partner and, when she's ready, they proceed to intercourse. They shun all stimulation, whether it is caresses, bodily contact or touches on the penis. To become even less excited, they try to think about something else or look elsewhere.

These avoidance tactics have many disadvantages. First, it is not very enjoyable for the man to participate in a sexual relationship without really getting involved, in other words not receiving anything and thinking about something else. Second, it is not very pleasant for the woman either. She must withhold her surges of affection and her sexual fantasies. In addition, when her partner is thinking about something else, she may feel isolated and unappreciated. Imagine for a moment what it would be like if your fiancée was always thinking about something else whenever you went to a restaurant with her. She would not talk to you; she would not be attentive to you. You would find this annoying. Third, thinking about something else in no way decreases the effects of direct stimulation on your penis which continues to increase your overall sexual excitement. Fourth, having your mind elsewhere stops you from detecting your excitement levels, observing your bodily reactions and applying the appropriate techniques. In other words, this takes away your means of preventing ejaculation! Finally, by not allowing yourself to be physically stimulated and thinking about something else, you risk having erectile difficulties beyond a certain age.

With the techniques and strategies outlined in this book, you and your partner will be able to let yourselves go completely during sexual relations. The two of you will be able to perceive and take pleasure in stimuli during foreplay and intercourse. You will be able to caress, kiss and stimulate each other without fear of unexpectedly provoking ejaculation.

Important note

Sexual excitement management methods

To reduce their sexual excitement, numerous men use aversive management methods. These methods consist of thinking about something unpleasant (which some therapists call cognitive distraction), pinching oneself, withdrawing suddenly from the vagina, hurting oneself, etc. These ways are neither elegant nor enjoyable, neither for the man nor for the woman. It is far better to use the different management techniques described in this book, which were developed to help you modulate your sexual excitement without spoiling your pleasure.

Being receptive to sexual stimuli has several advantages. First, sensing different touches leads to, in a paradoxical way, relaxation at the same time as a feeling of sexual excitement. You will be sexually excited but at the same time relaxed, which will enable you to remain below the point of no return. Second, you will have fun, which is a significant advantage. Third, sex with your partner will be reciprocal and not one-sided. This will provide you with moments of sharing and extraordinary communication. Fourth, receiving sexual stimuli, perceiving and savouring them, form the basis of your erectile capacity. If you are attentive to what is happening during the sexual encounter, you allow the neurophysiological processes of the erection to become activated and take place. From the age of 40, this condition becomes more and more necessary in the maintenance of sexual potency.

The pleasures of intercourse versus the pleasure of ejaculation

When you modulate your sexual excitement for 5, 10 or 15 minutes, you will not experience the same sensations as when you go towards ejaculation in 30 seconds. These sensations are less strong and the reason is simply that excitement is lower. Consequently, when you modulate your sexual excitement, you cannot expect to experience the same types of pleasure as when you let it skyrocket. These pleasures are more subtle, more delicate, more nuanced. To appreciate them, you must refine your ability to perceive them and discriminate among their different qualities. This takes a certain amount of time and learning. At first, you might find these pleasures unexciting and uninteresting. In the long run, you will learn to recognize their full value.

Important note

A fine wine!

We've compared love to art and sport. We can also do so with gastronomy and oenology. There are similarities, for example, between tasting a good wine and appreciating the subtleties of intercourse. In the case of wine, we admire its colour, we smell its bouquet, and we taste its flavours. We pause and, as we exhale, we delight in the memory of its aromas.

The same philosophy transposes into sexuality. We are taken by our partner's beauty. We commune with her femininity. We quiver at the sizzling touch of her skin.

By letting yourself absorb this mindset, you will become an extraordinary lover who takes his time and relishes the pleasures of love.

What you must remember from all of this is that you cannot obtain the intense pleasures connected with the upper part of the zone of modulation and at the same time extend intercourse. This is contradictory. If you want to delay your ejaculation, you must avoid continually carrying on at very high levels of excitement. These levels themselves are very enjoyable, but they inevitably lead to ejaculation. You must therefore be prepared to defer the strong sensations of imminent ejaculation. And, to that end, it is beneficial to learn to relish the subtle pleasures associated with the modulation of sexual excitement.

Exercises

Exercise 13. Relaxing different parts of the body

This exercise is described in the seventh session.

Exercise 12. The muscles of the perineum

This exercise is described in the sixth session.

Exercise 14. The movement of the pelvis while lying on the side

Objective: To perform the movement of the pelvis while lying on your side very slowly and with little muscular tension.

In order for you to execute the movement of the pelvis on your side, you have to use the same muscles as in the other positions, but the sensations you will experience will be different. Since you are resting on your hip, you must rotate your pelvis really well around its axis for this to work.

Make sure to bring your knees towards your chest in order to release the hip joint and enable you to make the forward pelvis movement. Do not contract your gluteals and do not accelerate the movement going forward.

Lie on your side, legs bent and thighs are raised towards your chest, lips slightly parted and eyes open.

- a Exhale and rotate your pelvis forward, counting to five (about 5 seconds). (Figure 3.31)
- b At the end of the exhalation, there is a stop of about one second. You make a micropause during this stop and you relax yourself before going back.
- c Inhale and rotate the pelvis backward, counting to five (about 5 seconds). (Figure 3.32)
- d At the end of the inhalation, there is a suspension. Make a micropause during this suspension in inhalation and relax yourself before going forward.

Repeat this exercise 30 times.

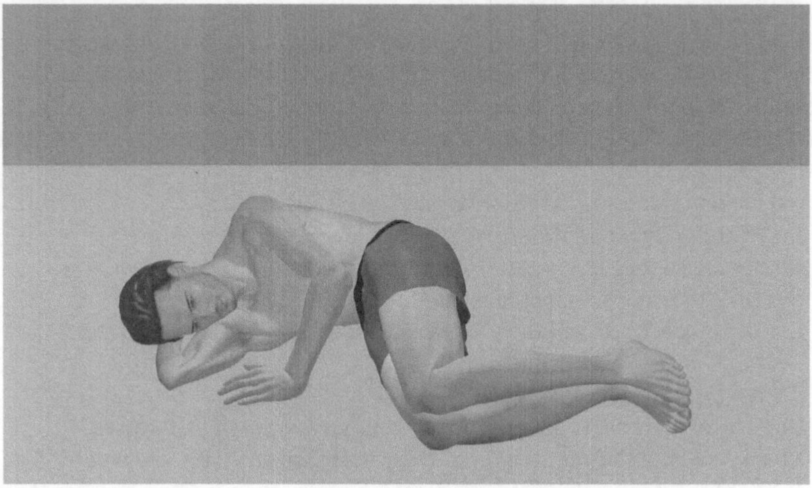

Figure 3.31 Movement of the pelvis forward while lying on the side

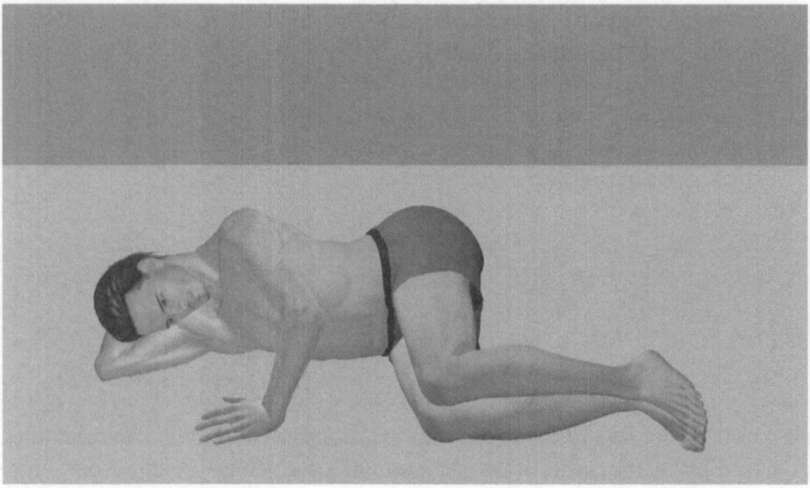

Figure 3.32 Movement of the pelvis backward while lying on the side

Exercise 15. The movement of the pelvis while lying on the side with and without the contraction of the muscles of the perineum

Objective: To perceive and relax the muscles in your perineum while moving your pelvis.

Lie on your side. Your legs should be bent and your thighs raised towards your chest. Your lips should be slightly parted and your eyes open. Do not worry if the muscles in your perineum relax quickly during this exercise. In fact it is difficult to keep these muscles contracted very long when you are not excited.

a Exhale and rotate your pelvis forward.
b Inhale into your stomach and rotate your pelvis backward.
c If you were engaged in sexual activity, you would be excited and this would make your perineal muscles contract.
  Contract them and keep them contracted while continuing to rotate your pelvis.
d Along the way, you would make an assessment of the situation.
  You would observe if the muscles in your perineum are contracted.
  You would feel the contraction of these muscles, and then you would relax them.
  Relax them now.
  Continue to execute the movement of the pelvis while breathing from the stomach and relaxing yourself.
e Accelerate the speed of your pelvis.
  As the penis would be stimulated by the vagina, the muscles in your perineum would contract immediately.
  Contract them now while continuing to move your pelvis.
f A little later, you would assess the situation again:
  "Are the muscles in my perineum contracted?"
  "Yes!" You would relax them.
  Relax them now.
  Also decrease the speed of your pelvis while relaxing yourself and breathing from the stomach.

Repeat this exercise three times.

You are now aware that to delay the moment of ejaculation, you can relax the muscles in your perineum, slow down the speed of your pelvis, breathe from your stomach and reduce the tone of all the muscles in your body. You could do all of these things at the same time or do them one at a time, whichever you prefer.

Exercises for the week

a) Exercises without sexual excitement

Perform the exercises without sexual excitement three times during the week. Set aside time and do them slowly, perceiving the sensations that accompany them.

Exercise 13. Relaxing different parts of the body
This exercise is described in the seventh session.

Exercise 12. The muscles of the perineum
This exercise is described in the sixth session.

Exercise 14. The movement of the pelvis while lying on the side
This exercise is described in this session.

Exercise 15. The movement of the pelvis while lying on the side with and without the contraction of the muscles of the perineum
This exercise is described in this session.

b) Exercises with sexual excitement

During sexual relations, adopt the position where the man is lying on his back and the woman is sitting on top of him. Make an effort to perceive and relax the muscles in your perineum, while continuing to move your pelvis and breathe from your stomach. From time to time, decrease the tone of the muscles in your body, while continuing to move.

Again this week, you will have intercourse for 10 minutes. This probably will not take place as vigorously as you'd like. But do not forget that you are building a foundation and there are steps to follow in order to obtain the desired results.

As always, you relax before each sexual engagement.

Suggestions for the single man

During masturbation, stroke your entire body and not just your genitals. This will put you in conditions similar to those which you will encounter during sexual relations with a woman. This will also help you develop your sensuality and improve your ability to modulate your sexual excitement. You will get the impression that your sexual excitement is spreading throughout your whole body, not concentrated in your genital organs, ready to explode.

We suggest you stimulate yourself by moving your pelvis as if you were penetrating a woman. Do this by breathing from your stomach, isolating the pelvis from your back, moving slowly, following the rhythm of your breathing, not using your gluteals and making pauses.

Suggestions for the woman

Many women think about a million things during sexual relations and, in fact, pay little attention to the stimuli being offered to them. Is this your case? Do you reflect on how you're going to dress your kids the next day? Do you tell yourself it is time to change the curtains in your bedroom? Do you finish a task for work in your mind? If you answered "yes" to any of these questions, rest assured that you are normal! Unlike men, it is very easy for women to think about a thousand things at once. However, what is an advantage in everyday life becomes a disadvantage in sexuality. If you want to have pleasure and reach orgasm, you must pay attention to what you like during the romantic encounter.

A good way to achieve this goal is to give yourself the time to be able to extract yourself from your daily routine and fall in love with your spouse all over again. Securing this special free time requires discipline and organization! It is only once you put order into your day-to-day affairs, but not in an obsessive manner, that you will have peace of mind and will be able to make the most of the present moment. Sensuality will then take its rightful place and you will totally abandon yourself to pleasure.

Suggestions for the couple

It is possible that your difficulty with prolonging the length of intercourse has stifled your sexual interactions into repetitive behaviours. If that is the case, it has surely resulted in a reduction in your sexual and romantic repertoire. To expand this repertoire and regain your freedom of expression, we suggest you explore new ways of acting. This exploration could begin with a discussion about your various preferences.

What are your emotional, romantic and erotic preferences? Have you shared them with your partner? What are the places, moments, situations and ambiences you cherish most? What attracts you to him or to her? Is it his/her attitude, words, actions, looks, touches, body, sexual attributes, qualities, hair, accessories, clothes? What sexually excites you? Is it the same thing that attracts you? What kind of encounters would you like to have with your partner? Playful, emotional, sensual, loving, romantic, passionate, languorous, erotic? What would you like to tell, do with or show to your partner?

Expressing your personal preferences to your spouse can turn out to be extremely exciting. Or telling him to find out what type of caresses you would like to receive. Or asking her to discover the most sensitive parts of your body. Sharing your fantasies, communicating your desires, revealing your secrets are excellent ways for you to get emotionally and sexually closer to your partner. This will equally permit you to derive more pleasure and satisfaction from your romantic and sexual life.

NINTH SESSION

Sexual information

The effect of sexual positions

Some positions contribute more to the arrival of ejaculation than others. The basic principle is the following: the more effort a position requires to be maintained, the more it increases the risk of ejaculating rapidly. The reason for this is when a man makes an effort to stay in a position, he contracts different muscles and the contraction of these muscles facilitates the onset of ejaculation.

Paradoxically, the position most likely to induce ejaculation is the one used by most couples. It is the position commonly called the "missionary" position in which the man is on top of the woman. There are several variations of this position. The most demanding of them is the one where the man rests on his hands and knees. In this position, the muscles located at the back of the arms (triceps), the chest muscles (pectorals) and the stomach muscles (abdominals) are contracted, which provokes a marked increase in muscular tension. Next, it is almost impossible to breathe from the stomach because the abdominal muscles are contracted; consequently, it is very difficult to lower muscular tension caused by sexual excitement with breathing. Finally, it is arduous to execute the forward-backward movement of the pelvis because of the limitations of the hip joint. This leads the man to perform the in-and-out movements of penetration while breathing from the rib cage, contracting the gluteal muscles and moving the back and pelvis as one unit. This therefore results in substantial muscular contractions.

Important note

The scientific attitude

It's important to approach your new sexual experiences with a scientific attitude and ask yourself the following two fundamental questions: "What did my partner and I do? What was the result?" From these observations, you will evaluate the effects of your new behaviours and decide whether to keep or change them. It is evident that you must apply a new technique numerous times before determining its effectiveness. Learning a bodily skill takes time. Only after several attempts will you master it and then be able to really evaluate its usefulness. Be careful not to get discouraged or give up too soon. The tips contained in this book are very effective but require practice to be assimilated. Patience and repetition are the watchwords to achieving your objectives.

The following version of the missionary position places less strain on the man's musculature. The man is all the same on top of the woman, resting on his knees, but this time he supports himself with his elbows rather than his hands. The advantage of this variant over the previous one is that the triceps do not have to contract to maintain the position. Furthermore, if the man rests his stomach and chest on his partner, his pectoral and abdominal muscles have to exert less effort.

Both variations of the position known as the "missionary" were analysed in detail because they are the ones most commonly used by couples. What you must remember from this study is that as soon as a position demands a certain amount of muscular effort to be maintained, it contributes to the onset of ejaculation.

In which positions is it easier for you to manage your sexual excitement? These are the ones that a man requires little effort to maintain. The best of them is the one in which the man lies on his back and the woman sits on him. Lateral positions where the man penetrates the woman from behind are also excellent.

Many couples like the man to be on top of the woman during intercourse. The position we will study in this session gives the man the opportunity to be on top of the woman with little stress on his muscles. It starts with the woman lying on her back, her two legs bent and spread out at least shoulder width apart, and her feet flat on the mattress. The man goes on top of her, between her legs, and penetrates her. She remains on her back while turning her pelvis and her legs to the left side. The man keeps his chest over the woman's chest as he turns his pelvis with legs bent to the right side. The right side of his pelvis rests on the mattress while the woman's left thigh is under his right hip. The man wraps the upper part of the woman's body in his arms. In this position, the man expends little energy to support his weight. He can also breathe from the stomach and move his pelvis with ease. In addition, the fact that the man is able to hold the woman's upper body against his chest retains the symbolic and emotional benefits of the position in which the man is on top of the woman.

These observations do not imply that you must always make love in positions that are less demanding on your musculature. You are perfectly free to add variety and fantasy to your sexual encounters. However, if you desire your sexual experience to last a long time, it is wise to start with a position that requires little muscular tension. Then, when you are sufficiently acclimatized to sexual excitement, you could move on to other positions.

Exercises

Exercise 13. Relaxing different parts of the body

This exercise is described in the seventh session.

Exercise 16. Muscular dissociation (first part)

Objective: To gain control over the muscle groups which play an important role in the rise of sexual excitement.

This exercise is relatively difficult and will require a lot of concentration. When you master it, your body control will increase substantially and it will be easier for you to manage your sexual excitement.

Lie on your back, legs stretched out and spread about shoulder width apart, lips slightly parted and eyes open.

- a Contract your gluteals.
- b While keeping your gluteals contracted, contract the muscles in your perineum.
- c While keeping your gluteals contracted, relax the muscles in your perineum.
- d Relax your gluteals.
- e Remember to breathe!

Repeat this exercise 10 times.

**

- a Contract the muscles in your perineum.
- b While you keep the muscles in your perineum contracted, contract your gluteals.
- c While you keep the muscles in your perineum contracted, relax your gluteals.
- d Relax the muscles in your perineum.
- e Remember to breathe!

Repeat this exercise 10 times.

Exercise 17. The study of the effects of positions where the man is on top of the woman

Objective: To become aware of muscular tension produced by different sexual positions.

Position yourself on your hands and knees, your pelvis raised about eight inches from the mattress, like during sexual intercourse (Figure 3.33). Hold this position for 1 minute. You will find that this position is very demanding in muscular terms. In addition, it restricts abdominal breathing and renders the execution of the movement of the pelvis very difficult.

(continued)

(continued)

a) Hold the position.
b) Become aware of the muscular tension at the back of your arms (triceps).
c) Become aware of the muscular tension in your chest area (pectorals).
d) Become aware of the muscular tension in your stomach area (abdominals).
e) Attempt to breathe from your stomach.
f) Try to rotate your pelvis.
g) Lie on your stomach and relax yourself.

**

This time position yourself on your elbows and knees, your pelvis raised eight inches from the mattress (Figure 3.34). Stay in this position for 1 minute. You will find that this position, just like the previous one, causes major muscular contractions. In addition, it makes abdominal breathing and the movement of the pelvis more arduous.

a) Hold the position.
b) Become aware of the muscular tension in your chest area (pectorals).
c) Become aware of the muscular tension in your stomach area (abdominals).
d) Attempt to breathe from your stomach.
e) Try to rotate your pelvis.
f) Lie on your stomach and relax yourself.

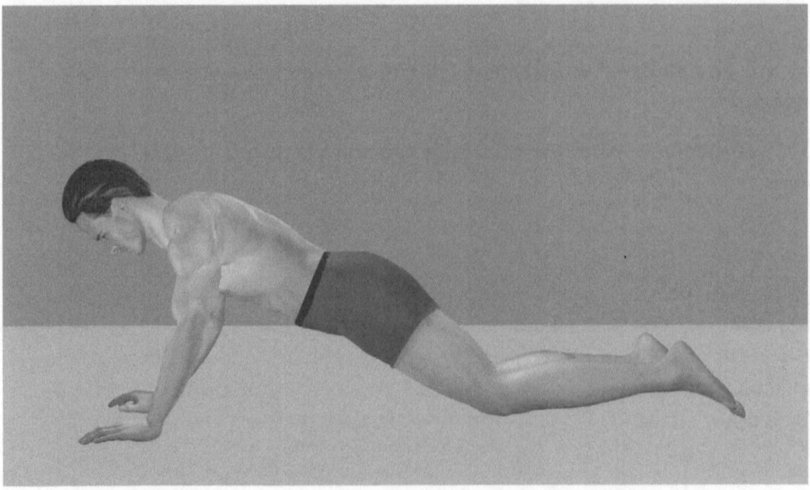

Figure 3.33 The man in the superior position resting on his hands and knees

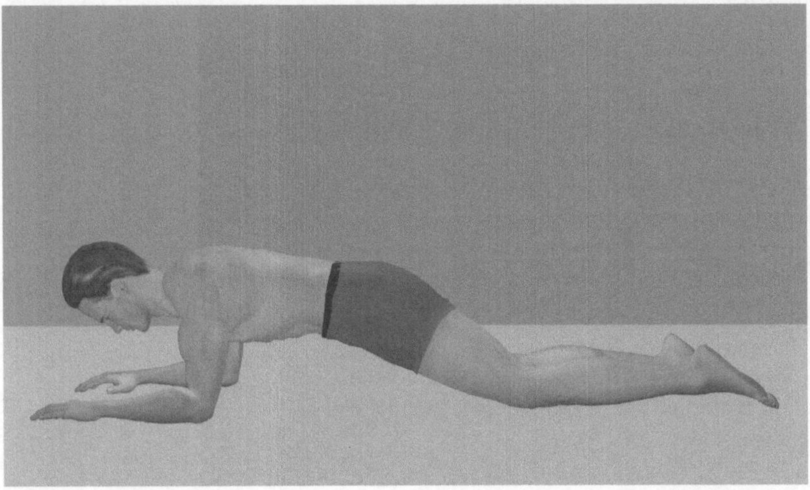

Figure 3.34 The man in the superior position resting on his elbows and knees

Exercise 18. The movement of the pelvis in the latero-superior position

Objective: To adopt a position where the man is on top of the woman and in which little muscular tension is generated.

To finish off you will learn how to move your pelvis in the latero-superior position. This position, in addition to helping you defer the moment of ejaculation, will prove conducive to the creation of intimacy between you and your partner.

Lie down on your right side, knees drawn up. Put your left leg over your right leg and turn your chest towards the mattress. Rest your head on your right arm, which is extended upward. Your eyes should be open and your mouth slightly open.

- a Exhale and rotate your pelvis forward for a count of five (about 5 seconds). Do not contract your gluteals and do not accelerate the movement going forward. (Figure 3.35)
- b At the end of the exhalation, there is a stop of about 1 second. Make a micropause during this stop and relax before going back.
- c Inhale and rotate your pelvis backward for a count of five (about 5 seconds). Completely release your stomach as you inhale. (Figure 3.36)
- d At the end of the inhalation, there is a suspension. Make a micropause during this suspension in exhalation and relax before proceeding.

Repeat this exercise 30 times.

(continued)

(continued)

**

Repeat the movement in the latero-superior position adding the contraction and relaxation of the muscles in your perineum.

a Exhale and rotate your pelvis forward.
b Inhale into your stomach and rotate your pelvis backward.
c If you were engaged in sexual activity, you would be excited and this would make the muscles in your perineum contract.
Contract these muscles and keep them contracted while continuing to move your pelvis.
d Along the way, you would assess the situation.
You would check to see whether the muscles in your perineum are contracted.
Feel the contraction of the muscles in your perineum and then release them.
Continue to execute the movement of the pelvis while breathing from your stomach and relaxing yourself.
e Now, accelerate the speed of your pelvis.
As the penis would be stimulated by the vagina, the muscles in your perineum would contract immediately.
Contract them while continuing to move your pelvis rapidly.
f A little later, you would assess the situation again:
"Are the muscles in my perineum contracted?"
"Yes!" You would relax them.
Relax them.
Decrease the speed of your pelvis as well while relaxing yourself and breathing from your stomach.
g Make a pause for 30 seconds.

Repeat this exercise five times.

Exercises for the week

a) Exercises without sexual excitement

Do the exercises without sexual excitement three times during the week in an atmosphere of calm and relaxation. You perceive and enjoy the emanating sensations.

Exercise 13. Relaxing different parts of the body
This exercise is described in the seventh session.

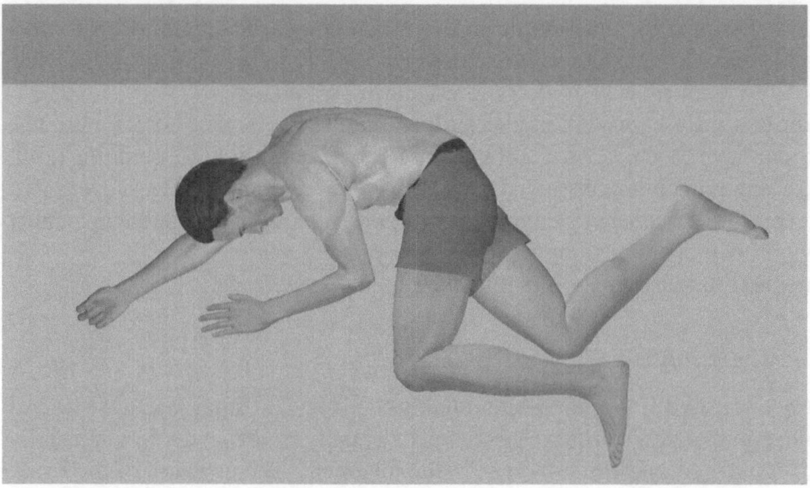

Figure 3.35 Movement of the pelvis forward in the latero-superior position

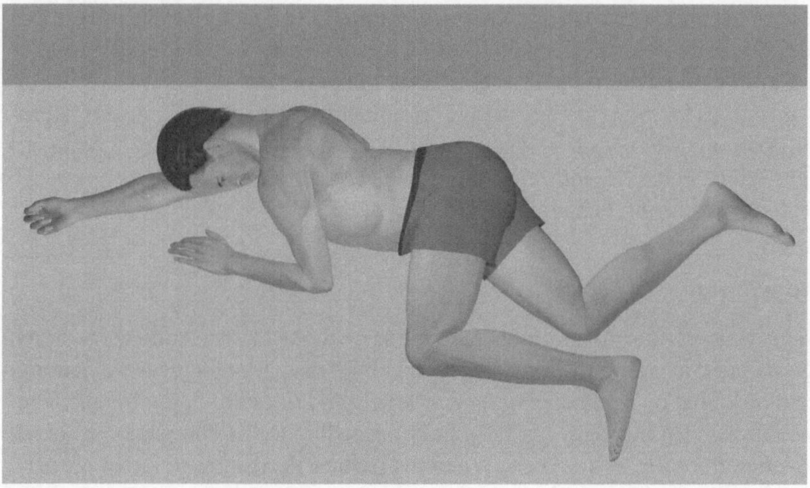

Figure 3.36 Movement of the pelvis backward in the latero-superior position

Exercise 16. Muscular dissociation (first part)
This exercise is described in this session.

Exercise 17. The study of the effect of positions where the man is on top of the woman
This exercise is described in this session.

Exercise 18. The movement of the pelvis in the latero-superior position
This exercise is described in this session.

b) Exercises with sexual excitement

Use the latero-superior position during sexual relations. Make an effort to perceive and relax the muscles in your perineum while continuing to move your pelvis. Allow your rib cage to decompress during exhalation.

Again this week, you will engage in penetrative intercourse for 10 minutes, even if you have to slow down and make a lot of pauses. In fact, from this point on I suggest having intercourse that extends beyond 10 minutes at least every two weeks. This will force you to let go of any notion you may have that the man must move vigorously without stopping inside his spouse's vagina.

Remember to relax yourself before each sexual experience.

For the single man

Do not be surprised if you ejaculate quickly the first few times you have sexual intercourse with a new partner. This happens equally to men who do not usually have difficulties in managing their sexual excitement. The newness of the situation, the emotional intensity and stress contribute to precipitating ejaculation. It is a matter of not worrying about it and considering it as something normal. You will not be the first or the last one to have to deal with this. You can view this situation as an opportunity to learn and improve yourself. Reflecting on the events that occurred, it will be possible for you to draw lessons from and to identify courses of action applicable towards your future sexual experiences.

It is possible, for practice, to engage in masturbatory activities in the latero-superior position. Move your pelvis from front to back while stimulating yourself with your hand. Perceive and relax the muscles in your perineum. Let your rib cage decompress during exhalation.

For the woman

Encourage your partner to prolong intercourse without having him worry about making you orgasm. A man who is concerned about his partner's pleasure does not pay attention to his own sexual excitement levels and does not apply his management techniques. He manages his behaviour according to his companion's sexual excitement and not that of his own. When his partner needs him to move quickly, he thrusts faster regardless of his own degree of sexual excitement. If at the start of intercourse, he follows his spouse's course of excitement rather than his own, he is extremely likely to ejaculate before she reaches orgasm. It is preferable in the beginning to work within the boundaries of male sexuality and start off slowly. Afterwards, when the man is acclimatized to the sensations and the symbolism of intercourse, you can speed up. But for this, he must be reassured that you accept that he cannot devote all of his attention and energy into trying to please you.

We suggest that you urge your partner to take his time and to proceed with sensuality rather than haste. Bring about the pauses yourself if he does not do them. This can be done by speaking or by simply stopping. Do not ask him to go faster until after 10 minutes of intercourse, and this acceleration must be gradual.

Suggestions for the couple

It is tempting to want to help the person you love and to offer him advice so that he can improve. But you have to be very careful. In fact, this good intention, while laudable, has hidden pitfalls that could cause more harm than good to your relationship. If you put on a different hat and become your spouse's therapist, you actually sow the seeds for long-term discord. This holds true for both the man and the woman.

How do you turn into your partner's therapist? By adopting aloofness, observing him, analysing his behaviour, making interpretations, pointing out his mistakes, telling him what to do, wanting to change him . . . This type of behaviour shifts the couple's equilibrium and instigates a power struggle. The therapist–patient relationship is not egalitarian and your "patient" will reject your suggestions in order to safeguard his role in the relationship. You will be frustrated because your advice will seem so good and the other partner will be frustrated because he will feel led by the nose. It is therefore essential not to assume a position of superiority – even if you see more clearly than your spouse – and to think together rather than to counsel him.

You will also need to show patience toward your spouse when he gets discouraged, does not learn as fast as you would like or loses interest in the programme. On the other hand, this does not prevent you from maintaining a positive attitude and congratulating him when he modifies a behaviour in the right direction. As for the person who is receiving advice, it is better to set aside your pride and be open-minded so as not to damage the relationship at all!

The most beneficial behaviours are to accept and encourage each other, demonstrate your affection and declare your love. These positive behaviours will help you weather the difficult times and progress more rapidly towards your goal.

Important note

The final stretch!

You have completed three quarters of your programme. Congratulations!

It is very likely however that you have not – apart from the imposed 10 minutes of intercourse – progressed one iota. This is completely normal. This is what happens when we teach these techniques to our patients. You must get through the entire programme to achieve success.

It is a bit like building a house. You must lay the foundation before the walls and the walls before the roof. As long as the roof is not in place, it will rain in the house.

A little patience goes a long way!

TENTH SESSION

Sexual information

Stimulation of the woman during intercourse

Over the course of this session, you will learn two ways to heighten your partner's excitement during intercourse without receiving too much stimulation yourself. The first way applies in the case where your partner pays attention to the sensations emanating from her internal genital organs. This approach is based on touches that give rise to movements facilitating the build-up of her excitement and pleasure.

One must first understand that when a woman receives vaginal stimulation through the intermediary of the penis, she can move in a manner to lessen or accentuate the perception of this stimulation. It is therefore important if she desires to obtain excitement and pleasure during intercourse that her body moves appropriately. The touches you will learn during this session head in this direction. They aim to facilitate within your partner a movement that is favourable to the perception of sensations in her vagina during intercourse. At the same time, they contribute to reducing the necessity of vigorous penile stimulation and thus help the man to keep his sexual excitement below the threshold of the point of no return. The man is no longer obliged to resort to fast and energetic movements of intercourse to stimulate the woman. He divides his involvement between vaginal stimulation and touches that elicit the appropriate movements in the woman.

The first thing a woman must do to facilitate the rise of her sexual excitement, when she is stimulated in the vaginal area, is to breathe from the abdomen. When she breathes in this way, her abdominal muscles relax and she perceives much more precisely the sensations coming from her internal genital organs. To help his partner breathe from the abdomen, the man can simply caress or massage her stomach during foreplay and intercourse when feasible (for example, in the side position, man behind the woman).

The second skill the woman must master is the execution, with her trunk, of a concave arc when she exhales and a convex arc when she inhales. When she executes the concave arc, her pelvis goes forward, her chest sinks inward and her head tilts back (Figure 3.37). When she carries out the convex arc, her pelvis shifts back, her back hollows and her head returns slightly forward (Figure 3.38). The concave arc occurs reflexively during orgasm. It is therefore called the "reflex arc". When executed voluntarily, the concave arc – because it takes the same neuromuscular pathways as those of the reflex arc – facilitates the progression of sexual excitement and pleasure.

The man can guide the woman to execute the movement of the concave arc. When she breathes out, he can either rotate her pelvis forward using his hands, incline her rib cage forward (while sliding his hand on her sternum from top to bottom) or tilt her head back (while caressing the nape of her neck from top to bottom).

There are, however, women who are not keen on this approach and who respond primarily to clitoral stimulation. In that case, you can caress your partner's clitoris with your fingers while keeping your pelvis immobile. This way you will be less stimulated and she will be more so. It is also possible that she will prefer, like many women who know their bodies well, to touch herself. The stimulation of the clitoris can be combined with that of other erogenous zones such as the breasts, neck, lips, sides and anus. This provokes both an accumulation and synergy of nerve impulses involved in the rise of her excitement and pleasure.

Such an approach, focused on the clitoris, makes obtaining an orgasm easier. It has the disadvantage, however, of being restrictive on the interactive, emotional

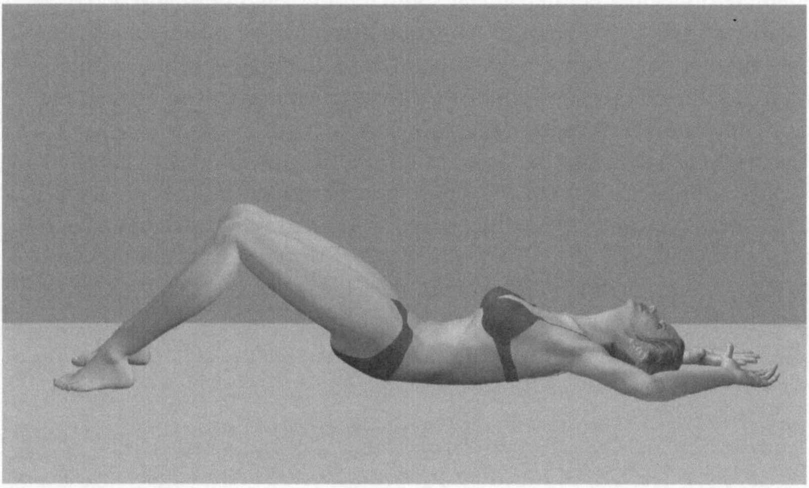

Figure 3.37 A woman executing the concave arc

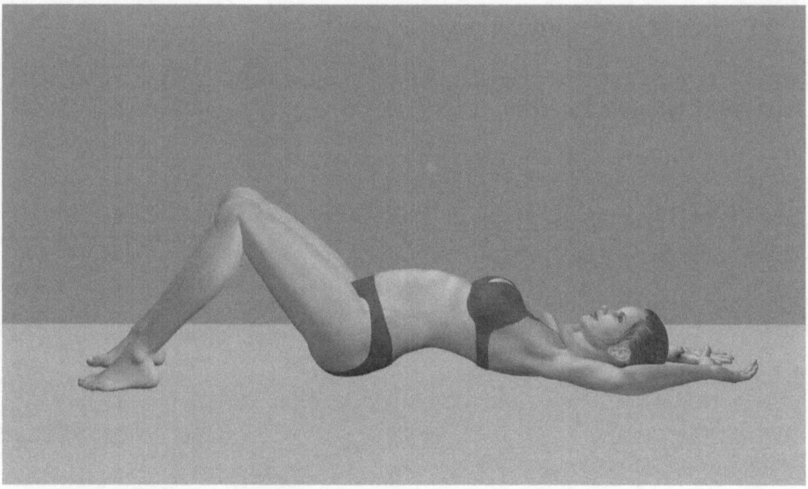

Figure 3.38 A woman executing the convex arc

and symbolic levels. In general, women report that clitoral stimulation is more intense on the physiological level, but less nourishing on the emotional level. It is up to the couple to identify what they desire and to be aware of the implications.

Important note

The woman's orgasm

The female orgasm is not dependent solely on the length of intercourse or the quality of penile stimulation. It rests on a number of factors such as the amount of attention the man pays to his spouse, the quality of the couple's relationship, the ambience in which the romantic encounter takes place, the type of approach, the duration of foreplay, etc.

The woman's orgasm also depends on multiple conditions within herself and over which the man has no power: hormonal influences, sexual maturity, bodily awareness, codification of stimuli as erotic, perception and enjoyment of stimuli codified as erotic, mastery of physical skills, the ability to let go, etc. The man and woman therefore each hold their share of responsibility in the quest for the female orgasm.

Exercises

Exercise 13. Relaxing different parts of the body

This exercise is described in the seventh session.

Exercise 16. Muscular dissociation (second part)

Objective: To acquire control over the muscle groups which play an important role in the rise of sexual excitement.

Lie on your back, legs stretched out and spread at least shoulder width apart, lips slightly parted and eyes open.

a) Contract your abdominals (pull in your stomach).
b) While keeping your abdominals contracted, contract the muscles in your perineum.
c) While keeping your abdominals contracted, relax the muscles in your perineum.
d) Relax your abdominals.
e) Remember to breathe!

Repeat this exercise 20 times.

**

a Contract the muscles in your perineum.
b While keeping the muscles in your perineum contracted, contract your abdominals.
c While keeping the muscles in your perineum contracted, relax your abdominals.
d Relax the muscles in your perineum.
e Remember to breathe!

Repeat this exercise 20 times.

Exercise 19. Movement of the pelvis in the superior position

First part: Technique and breathing

Objective: To prolong the length of intercourse when the man is in the superior position.

This position is by far the most difficult. It causes a considerable amount of muscular tension and makes the movement of the pelvis and abdominal breathing quite challenging to do. It requires a lot of effort at the beginning and only becomes natural with sustained regular practice. Since it is very demanding, you will learn it in a progressive manner. In order to reassure you, know that it is less difficult when you support yourself on your partner's pelvis and stomach during sexual intercourse. Do not hesitate to use a mirror to correct your position.

First step

To master the movement of the pelvis, you should repeat the pelvis movement exercise with support as seen in the second session.

Position yourself on the floor, resting on your hands and knees. Your arms and thighs should be perpendicular to the floor. Spread your legs shoulder width apart, breathe through your mouth and keep your eyes open.

a Exhale and, at the same time, arch your back and rotate your pelvis forward counting to five (around 5 seconds).
(Figure 3.39).
Really feel the movement your pelvis makes forward.
b At the end of the exhalation, there is a stop for about 1 second.
Make a micropause during this stop following exhalation and relax yourself before recommencing.
c Inhale and, at the same time, hollow your back and rotate your pelvis backward counting to five (about 5 seconds).

(continued)

(continued)

(Figure 3.40).
Really feel the movement your pelvis makes backward.

d At the end of the inhalation, there is a suspension.
Make a micropause during this suspension in inhalation and relax yourself before starting again.

Repeat this exercise 30 times.

Figure 3.39 Movement of the pelvis forward with support

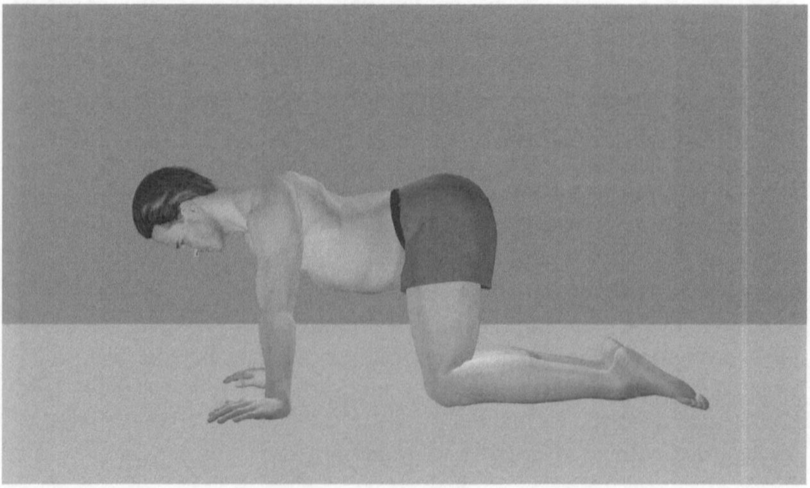

Figure 3.40 Movement of the pelvis backward with support

Second step

Rest on your elbows and knees. Your arms should be perpendicular and your thighs oblique in relation to the floor. Your legs should be spread shoulder width apart, your mouth partially open and your eyes open. This position is halfway between the position on hands and knees and the superior position. It will allow you to transition between these two positions.

a Exhale and, at the same time, you round your back and rotate your pelvis forward counting to five (about 5 seconds).
(Figure 3.41).
Really feel the movement your pelvis makes forward.

b At the end of the exhalation, there is a stop for about 1 second.
Make a micropause during this stop and relax yourself before recommencing.

c Inhale and, at the same time, hollow your back and rotate your pelvis backward counting to five (about 5 seconds).
(Figure 3.42).
Really feel the movement your pelvis makes backward.

d At the end of the inhalation, there is a suspension.
Make a micropause during this suspension in inhalation and relax yourself before starting off again.

Repeat this exercise 15 times.
Rest.
Repeat this exercise 15 times.

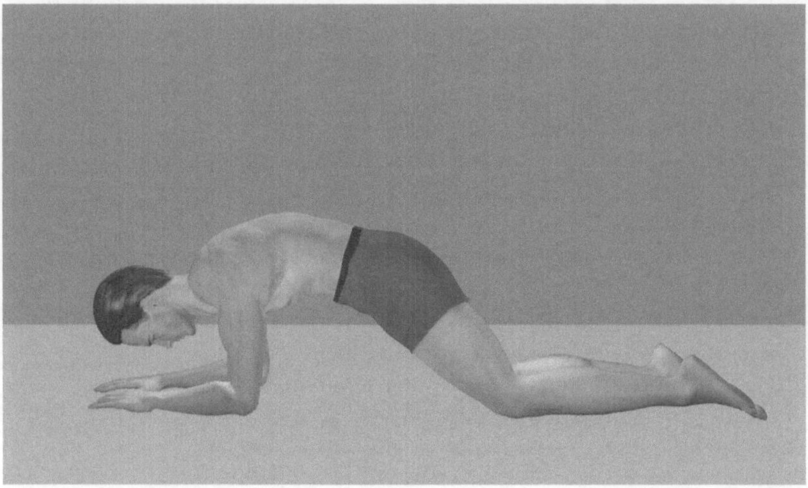

Figure 3.41 Movement of the pelvis forward resting on your elbows and knees

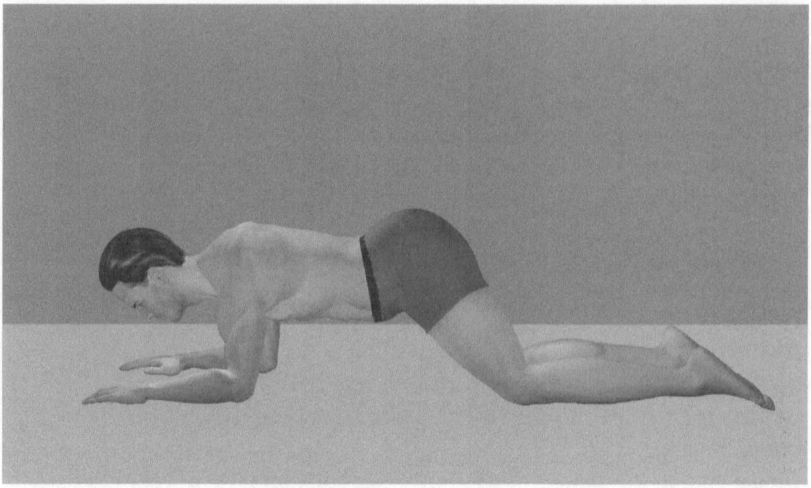

Figure 3.42 Movement of the pelvis backward resting on your elbows and knees

Third step

Place yourself in the superior position resting on your elbows and knees. Your arms should be perpendicular and your thighs oblique in relation to the floor. Your legs should be spaced shoulder width apart, your mouth partially open and your eyes open. As in the position on your hands and knees, you must arch your back even if in this position the range of motion is smaller.

a Exhale and, at the same time, arch your back and rotate your pelvis forward counting to five (about 5 seconds).
(Figure 3.43).
Really feel the movement your pelvis makes forward.

b At the end of the exhalation, there is a stop for about 1 second.
Make a micropause during this stop and relax yourself before recommencing.

c Inhale and, at the same time, hollow your back and rotate your pelvis backward counting to five (about 5 seconds).
(Figure 3.44).

d At the end of the inhalation, there is a suspension.
Make a micropause during this suspension in inhalation and relax yourself before starting off again.

Repeat this exercise 10 times.
Rest.
Repeat this exercise 10 times.
Rest.
Repeat this exercise 10 times.

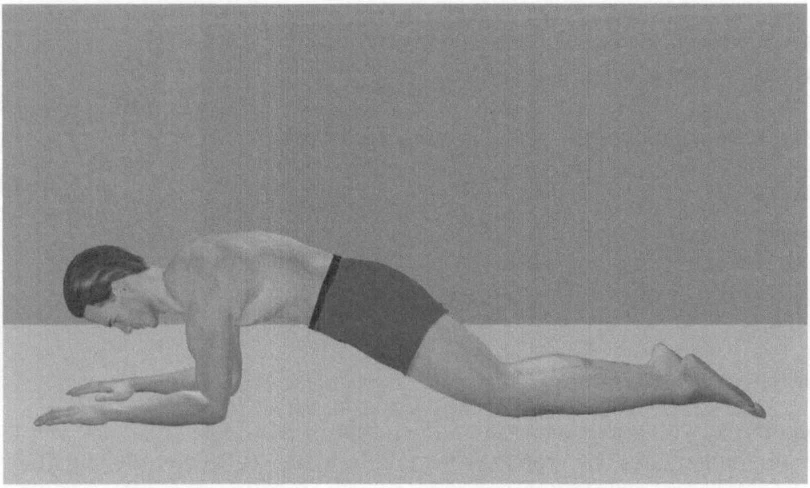

Figure 3.43 Movement of the pelvis forward in the superior position

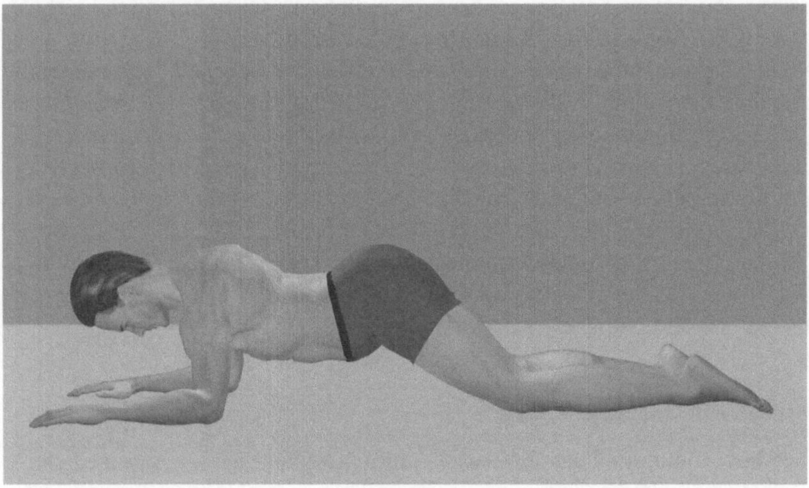

Figure 3.44 Movement of the pelvis backward in the superior position

Exercises for the week

a) Exercises without sexual excitement

These exercises should be executed in a calm and pleasant environment three times during the week.

Exercise 13. Relaxing different parts of the body
This exercise is described in the seventh session.

Exercise 16. Muscular dissociation (second part)
This exercise is described in this session.

Exercise 19. Movement of the pelvis in the superior position
First part: Technique and breathing
First step
Second step
Third step
This exercise is described in this session.

b) Exercises with sexual excitement

You can discuss with your partner the different facets of female eroticism. What type of stimulation does she prefer? Is there a desirable sequence of stimulation for her sexual fulfilment? Would she like to explore new avenues with you?

Gradually, you will begin to ease her into new ways of moving – or add to what she is already doing – by drawing inspiration from suggestions made throughout this session: abdominal breathing, forward-backward movement of the pelvis, inclination of the rib cage forward and tilting the head back (concave arc). You will want to ensure that the movements of penetration are slow and that your penis presses against the vaginal wall, whether it is the front, the back, the sides or the bottom. You can also take an approach that is more focused on your partner's clitoris and caress it with your fingers while reducing the speed of your pelvis or keeping it motionless during intercourse.

You will have sexual intercourse in the superior position. Since this is the position in which it is most difficult to manage your sexual excitement, it would be a good idea for you to take at least 5 minutes to acclimatize to sexual stimulation in positions that are less demanding before moving on to this position.

Suggestions for the single man

Many men have mentioned that they waited until the end of the programme before engaging in sexual relations with a new partner. They then proceeded according to the guidelines outlined in this programme and were able to significantly prolong the length of intercourse. It is obvious that to succeed, they had to put aside their old ways of doing things and act on the new principles that they learnt. Several also found that it was easier with their new companion. Their sexual interactions were no longer encumbered by inadequate and inflexible strategies arising from their past difficulty as was the case with their former partner.

This does not mean you have to wait until the end of the programme before participating in sexual activities with a new person. However, it is important to remember that you will not obtain conclusive results until you master all of the techniques. And furthermore, like all men, it will always remain difficult for you to prolong intercourse the first few times during a new encounter.

If you do not have a partner, you will be unable to practise in the superior position. You can then go back to using the latero-superior position during activities with sexual excitement.

Suggestions for the woman

It would be interesting for you to explore the subtleties of clitoral and vaginal eroticisms. Below is some information that will help you better understand each one of these eroticisms.

The clitoris is rich in superficial nerve endings and responds well to gentle tactile stimulation. To be effective, this stimulation must be applied in the right area, at the right speed, at the right intensity and in a relatively continuous manner. In addition, to heighten her excitement, the woman must focus on the sensations stemming from this part of her anatomy. Her body responds by immobilizing and contracting strongly. Her breathing is high and rapid. The woman will even hold her breath to increase the pressure inside her rib cage and intensify her degree of excitement. Her sexual tension is also amplified by the voluntary, intense and sustained contraction of her buttock, perineum, stomach, arm and leg muscles. The path of her excitement curve is largely determined by the manner in which the stimulation is applied and by her breathing rhythm. Her pleasure is closely associated with the rise and release of her sexual excitement. As far as her satisfaction goes it is very much linked to the liberation and appeasement following this discharge.

The vagina possesses nerve endings that respond to pressure. The most sensitive areas are located at the entrance and at the bottom of the anterior wall as well as the entrance of the posterior wall. To be effective, the stimulation of the vagina requires pressure of the penis against its walls. This contact is obtained through appropriate penetration angles as well as specific movements of the woman's pelvis and that of her partner. The vaginal sensations are enriched by emotions and feelings arising from interactions with the man. The woman's field of consciousness awakens to what is happening inside and outside of her. The perception of stimuli stemming from the context, her spouse, her vagina, her entire body and her mind nourish her sexual and sentimental experience. Vaginal eroticism adapts well in the beginning to a voluptuous way of behaving, deep breathing and fluid body movement. Physical and emotional abandon participate in the rise of pleasure and excitement. The sexual excitement curve follows a wave-like path. This path is created by the alternation of the speed and the intensity of pelvic movements. The woman's pleasure is diverse and is based on a variety of factors, such as the type of ambience, the quality of sensorial exchanges with her partner, the sharing of feelings, listening to her body, paying a special attention to her vagina, her way of moving, her physiological responses and her ability to let go. Vaginal eroticism does not exclude clitoral stimulation during foreplay. However, seeing that in intercourse the emphasis is placed on the sensations and emotions arising from the vaginal stimulation and pelvic movement, it is important to make the transition from the clitoris to the vagina prior to intromission, if you desire to fully enjoy the experience related to intercourse.

Orgasm by clitoral stimulation is more intense and easier to achieve. Orgasm through coital stimulation is felt more globally and is emotionally richer. Each eroticism has its requirements and characteristics, its qualities and limitations. Both have advantages and disadvantages and necessitate particular training on the part of the man and the woman.

Suggestions for the couple

How have you adapted to intercourse of short duration? You have now reached the stage where you can discuss the strategies you have each developed in order to adjust to this situation. You have learnt different things over the course of this programme and you now have a better understanding of how a man proceeds to ejaculate shortly after the beginning of intercourse or, conversely, how he can behave in order to prolong the duration of sexual activities with his companion. You also know the things you did to prevent ejaculation from occurring too soon, to give pleasure to your partner or to conceal your disappointment. By sharing the various methods you have used to manage this problem, you will better understand your sexual dynamics and will progress much faster.

What concessions have you made? Have you accepted the situation in silence? Have you resigned yourself to the fact? Have you held back your sexual desires? Have you put your needs and your spontaneity on the back burner? How have you compensated for your weaknesses? What methods have you used to delay the onset of ejaculation? What actions have you taken? What kind of attitude have you adopted? Have you been aggressive in the hope that your partner would understand and react? Have you refused sexual and emotional contact in order not to experience additional frustration? Have you avoided making advances for fear of being rejected again? This frank discussion will help you understand each other and allow you to eliminate behaviours that, if they held any meaning in the past, can harm your progress and happiness today.

ELEVENTH SESSION

Sexual information

The field of consciousness

It is of vital importance to know that the more a man's sexual excitement increases, the more his field of consciousness shrinks. When he approaches the zone of ejaculatory imminence, a man loses contact with a large part of the outside world. Only a few sexual stimuli remain present in his mind. He no longer notices the room's décor, he no longer hears the noises around him and he ignores the surrounding doors. Within his inner universe, he only experiences pleasant sensations. He forgets his financial troubles; he does not feel his back pain anymore and . . . he stops thinking about checking his excitement levels and applying his management techniques! Focused on the sexual stimuli he likes and captivated by the escalating pleasure, he neglects to manage his sexual excitement and heads toward ejaculation without realizing it. It is only after having ejaculated that he remembers he could have acted otherwise.

If we look at this from an evolutionary perspective, we can say that the human race still possesses, despite numerous changes brought about by time and culture, excellent mechanisms dedicated to reproduction. When a man gets excited, he moves faster, his muscular tension increases, his breathing quickens, his pleasure heightens and he becomes less aware of the consequences of his actions. He naturally moves toward ejaculation and fertilization. If the opposite happened, if making love became more and more painful and unpleasant as sexual excitement soared, individuals would flee from this situation and the difficulty with prolonging intercourse would not even arise. Consequently, if a man desires to delay the moment of his ejaculation, he must keep his excitement below a certain level. This way his field of consciousness will not shrink too much and he will not neglect to apply his management techniques. Since this notion is subjective, it is up to each man to determine how excited he can get while maintaining a sufficiently open perceptual field to continue managing his sexual excitement.

The phenomenon of the narrowing of the field of consciousness plays out even more among men who have a habit of getting lost or immersed in the perception of their preferred stimulus. As soon as they focus on this stimulus, they see nothing else and their excitement increases sharply. In others, the feeling of love has the same effect. They admire their partner so much that when they allow themselves to be mesmerized by her during sexual relations, the resulting emotional charge potentiates their sexual excitement astronomically.

If you have a tendency to reduce the environment to the size of your preferred erotic stimulus, an excellent technique exists to counter this propensity. It consists of stepping back and broadening your perspective. For example, if seeing your partner's breasts arouses you a great deal, you can put some distance between yourself and them. While continuing to admire them, you can enlarge your perceptual field by distancing yourself slightly and paying attention to other aspects such as your partner's face, her emotions, feelings, personality, touches, skin, the setting, context, ambience, etc. Instead of letting yourself be overwhelmed by the sight of this part of her body, you will lower the intensity of your sexual excitement and enrich the substance of your romantic encounter.

If your love for your partner extends across the universe, if you let yourself become overwhelmed by your feelings toward her, an effective technique lies in giving these feelings a shape. You can, for example, encircle them inside a bubble. Then you play with this bubble – make it smaller, move it upward, bring it downward, pull it closer, push it farther, change its colour, etc. – as you continue to perceive the surrounding reality, including your partner. Everything will become relative and your feelings will no longer exert the same effect on your excitement. The feelings of human beings are extensible and compressible. The more you let them grow, the more they prove overwhelming, especially when you have difficulty prolonging the length of intercourse.

Mastering the fear of failure

The fear of ejaculating too fast and frustrating one's partner can influence the onset of ejaculation. In fact, ejaculation is provoked by the activation of the same branch of the nervous system which is called upon when an individual is anxious, namely the sympathetic nervous system. When this system is sufficiently activated by a combination of excitement and anxiety, it is extremely likely that it will trigger ejaculation.

The appearance and rise of sexual excitement are ensured by the parasympathetic nervous system. When the degree of excitement is high enough, the sympathetic nervous system takes over and prompts ejaculation. Therefore, if a man feeds fears during sexual relations, his sympathetic nervous system will be doubly stimulated and the possibility of him ejaculating prematurely will be increased.

In addition, an anxious man risks having his sympathetic nervous system become very active even if he is only slightly sexually excited. Because he is not too excited, the body's indicator signals for high degrees of sexual excitement do not appear. Not having these body signals to get his bearings, his ability to manage his sexual excitement is diminished and he could ejaculate rapidly without being able to anticipate it.

To cope with their anxiety, human beings have at their disposal physical and psychological means. Traditional physical methods include abdominal breathing and the reduction of muscular tension. Fortunately, these are the same methods that you use to manage your sexual excitement. So when you breathe from your stomach and relax your muscles in order to delay the arrival of your ejaculation, you deal with your anxiety at the same time.

As for psychological means, there are many. We will examine cognitive competition, dedramatization and the use of realistic criteria. Cognitive competition is based on the functional limitation of the mind being unable to think about several things at once. When you are focusing on sexual stimuli, paying attention to your excitement level or applying your management techniques, there remains little room in your mind for anxiogenic and defeatist thoughts. In other words, when you think about sexuality you cannot think about a lot of other things. In these conditions, it is more difficult to worry and activate the sympathetic nervous system.

Dedramatization consists of not exaggerating the consequences that may occur if your spouse is not sexually satisfied. By not blowing these life difficulties out of proportion, you give yourself a chance of being calmer and more proficient at managing your excitement. It is obviously frustrating for a woman to have her sexual desires cut short by her partner ejaculating soon after the beginning of intercourse. But it is not a major catastrophe and she will not be penalized for life.

The same goes if she leaves you because of your inability to prolong sexual intercourse. You will probably be sad and discouraged. But once again, it is not the end of the world. You will not disintegrate. You will not be shunned by the whole female population. The labour market will not be forever closed to you. You will not be rejected by the entire universe! You should not over dramatize the difficult events in your sexual life and your relationship as a couple. This way, you will be less tormented by the prospect of failure. Your sympathetic nervous system will be less activated and you will manage your excitement more easily.

Finally, it is fundamental not to impose on yourself unrealistic performance criteria. If you can better manage your excitement six to seven times out of ten, that's excellent. If you demand perfection, you will become anxious and it will be more difficult for you to defer the moment of your ejaculation.

It would be useful to talk about your mutual expectations with your partner. What vision do you each have of a pleasant sexual life? Do either of you have a tendency to be demanding? What would you like to change and what would you like to keep from your current interactions? Perhaps you have a misconception about what your partner desires. There is nothing wrong with finding out what the other person thinks.

Important note

The journey is as interesting as the destination

It is possible to travel in different ways. For example, when you take a trip to the ocean, you can hop on the highway, drive 80 miles an hour and jump into the water as soon as you get there. You can also drive along small country roads and take all your time. You stop at various locations and contemplate the landscape. You sample regional culinary specialties and chat with the locals. You admire the architecture of the villages and visit a small museum. At four o'clock in the afternoon, you arrive at the seaside. You drop your bags off at the hotel and after that head to the beach. You walk on the fine sand and then slowly make your way into the warm and welcoming water. The sun sets and you return to your hotel. You had just as much fun travelling to your destination as you did swimming! The same goes for sexual activities. You can rush toward the strong sensations of ejaculation or take your time and savour all the subtleties of intercourse. This is what will make the difference between a short sexual encounter and a long-lasting one.

Exercises

Exercise 13. Relaxing different parts of the body

This exercise is described in the seventh session.

Exercise 16. Muscular dissociation (third part)

Objective: To acquire control over the muscular groups which play an important role in the rise of sexual excitement.

This exercise is very difficult. Moreover, mastering it is not essential for the programme to work well. But even if you do not accomplish the exercise completely, the mere fact of focusing and contracting and releasing your muscles will help you increase your capacity to manage your excitement.

Lie on your back, your legs spaced out at least the width of your shoulders, your lips slightly parted and your eyes open.

a Contract your abdominals.
b While keeping your abdominals contracted, contract your gluteals.
c While keeping your abdominals and gluteals contracted, contract the muscles in your perineum.
d While keeping your abdominals and gluteals contracted, release the muscles in your perineum.
e While keeping your abdominals contracted, release your gluteals.
f Release your abdominals.
g Check to see if all your muscles are relaxed.
h Remember to breathe!

Repeat this exercise 20 times.

**

a Contract your gluteals.
b While keeping your gluteals contracted, contract the muscles in your perineum.
c While keeping your gluteals and the muscles in your perineum contracted, contract your abdominals.
d While keeping your gluteals and the muscles in your perineum contracted, release your abdominals.
e While keeping your gluteals contracted, release the muscles in your perineum.
f Release your gluteals.
g Check to see if all your muscles are relaxed.
h Remember to breathe!

Repeat this exercise 20 times.

Exercise 19. Movement of the pelvis in the superior position

First part: Technique and breathing

- First step
- Second step
- Third step.

This exercise is described in the tenth session.

Second part: Intensity

Objective: To execute the movement of the pelvis in the superior position with minimal muscular tension.

In this exercise, you will execute the forward-backward movement of your pelvis in the superior position (Figure 3.43) with and without using your gluteal muscles.

Assume the superior position resting on your elbows and knees. Your arms should be perpendicular and your thighs oblique in relation to the floor. Your legs should be spread shoulder width apart, your mouth partially open and your eyes open.

a Exhale while rotating your pelvis forward and contracting your gluteals (during sexual intercourse, you must avoid contracting your gluteals).
b Feel the contraction of your gluteals (in order to know what not to do during sexual relations).
c Inhale while rotating your pelvis backward (your gluteals automatically release).

Do 10 repetitions.
Rest 1 minute.
Do 10 repetitions.
Rest 1 minute.

**

a Exhale while rotating your pelvis forward without contracting your gluteals (during sexual intercourse, this is the way it must be done).
b Feel the relaxation of your gluteal muscles (in order to know what to do during sexual relations).
c Inhale while rotating your pelvis backward.

Do 10 repetitions.
Rest 1 minute.
Do 10 repetitions.
Rest 1 minute.

Third part: speed

Objective: To execute the movement of the pelvis in the superior position very slowly.

Assume the superior position resting on your elbows and knees. Your arms should be perpendicular and your thighs oblique in relation to the floor. Your legs should be spaced shoulder width apart, your mouth partially open and your eyes open.

- a Inhale and rotate your pelvis backward counting to five (about 5 seconds).
- b At the end of the inhalation, there is a suspension. Make a micropause during this suspension in inhalation and relax yourself before continuing.
- c Exhale and rotate your pelvis forward counting to five (about 5 seconds).
- d At the end of the exhalation, there is a stop for about 1 second. Make a micropause during this stop and relax yourself before going back.
- e Slowly increase the speed of your movement.
- f Go as fast as possible. (five repetitions)
- g Reduce the speed of your movement.
- h Move as slowly as possible. (five repetitions)

Rest.
Repeat this exercise once.
Rest.
Repeat this exercise once.

Fourth part: Vigour

Objective: To execute the movement of the pelvis in the superior position very vigorously.

It is possible to display strength and vivacity without being tense. Through this exercise, you will learn to perform strong movements of intercourse without precipitating the arrival of your ejaculation. You will be very virile and will be able to give your partner more pleasure while continuing to manage your sexual excitement.

These vigorous movements executed in this way enable to release all your sexual potency without the risk of provoking an unexpected ejaculation. You must, however, take care not to contract your gluteals going forward and to fully relax your entire body each time you go back.

Assume the superior position resting on your elbows and knees. Your arms should be perpendicular and your thighs oblique in relation to the floor. Your legs should be spaced shoulder width apart, your mouth slightly open and your eyes open.

a Inhale and rotate your pelvis backward counting to five (about 5 seconds).
b At the end of the inhalation, there is a suspension.
Make a micropause during this suspension in inhalation and relax yourself before continuing.
c Exhale and rotate your pelvis forward very quickly and very vigorously (without contracting your gluteals muscles).
d At the end of the exhalation, there is a stop for about 1 second.
Make a micropause during this stop and relax yourself before going back.
e Inhale and rotate your pelvis very slowly backward while relaxing as much as you can.
f At the end of the inhalation, there is a suspension.
Make a micropause during this suspension in inhalation and relax yourself before continuing forward.
g Exhale and rotate your pelvis forward very quickly and very vigorously (without contracting your gluteals muscles).
h At the end of the exhalation, there is a stop for about 1 second. Make a micropause during this stop and relax yourself before going back.

Repeat this exercise 15 times.
Rest.
Repeat this exercise 15 times.

Exercises for the week

a) Exercises without sexual excitement

You perform the exercises without sexual excitement three times during the coming week. Choose a calm location where you will not be disturbed.

Exercise 13. Relaxing different parts of the body
This exercise is described in the seventh session.

Exercise 16. Muscular dissociation (third part)
This exercise is described in this session.

Exercise 19. Movement of the pelvis in the superior position
First part: Technique and breathing
First step
Second step
Third step
This exercise is described in the tenth session.

Exercise 19. Movement of the pelvis in the superior position
Second part: Intensity
Third part: Speed
Fourth part: Vigour
These exercises are described in this session.

b) Exercises with sexual excitement

Take note of what is happening inside of your mind when your sexual excitement mounts and you experience more pleasure. Do you still pay attention to your excitement levels? Do you neglect to apply your management techniques? If that is the case, it is essential in the future that you navigate at lower levels of excitement. Your field of consciousness will not be overpowered by pleasure and you will be better able to manage your sexual excitement.

If the fear of ejaculating too quickly haunts you, do not forget that applying the advice you received to manage your sexual excitement is a powerful antidote against anxiety-fuelled thoughts. By focusing on sexual stimuli, having pleasure, checking your excitement levels and applying your management techniques, you will leave less room in your mind for unnecessary worries and expectations. You will fully enjoy the present moment and will be better able to modulate your sexual excitement.

During this session, you learnt how to execute the movement of the pelvis at high speed and with great vigour. However, it is not recommended at this time to do this during sexual relations. It is better instead that you wait a few months before moving to this level of difficulty. It is preferable that you consolidate your bases and that you progress slowly but surely. Make sure you are able to last 10 minutes in the superior position – making pauses, leaning on the bed or your partner, moving slowly and applying your techniques – before accelerating and intensifying your movements.

Suggestions for the single man

During your masturbatory activities, observe what is taking place in your mind as your sexual excitement climbs. Are you focusing on the stimuli and sensations? Do you let yourself get swept away by the pleasure to the detriment of your capacity to perceive your excitement levels and use your techniques? If the answer is yes, try to stay in the middle of the zone of the modulation of sexual tension in order to retain your ability to manage your excitement and pleasure.

What was said on the subject of fear of failure applies to you as well. Some of you had past experiences of rejection on the part of one or several demanding, sometimes even overbearing partners. It is important to forget these events and to concentrate on your new ways of thinking and acting. You now possess effective techniques and proven strategies for managing your sexual excitement. All you have to do is put them into practice as they appear. They will help you conquer your fears while allowing you to modulate your sexual tension.

During masturbation, apply, in various positions, the techniques you have learnt to date.

Suggestions for the woman

Some women, through the criticisms, disparaging remarks and ultimatums that they hurl at their partner, contribute to increasing their partner's anxiety. And without realizing it, they are at the origin of why he ejaculates even faster. Without a doubt there exist egocentric men who accord no importance to the pleasure of their partner. It is also true that, to counteract their difficulty with prolonging intercourse, many men use strategies that are hardly erotic and very unsatisfying for their spouse. But most men are well intentioned, even if they are often awkward, and their first thought is not to frustrate their partner; on the contrary.

If this is your case, it will be more beneficial that – instead of getting vexed over your spouse's awkwardness and reprimanding him – you show some indulgence and put the knowledge you have acquired in this book to good use. The climate of tolerance you will establish will contribute to reducing the stress your partner is imposing on himself and will help him to better manage his sexual excitement.

Suggestions for the couple

There will be times when your sexual activities will be less than titillating, sometimes even mundane and boring. An absence of desire, a lacklustre ambience, omitted foreplay, lack of energy, sexual excitement that is either too low or too high, consuming preoccupations, mechanical movements, emotional disconnection, insufficient communication as well as dull postludes make up the share of the sex life of all couples. This is normal and it is best to just accept it for what it is. You will have experiences of varying significance depending on the situations and circumstances. However, if the quality of your sexual activities rank for the most part below five on a scale of 0 to 10 (0 indicating a very disappointing activity and 10 designating an extremely satisfying activity), there is room for improvement. Routine has perhaps settled in and it is time for some reflection.

Your sexuality demands that you take care of it. What is your lifestyle? Do work and family life take precedence over your love and sexual lives? What are your priorities? How do you manage your time? Does the routine of everyday life overrun your time and schedule to the point where intimacy and romance have lost their place? These are some questions that will help you find solutions and redirect the course of your emotional and erotic life if need be.

TWELFTH SESSION

Sexual information

Self-confidence

Having confidence in yourself is essential in order for you to be able to manage properly your sexual excitement. But where does this confidence to succeed come from? Certainly not from exhortations or words of encouragement! Even if you were told that you have the required potential and possess all the techniques to make it happen, this would not necessarily convince you. So where does self-confidence come from? The answer is simple: from experience and wisdom.

Experience comes from putting into practice the knowledge, techniques and strategies you have learnt within this programme. You adopt a new behaviour and observe the results it produces. When you achieve your goal several times, the success obtained proves that you are able to do it. All that remains is for you to admit it! This is how you will gain confidence in your new abilities. What you must first do is test the information in this programme and note the effects. Then you acknowledge these effects for what they are and deduce that you are the one who, through your efforts, has produced them. When you achieve the desired changes, when you manage your excitement, do not hesitate to tell yourself: "Yes, I did it! Yes, I succeeded!" Reality at that moment indicates that you have reached your objectives and that you could do it again. Thus confidence in yourself will be born.

As for wisdom, it arises out of a realistic and tolerant attitude that you develop towards yourself. If you impose upon yourself the requirement to accomplish extraordinary sexual performances, you will fail and you will not develop a healthy level of self-confidence. Clinical practice reveals that there are some men who after having greatly increased the duration of their lovemaking still have the impression of suffering from a sexual dysfunction. Even if they have intercourse with a duration superior to that of 90 per cent of men, they still consider themselves "premature ejaculators". And why? Because they persist in wrongly believing that "normal" individuals are not obliged to make pauses, use techniques or employ strategies. They still push themselves to perform like supermen. Since they are not able to do this – no human being can in fact do so – they continue to perceive themselves as inadequate and lack confidence in themselves. You have now acquired all the knowledge and techniques to behave better than the majority of men. If you are compassionate towards yourself, you will develop this self-confidence and you will feel a lot more comfortable during sexual relations.

Exercises

Exercise 13. Relaxing different parts of the body

This exercise is described in the seventh session.

Exercise 16. Muscular dissociation (fourth part)

Objective: To acquire control over the muscular groups which play an important role in the rise of sexual excitement.

This exercise is very difficult. Moreover, mastering it is not essential for the programme to work well. But even if you do not accomplish the exercise completely, the mere fact of focusing on contracting and releasing your muscles will help you better modulate your sexual excitement.

Lie on your back, legs stretched out and spread at least shoulder width apart, lips slightly parted and eyes open.

a Contract the muscles in your perineum.
b While keeping the muscles in your perineum contracted, contract your abdominals.
c While keeping the muscles in your perineum and your abdominals contracted, contract your gluteals.
d While keeping the muscles in your perineum and your abdominals contracted, release your gluteals.
e While keeping the muscles in your perineum contracted, release your abdominals.
f Release the muscles in your perineum.
g Check to see if all your muscles are relaxed.
h Remember to breathe!

Repeat this exercise 20 times.

**

a Contract your abdominals.
b While keeping your abdominals contracted, contract the muscles in your perineum.
c While keeping your abdominals and the muscles in your perineum contracted, contract your gluteals.
d While keeping your abdominals and the muscles in your perineum contracted, release your gluteals.
e While keeping your abdominals contracted, release the muscles in your perineum.
f Release your abdominals.
g Check to see if all your muscles are relaxed.
h Remember to breathe!

Repeat this exercise 20 times.

Exercise 19. Movement of the pelvis in the superior position

First part: Technique and breathing

- First step
- Second step
- Third step.

This exercise is described in the tenth session.

Second part: Intensity
Third part: Speed
Fourth part: Vigour

These exercises are described in the eleventh session.

Exercise 20. Integration of techniques

Objective: To execute the movement of the pelvis in the superior position while integrating the different techniques to manage sexual excitement.

Assume the superior position resting on your elbows and knees. Your arms should be perpendicular and your thighs oblique in relation to the floor. Your legs should be spaced shoulder width apart, your mouth half-open and your eyes open.

a Inhale and rotate your pelvis backward counting to five (around 5 seconds).
b At the end of the inhalation, there is a suspension.
Make a micropause during this suspension in inhalation and relax yourself before continuing.
c Exhale and rotate your pelvis forward counting to five (around 5 seconds).
d At the end of the exhalation, there is a stop for about 1 second.
Make a micropause during this stop and relax yourself before going back.
e Gradually accelerate the speed of your movement.
f Go as fast as possible.
g Reduce the speed of your movement.
h Move as slowly as possible.
i Exhale and rotate your pelvis forward once very quickly and very vigorously.

j At the end of the exhalation, there is a stop for about 1 second. Make a micropause during this stop and relax yourself before going backward.
k Inhale and rotate your pelvis very slowly backward while relaxing as much as you can.
l At the end of the inhalation, there is a suspension. Make a micropause during this suspension in inhalation and relax yourself before continuing forward.
m Speed up. Your movements become more and more rapid and energetic.
n Slow down. Your movements are performed more and more slowly and in a more and more relaxed manner.
o Imagine that you make a pause, both you and your partner.
p Adopt the latero-superior position.
q Relax yourself and breathe.
r Imagine that your partner is starting to move.
s Remain immobile.
t The muscles in your perineum would contract. Contract them.
u You would verify this: "Are they contracted?"
v You would not be sure. You would contract them very slightly. Go ahead, contract them.
w You would release them right away. Release them.
x Breathe from your abdomen.
y Relax all of your muscles.
z Congratulate yourself for doing so well!

Repeat this exercise three times.

Exercises for the week

a) Exercises without sexual excitement

During the week, you will practise these exercises on three separate occasions. As always, do them in a location conducive to concentration and learning.

Exercise 13. Relaxing different parts of the body
This exercise is described in the seventh session.

Exercise 16. Muscular dissociation (fourth part)
This exercise is described in this session.

Exercise 19. Movement of the pelvis in the superior position
First part: Technique and breathing

First step
Second step
Third step
This exercise is described in the tenth session.

Exercise 19. Movement of the pelvis in the superior position
Second part: Intensity
Third part: Speed
Fourth part: Vigour
These exercises are described in the eleventh session.

Exercise 20. Integration of techniques
This exercise is described in this session.

b) Exercises with sexual excitement

Integrate into your sexual activities all of the techniques and strategies that you have learnt in this programme. Take your time and observe the effect they have on your sexual excitement. If some movements remain difficult to execute, you can repeat them without sexual excitement in order to ensure assimilation. You will find included in Appendix 1 a summary of the methods you can employ to modulate your sexual excitement and delay the arrival of your ejaculation.

Suggestions for the single man

This week, you will integrate into your sexual activities all of the techniques and strategies described in this book. You will find them summarized in Appendix 1. To facilitate the transition from sexual activities alone to sexual activities with a partner, try to imagine erotic scenes that are as close as possible to reality.

If a certain amount of time passes between the end of this programme and the meeting of a new partner, it will be wise to reread the key passages of this book and repeat the exercises. These are bodily skills and it is very easy to lose mastery of them and to return to old habits without even realizing it.

When you will meet a new partner, you will have a better chance of success by proceeding in the following manner:

1 It is preferable not to demand of yourself to succeed the first few times and to be tolerant with yourself. Most men who meet a new partner ejaculate quickly at the beginning. It is almost inevitable and women are used to that. You will be no different than others. If your ejaculation occurs sooner than desired it will not be considered unusual. Things will go much better if you do not think you still have a problem or feel that you are starting the relationship badly because you ejaculate quickly initially.

2 Like an artist or an athlete, you will benefit from reviewing and repeating the strategies and techniques several times on your own at home – with and without sexual excitement – before interacting sexually with a woman.
3 It is important to apply the techniques and strategies described in this manual with your new partner immediately. They work! It is better not to cling to the 'safety' of old habits and repeat ineffective behaviours from the past.
4 It is advantageous to experiment with your techniques while adopting a scientific attitude: this includes putting your new ways of doing into action, observing the effects on your body and noting the results.
5 It helps to congratulate yourself on the progress you make and is useless to blame yourself if you do not succeed at everything right away. You can applaud any new discovery, observation or modification you make, however small it may be.

When you will be with a new partner, you will approach sexual relations on an entirely different basis than previously. Your behaviours will be different. Your way of managing your sexual excitement will have changed. As a result, you will be in a position to extend the length of intercourse. Your new companion will not react in the same way as other women you have known because you will no longer act in the same way you did before. Your past will be behind you. Everything will be easier. It is therefore advisable that your attitude measures up to your new skills and that you now see yourself as someone who has the ability to prolong the length of intercourse.

Suggestions for the woman

Congratulations, you successfully got through this quite technical and not very romantic read! We hope you do not feel guilty about your spouse's difficulty with prolonging intercourse and that you do not blame him either. Male sexuality has a biological reality (the ejaculatory reflex) which, if it promotes the reproduction of the human species, imposes restrictions on the man and woman's spontaneity. It is commendable of you to help your spouse, often without him even knowing it, to circumvent the difficulties and disadvantages that result from this limitation.

As for your sexuality, it is also subject to learning. We have given you a few avenues for development in this book. It is up to you to continue to explore and experiment. Female sexuality is a potential to realize and, if you devote time to it, you will discover a universe of infinite riches.

Suggestions for the couple

What does the future hold for you? Probably some surprises! The surprise of realizing that the changes you introduced exceed all of your expectations. And equally surprising is seeing that you can lose your newly acquired skills and quickly end up back where you started. If this is the case, do not panic and do not blame your partner, but reflect . . . together as a couple. What happened? What did you observe?

Was there an interruption of sexual activity due to pregnancy, illness, a trip or a demanding career? These prolonged breaks are often the cause of the loss of mastery of basic skills. In order to avoid a relapse, it is important for you to be vigilant after these break periods and to return to the principles taught in this book.

There will always be times when ejaculation will occur soon after the start of intercourse. Most couples face this reality. Do not get discouraged and do not believe that you have returned to the starting point. However, if you get the impression that the length of intercourse is again becoming too short, create your own statistics in order not to confuse temporary frustration with the return to previous habits. In a month, how many times did ejaculation occur sooner than desired? Two times? Eight times? If the answer is more than four times out of ten, you can begin to examine what you can change. If it is less than four times out of ten, you fall within the average and there is no reason to worry. It is part of the normal variation of life.

Part of the success depends on the considerate participation of the woman. Once she accepts this male limitation, namely the impossibility to control the ejaculatory reflex, the doors to sharing and cooperation between her and her partner then open.

On the other hand, when the man expresses his feelings, discusses sexuality and . . . shows some humour, he puts into place the means to overcome the difficulties that a too-brief intercourse can impose on the couple.

Considering your significant other an intimate friend – a confidant with whom you can share your emotions on the subject of sexuality – and working together will help you tremendously in making progress. This will allow you to take pleasure in a more enjoyable sexual experience and walk through life more serenely.

What's next?

Way to go! You have completed your programme! You now have a variety of knowledge, techniques and strategies that will enable you to prolong the length of intercourse and enjoy a more pleasurable sexual experience for both you and your partner.

The results you will obtain depend on several factors; the most important remain your degree of involvement and your diligence. The techniques and strategies you've seen were taught to thousands of men and have proven to be very effective for a considerable number of them. The more you use and refine them, the more you will increase your ability to manage your excitement. With repeated practice, you will develop new habits, become more skilled and raise your self-confidence.

The programme elements which generate the greatest success are not the same for every individual. Some men say they have to apply all the techniques they learnt to the letter in order to manage their sexual excitement. Others declare that the breathing is what makes the difference. Several mention relaxing the muscles of the perineum. The fact of having explained to their partner the functioning of the male physiology and having integrated into their sexual activities the strategies this reality imposes has helped many. In Appendix 1, you will find summarized all the management techniques and strategies described in this programme. Reviewing this summary periodically will help you keep in mind the essentials of what you must do to modulate your sexual excitement.

The important thing is to experiment and to see what works best for you. If you examine the way your body responds when it is sexually excited, this will give you invaluable information to introduce changes to the way you act. Your worst enemy will always be the excessive expectations you harbour in your mind. They will prevent you from perceiving what is happening inside of you and from drawing useful lessons. These expectations are oppressive when they involve a sexual performance obligation. When you repeat phrases such as "a normal man does not make pauses" or "my erection must always be 100 per cent firm", you create demands that impede the adoption of a tolerant and scientific attitude.

I recommend that you regularly observe the links which form between your thoughts, your movements, the actions of your partner and the direction your excitement takes. From the techniques and knowledge you have acquired in this programme and the personal discoveries that you will make, you could initiate changes and study their effects. If they are satisfactory, you could keep them. If they do not produce the expected results after a sufficient trial period, you could apply a new technique or a different strategy. The idea is to explore new ways of doing rather than imposing a strict line of conduct upon yourself.

It is essential to continue repeating your exercises inside and outside of sexual activities. This programme is based on learning skills. Their mastery declines very quickly. It is the major disadvantage of this type of approach. One month without practice and old habits come creeping back, and at a crazy speed. You will no longer do the movements very well, you will lose control of your excitement and you will once again ejaculate sooner than you desire. This may seem alarmist, but clinical experience shows that negligence at this level is not very beneficial and that a little effort will help you a great deal. You will find in Appendix 2 the list of exercises from all of the sessions.

It has been a pleasure for me to pass along this knowledge to you which is the fruit of my research and clinical experience combined with scientific thinking and wisdom handed down from one generation to the next for hundreds of years. I am indebted to my predecessors and I hope that, in turn, you will fully benefit from my contribution. I wish you all the best and lots of happiness!

Notes

1 These reactions have been described in detail in the first chapter of this book in the section entitled *Sexological causes*.

2 Graph 3.1 was already presented in the section *Sexological causes* in the first chapter of this book. It is reproduced here for the sake of clarity.

Appendix 1

Summary of management techniques and strategies

To manage your sexual excitement and prolong the length of intercourse you can use the following techniques and strategies.

Techniques

- Relaxing yourself before beginning any sexual activity.
- Paying attention to your levels of sexual excitement and your bodily reactions during foreplay and intercourse.
- Keeping your body posture open (eyes, mouth, legs) when possible.
- Breathing from your abdomen.
- Exhaling while rotating your pelvis forward (penetration).
- Inhaling while rotating your pelvis backward (withdrawal).
- Performing micropauses at the end of each movement of the pelvis (forward and back).
- Relaxing your gluteal muscles.
- Releasing the muscles in your perineum.
- Lowering the tone of all the muscles in your body.
- Slowing down the speed of your movements.
- Not trying to hold back your ejaculation as you approach the point of no return, instead letting yourself go and relaxing.
- Emergency formula: making a pause, loosening all the muscles in your body, relaxing the muscles in your perineum, breathing from your abdomen.

Strategies

- Maintaining an ejaculatory frequency corresponding to your physiological needs.
- Engaging in lengthy foreplay.
- Accepting and appreciating your partner's caresses.
- Experimenting with high levels of excitement during foreplay so you will know how to manage them during intercourse.
- Acclimatizing yourself to sexual sensations.
- Accepting erectile fluctuations.

- Considering the characteristics of female sexuality during foreplay and intercourse.
- Avoiding intense and continuous sexual stimulation; varying the intensity of stimulation (modulation of stimulation).
- Determining the amount of stimulation you can receive (only you can do this).
- Penetrating your partner when both you and her are at a moderate level of excitement.
- Adopting sexual positions that put little strain on the musculature of your body (i.e. the man lying on his back) at the beginning of intercourse.
- Making a pause at the beginning of intercourse.
- Making pauses during intercourse to allow your excitement to come back down.
- Navigating in the middle of the zone of the modulation of sexual excitement during intercourse (to keep a certain distance from the zone of ejaculatory imminence).
- Not thinking about something else in an attempt to decrease your excitement, but on the contrary, paying attention to your partner and to what you find pleasurable about the sexual experience.
- Savouring the subtle pleasures of intercourse (not only the strong sensations of intense excitement and ejaculation).
- Recognizing that the more excited you get, the more your field of consciousness shrinks, and the less you are able to manage your excitement.
- Reducing the fear of ejaculating too soon by applying the techniques and strategies in this programme and subscribing to realistic performance criteria.

Appendix 2
List of exercises

You will find here as a memory aid the complete list of exercises described in the programme, including their number and the session in which they are presented.

First session

Exercise 1. Identifying the breathing process in a state of relaxation with the help of hands (first session).

Exercise 2. Identifying the breathing process in a state of relaxation without the help of hands (first session).

Exercise 3. Reversal of the breathing process when in a state of excitement (slow speed).
First part: Technique (first session)
Second part: Simulation exercise (first session).

Second session

Exercise 2. Identifying the breathing process in a state of relaxation without the help of hands (first session).

Exercise 3. Reversal of the breathing process when in a state of excitement (slow speed).
First part: Technique (first session)
Second part: Simulation exercise (first session).

Exercise 4. Reversal of the breathing process when in a state of excitement (fast speed) (second session).

Exercise 5. Movement of the pelvis with support.
First part: Technique (second session)
Second part: Breathing (second session).

Third session

Exercise 2. Identification of the breathing process in a state of relaxation without the help of hands (first session).

Exercise 3. Reversal of the breathing process when in a state of excitement (slow speed).
First part: Technique (first session)
Second part: Simulation exercise (first session).

Exercise 6. Reversal of the breathing process when in a state of excitement in the zone of ejaculatory imminence (third session).

Exercise 5. Movement of the pelvis with support.
First part: Technique (second session)
Second part: Breathing (second session).

Exercise 5. Movement of the pelvis with support.
Third part: Intensity (third session)
Fourth part: Speed (third session).

Fourth session

Exercise 2. Identification of the breathing process in a state of relaxation without the help of hands (first session).

Exercise 3. Reversal of the breathing process when in a state of excitement (slow speed).
First part: Technique (first session)
Second part: Simulation exercise (first session).

Exercise 7. Reversal of the breathing process when in a state of excitement in the zone of ejaculatory imminence in relation to the principle of letting go (fourth session).

Exercise 5. Movement of the pelvis with support.
First part: Technique (second session)
Second part: Breathing (second session).

Exercise 5. Movement of the pelvis with support.
Fifth part: Sensuality (fourth session).

Exercise 8. Movement of the pelvis in a standing position.
First part: Technique (fourth session)
Second part: Breathing (fourth session).

Fifth session

Exercise 8. Movement of the pelvis in a standing position.
First part: Technique (fourth session)
Second part: Breathing (fourth session).

Exercise 9. The gluteal muscles (fifth session).

Exercise 8. Movement of the pelvis in a standing position.
Third part: Intensity (fifth session)
Fourth part: Speed (fifth session)

Sixth session

Exercise 10. Movement of the pelvis while lying on the back.
First part: Technique (sixth session)
Second part: Breathing (sixth session).

Exercise 11. Contraction and relaxation of the gluteal muscles while lying on the back (sixth session).

Exercise 12. The muscles of the perineum (sixth session).

Seventh session

Exercise 13. Relaxation of different parts of the body (seventh session).

Exercise 12. The muscles of the perineum (sixth session).

Exercise 10. Movement of the pelvis while lying on the back.
First part: Technique (sixth session)
Second part: Breathing (sixth session).

Exercise 10. Movement of the pelvis while lying on the back.
Third part: Intensity (seventh session)
Fourth part: Speed (seventh session).

Eighth session

Exercise 13. Relaxation of different parts of the body (seventh session).

Exercise 12. The muscles of the perineum (sixth session).

Exercise 14. The pelvis while lying on the side (eighth session).

Exercise 15. Movement of the pelvis while lying on the side with and without contraction of the muscles of the perineum (eighth session).

Ninth session

Exercise 13. Relaxation of different parts of the body (seventh session).

Exercise 16. Muscular dissociation (first part) (ninth session).

Exercise 17. Studying the effect of positions where the man is on top of the woman (ninth session).

Exercise 18. Movement of the pelvis in the latero-superior position (ninth session).

Tenth session

Exercise 13. Relaxation of different parts of the body (seventh session).

Exercise 16. Muscular dissociation (second part) (tenth session).

Exercise 19. Movement of the pelvis in the superior position.
First part: Technique and breathing.
First step (tenth session)
Second step (tenth session)
Third step (tenth session).

Eleventh session

Exercise 13. Relaxation of different parts of the body (seventh session).

Exercise 16. Muscular dissociation (third part) (eleventh session).

Exercise 19. Movement of the pelvis in the superior position.
First part: Technique and breathing.
First step (tenth session)
Second step (tenth session)
Third step (tenth session).

Exercise 19. Movement of the pelvis in the superior position.
Second part: Intensity (eleventh session)
Third part: Speed (eleventh session)
Fourth part: Vigour (eleventh session).

Twelfth session

Exercise 13. Relaxation of different parts of the body (seventh session).

Exercise 16. Muscular dissociation (fourth part) (twelfth session).

Exercise 19. Movement of the pelvis in the superior position.
First part: Technique and breathing.
First step (tenth session)
Second step (tenth session)
Third step (tenth session).

Exercise 19. Movement of the pelvis in the superior position.
Second part: Intensity (eleventh session)
Third part: Speed (eleventh session)
Fourth part: Vigour (eleventh session).

Exercise 20. Integration of different techniques (twelfth session).

References

Abraham, G. *Sexologie Clinique*. Paris: Édition Doin, 1967.

Abraham, K. Ejaculatio Praecox. In E. Jones (Ed) *Selected Papers on Psychoanalysis*, London: Hogarth Press, pp. 280–304, 1949.

Althof, S. E. Prevalence, Characteristics and Implications of Premature Ejaculation/Rapid Ejaculation. *The Journal of Urology*, 175, 842–848, 2006.

Althof, S. E., Abdo, C. H., Dean, J., Hackett, G., McCabe, M., McMahon, C. G., Rosen, R. C., Sadovsky, R., Waldinger, M., Becher, E., Broderick, G. A., Buvat, J., Goldstein, I., El-Meliegy, A. I., Giuliano, F., Hellstrom, W. J., Incrocci, L., Jannini, E. A., Park, K., Parish, S., Porst, H., Rowland, D., Segraves, R., Sharlip, I., Simonelli, C. and Tan, H. M. International Society For Sexual Medicine's Guidelines for the Diagnosis and Treatment of Premature Ejaculation. *The Journal of Sexual Medicine*, 7, 2947–69, 2010.

Althof, S. E., Levine, S. B., Corty, E. W., Risen, C. B., Stern, E. B. and Kurit, D. M. A Double-bind Crossover Trial of Clomipramine for Rapid Ejaculation in 15 Couples. *Journal of Clinical Psychiatry*, 56, 402–407, 1995.

Althof, S., Rosen, R., Symonds, T., Mundayat, R., May, K. and Abraham, L. Development and Validation of a New Questionnaire to Assess Sexual Satisfaction, Control and Distress Associated with Premature Ejaculation. *The Journal of Sexual Medicine*, 3, 465–475, 2006.

American Psychiatric Association. *Diagnostic and Statistical Manual of Mental Disorders (Fifth Edition) (DSM-5)*. Washington, DC: American Psychiatric Association, 2013.

Arafa, M. and Shamloul, R. Efficacy of Sertraline Hydrochloride in Treatment of Premature Ejaculation: a Placebo-controlled Study Using a Validated Questionnaire. *International Journal of Impotence Research*, 18, 534–538, 2006.

Arafa, M. and Shamloul R. Development and Evaluation of the Arabic Index of Premature Ejaculation (AIPE). *The Journal of Sexual Medicine*, 4, 1750–1756, 2007.

Aschka, C., Himmel, W., Ittner, E. and Kochen, M. M. Sexual Problems of Male Patients in Family Practice. *The Journal of Family Practice*, 50, 773–778, 2001.

Assalian, P. Clomipramine in the Treatment of Premature Ejaculation. *The Journal of Sex Research*, 24, 213–214, 1988.

Assalian, P. Premature Ejaculation: Is It Really Psychogenic? *Journal of Sex Education and Therapy*, 20, 1–4, 1994.

Assalian, P. Guidelines for the Pharmacotherapy of Premature Ejaculation. *World Journal of Urology*, 23, 127–129, 2005.

Astbury-Ward, E. From Kama Sutra to Dotcom: The History, Myth, and Management of Premature Ejaculation. *Sexual & Relationship Therapy*, 17, 367–380, 2002.

Atikeler, M. K., Gecit, I. and Senol, F. A. Optimum Usage of Prilocaine-Lidocaine Cream in Premature Ejaculation. *Andrologia*, 34, 356–359, 2002.

Athanasiadis, L. Premature Ejaculation: Is it a Biogenic or a Psychogenic Disorder? *Sexual and Marital Therapy*, 13, 241–255, 1998.

Aversa, A., Pili, M., Francomano, D., Bruzziches, R., Spera, E., La Pera, G. and Spera, G. Effects of Vardenafil Administration on Intravaginal Ejaculatory Latency Time in Men with Lifelong Premature Ejaculation. *International Journal of Impotence Research*, 21, 221–227, 2009.

Aycock, J. The Medical Management of Premature Ejaculation. *Journal of Urology*, 62, 361–362, 1949.

Bandler,R. and Grinder, J. *The Structure of Magic*. Palo Alto, CA: Science and Behavior Books, 1975.

Barnes, T. and Eardley, I. Premature Ejaculation: The Scope of the Problem. *Journal of Sex and Marital Therapy*, 33, 151–170, 2007.

Basile-Fasolo, C., Mirone, V., Gentile, V., Parazzini, F. and Ricci, E. Premature Ejaculation: Prevalence and Associated Conditions in a Sample of 12,558 Men Attending the Andrology Prevention Week 2001. A Study of the Italian Society of Andrology (SIA). *The Journal of Sexual Medicine*, 2, 376–382, 2005.

Beaudry, M. and Boisvert, J. M. *Psychologie du couple: Quand la science se met à parler d'amour*. Montréal: Méridien, 1988.

Bennet, D. Treatment of Ejaculatio Praecox with Monoamine-oxidase Inhibitors. *The Lancet*, 2, 1309, 1961.

Benson, G. Male Sexual Function: Erection, Emission and Ejaculation. In E. Knobil and J. D. Neil (Eds). *The Physiology of Reproduction*. New York: Raven Press, 1988.

Bergler, E. Premature Ejaculation. *International Journal of Sexology*, 4, 14–26, 1950.

Berkovitch, M., Keresteci, A. G. and Koren, G. Efficacy of Prilocaine-Lidocaine Cream in the Treatment of Premature Ejaculation. *Journal of Urology*, 154, 1360–1361, 1995.

Biri, H., Isen, K., Sinik, Z., Onaran, M., Kupeli, B. and Bozkirli, I. Sertraline in the Treatment of Premature Ejaculation: a Double-blind Placebo Controlled Study. *International Urology Nephrology*, 30, 611–615, 1998.

Boutot, B. Éjaculation prématurée: Les différents traitements et leur évaluation. Revue de littérature. *Cahiers de sexologie clinique*, 17, 43–51, 1991.

Brody, S. and Weiss, P. Vaginal Orgasm is Associated with Vaginal (Not Clitoral) Sex Education, Focusing Mental Attention on Vaginal Sensations, Intercourse Duration and a Preference for a Longer Penis. *The Journal of Sexual Medicine*, 7, 2774–2781, 2010.

Burger, A. L. and Jacobson, N. S. The Relationship Between Sex Role Characteristics, Couple Satisfaction and Problem-Solving Skills. *American Journal of Family Therapy*, 7, 52–61, 1979.

Busato, W. and Galindo, C. C. Topical Anaesthetic Use for Treating Premature Ejaculation: A Double-Blind Randomized, Placebo-controlled Study. *British Journal of Urology International*, 93, 1018–1021, 2004.

Butler, C. A. New Data about Female Sexual Response. *Journal of Sex and Marital Therapy*, 2, 40–46, 1976.

Buvat, J. Pathophysiology of Premature Ejaculation. *The Journal of Sexual Medicine*. 8 (suppl 4), 316–327, 2011.

Byers, E. S. et Grenier, G. Premature or Rapid Ejaculation: Heterosexual Couples' Perceptions of Men's Ejaculatory Behavior. *Archives of Sexual Behavior*, 32, 261–270, 2003.

Caird, W. and Wincze, J.P. *Sex Therapy: A Behavioral Approach*. New York: Harper & Row, 1977.

Carani, C., Isidori, A. M., Granata, A., Carosa, E., Maggi, M., Lenzi, A. and Jannini, E. A. Multicenter Study on the Prevalence of Sexual Symptoms in Male Hypo- and Hyperthyroid Patients. *The Journal of Clinical Endocrinology & Metabolism*, 90, 6472–6479, 2005.

Carson, C., Glasser, D., Laumann, E., West, S. L. and Rosen, R. C. Prevalence and Correlates of Premature Ejaculation Among Men Aged 40 Years and Older: A United States Nationwide Population-based Study. Program and abstracts from the *American Urological Association 98th Annual Meeting*, April 26–May 1, Chicago, Illinois, Abstract 1249, 2003.

Chatton, D. Personal communication, 2008.

Chen, J., Mabjeesh, N. J., Matskin, H. and Greenstein, A. Efficacy of Sildenafil as Adjuvant Therapy to Selective Serotonin Reuptake Inhibitor in Alleviating Premature Ejaculation. *Urology*, 61, 197–200, 2003.

Chen, J, in Jannini, E. A., McMahon, C., Chen, J., Aversa, J. A. and Perelman, M. The Controversial Role of Phosphodiesterase Type 5 Inhibitors in the Treatment of Premature Ejaculation. *The Journal of Sexual Medicine*, 8, 2135–2143, 2011.

Collier F. La femme de l'éjaculateur prématurée. Symposium: L'éjaculation prématurée. *Congrès AIHUS*, Marseille, 2006.

Colpi, G. M., Fanciullacci, F., Beretta, G., Negri, L. and Zanollo, A. Evoked Sacral Potentials in Subjects with True Premature Ejaculation. *Andrologia*, 18, 583–586, 1986.

Cooper, A. J. A Clinical Study of "Coital Anxiety" in Male Potency Disorders. *Journal of Psychosomatic Research*, 13, 143–147, 1969a.

Cooper, A. J. Clinical and Therapeutic Studies in Premature Ejaculation. *Comprehensive Psychiatry*, 10, 285–295, 1969b.

Cooper, A. and Magnus, R. A Clinical Trial of the Beta Blocker Propranolol in Premature Ejaculation. *Journal of Psychosomatic Research*, 28, 331–336, 1984.

Coretti, G., Pierucci, S., De Scisciolo, M. and Nisita, C. Comorbidity between Social Phobia and Premature Ejaculation: Study on 242 Males Affected by Sexual Disorders. *Journal of Sex and Marital Therapy*, 32, 183–187, 2006.

Corona, G., Mannucci, E., Petrone, L., Ricca, V., Balercia, G., Giommi, R., Forti, G. and Maggi, M. Psycho-Biological Correlates of Free-Floating Anxiety in Male Patients with Sexual Dysfunctions. *Journal of Andrology*, 27, 86–93, 2005.

Costa P. Actualités épidémiologiques. Symposium: L'éjaculation prématurée. Congrès AIHUS, Marseille, 2006.

Crépault, C. and Desjardins, J. Y. *La complémentarité érotique*. Ottawa: Novacom, 1978.

Damrau, F. Premature Ejaculation: Use of Ethyl Aminobenzoate to Prolong Coitus. *Journal of Urology*, 89, 936–939, 1963.

DeAmicis, L. A., Goldberg, D. C., LoPiccolo, J., Friedman, L. and Davies, L. Clinical Follow-up of Couples Treated for Sexual Dysfunction. *Archives of Sexual Behavior*, 14, 467–489, 1985.

de Carufel, F. L'approche sexo-corporelle et la fonctionnalité sexuelle. *Cahiers des Sciences Familiales et Sexologiques*, *13*, 109–119, 1990.

de Carufel, F. Comparaison d'un traitement béhavorial et d'un traitement sexo-corporel de l'éjaculation précoce. *Thèse de doctorat. Département de psychologie de l'Université du Québec à Montréal*, 1996.

de Carufel, F. Les zones de la courbe d'excitation sexuelle de l'homme. *Réalités en Gynécologie-Obstétrique/Sexologie*, 1, 1, 8–18, 2007.

de Carufel, F. *L'éjaculation prématurée. Compréhension et traitement par la thérapie sexofonctionnelle*. Louvain: Presses universitaires de Louvain, 2009.

de Carufel, F. and Trudel, G. Effects of a New Functional-sexological Treatment for Premature Ejaculation. *Journal of Sex & Marital Therapy*, *32*, 97–114, 2006.

de Carufel, F. and De Sutter, P. (under the pen names of Carr, F. & Sutter, P.) *Confidential File 101*. New York: Anglehart Press, 2001.

De Sutter, P., Reynaert, C., Van Broeck, N. and de Carufel, F. Traitement de l'éjaculation précoce par une approche bibliothérapeutique cognitivo-comportementale sexologique. *Journal de Thérapie Comportementale et Cognitive*, 12, 4, 131–136, 2002.

Desjardins, J. Y. L'approche sexo-corporelle: fondements théoriques et champs d'applications. *Psychothérapies*, 1, 51–58, 1986.

Desjardins, J. Y. Approche sexo-corporelle. In M. El Féki (Éd.) *La sexothérapie*. Bruxelles: De Boeck, 2007.

Didonna, F. (Ed.) *Clinical Handbook of Mindfullness*. New York: Springer, 2009.

Dintrans, J. R. Les troubles sexuels. In B. Samuel-Lajeunesse et al. (Éds) *Manuel de thérapie comportementale et cognitive (Second Edition)* Paris: Monod, 2004.

Dinsmore, W. W., Hackett, G., Goldmeier, D., Waldinger, M., Dean, J., Wright, P., Callander, M., Wylie, K., Novak, C., Keywood, C., Heat, P. and Wyllie, M. Topical Eutectic Mixture for Premature Ejaculation (TEMPE): a Novel Aerosol-delivery Form of Lidocaine-Prilocaine for Treating Premature Ejaculation. *British Journal of Urology International*, 99, 369–375, 2006.

Dunn, K. M., Croft, P. R. and Hackett, G. I. Sexual Problems: A Study of the Prevalence and Need for Health care in the General Population. *Family Practice*, 15, 519–524, 1998.

Dunn, K. M., Croft, P. R. and Hackett, G. I. Association of Sexual Problems with Social, Psychological and Physical Problems in Men and Women: A Cross Sectional Population Survey. *Journal of Epidemiology and Community Health*, 53, 144–148, 1999.

Eaton, H. Clomipramine (Anafranil) in the Treatment of Premature Ejaculation. *Journal of International Medical Research*, 1, 432–434, 1973.

Ekmekcioglu, O., Inci, M., Demerci, D. and Tatlisen, A. Effects of Sildenafil Citrate on Ejaculation Latency, Detumescence time, and Refractory Period: Placebo-controlled, Double-Blind, Crossover Laboratory Setting Study. *Urology*, 65, 347–352, 2005.

El Féki, M. Approche sexo-cognitivo-comportementale. In M. El Féki (Éd.) *La sexothérapie*. Bruxelles: De Boeck, 2007.

El Féki, M. Approche sexosystémique. In M. El Féki (Éd.) *La sexothérapie*. Bruxelles: De Boeck, 2007.

El-Sakka, A. Premature Ejaculation in Non-Insulin Dependant Diabetic Patients. *International Journal of Andrology*, 26, 329–334, 2003.

Épictetus. *Enchiridion*. Dover: Thrift Editions, 2004.

Fava, M., Judge, R., Hoog, S. L., Nilsson, M. E. and Koke, S. C. Fluoxetine versus Sertraline and Paroxetine in Major Depressive Disorder: Changes in Weight with Long-Term Treatment. *Journal of Clinical Psychiatry*, 61, 863–867, 2000.

Fenichel, O. *The Psychoanalytic Theory of Neurosis*. New York: Norton, 1945.

Ferenczi, S. The Analytic Interpretation and Treatment of Psychosexual Impotence. In *Sex and Psychoanalysis*. New York: Dover Publication,1956.

Figueira, I., Possidente, E., Marques, C. and Hayes, K. Sexual Dysfunction: A Neglected Complication of Panic Disorder and Social Phobia. *Archives of Sexual Behavior*, 30, 369–376, 2001.

Fisher, H. *Anatomy of Love: The Natural History of Monogamy, Adultery, and Divorce*. New York: W. W. Norton & Company, 1992.

Fisher, S. *The Female Orgasm*. New York: Basic Books, 1973.

Forster, P. and King, J. Fluoxetine for Premature Ejaculation. *American Journal of Psychiatry*, 151, 1523, 1994.

Fugl-Meyer, A. R., Sjogren, K. and Fugl-Meyer, K. S. Sexual Disabilities, Problems, and Satisfaction in 18–74 Year Old Swedes. *Scandinavian Journal of Sexology*, 3, 79–105,1999.

Gebhard, C. Factors in Marital Orgasm. In J. LoPiccolo and L. LoPiccolo (Eds). *Handbook of Sex Therapy*. New York: Plenum Press, 1978.

Gentry, D. L. The Treatment of Premature Ejaculation Through Brief Therapy. *Psychotherapy: Theory, Research and Practice*, 15, 32–34, 1978.

Giuliano, F. and Clement, P. Serotonin and Premature Eejaculation: From Physiology to Patient Management. *European Urology*, 50, 454–466, 2006.

Giuliano, F. Neurophysiology of Erection and Ejaculation. *The Journal of Sexual Medicine*, 8 (suppl 4), 310–315, 2011.

Godpodinoff, M. L. Premature Ejaculation: Clinical Subgroups and Etiology. *Journal of Sex & Marital Therapy*, 15, 130–134, 1989.

Golden, J. S., Price, S., Heinrich, A. G. and Lobitz, W. C. Group vs. Couple Treatment of Sexual Dysfunctions. *Archives of Sexual Behavior*, 7, 593–603, 1978.

Goodman, R. E. An Assessment of Clomipramine (Anafranil) in the Treatment or Premature Ejaculation. *Journal of International Medical Research*, 8, 35–39, 1980.

Grenier, G. and Byers, S. Evaluating Models of Premature Ejaculation: A Review. *The Canadian Journal of Human Sexuality*, 1, 115–122, 1992.

Grenier, G. and Byers, S. Operationalizing Premature or Rapid Ejaculation. *The Journal of Sex Research*, 38, 369–378, 2001.

Gross, S. W. *A Practical Treatise on Impotence, Sterility and Allied Disorders of the Male Sexual Organs*. Philadelphia: Henry C. Lea's Son & Co. 1881.

Haavio-manila, E. and Kontula, O. *Sexual Trends in the Baltic Sea Area*. Helinski: Family Federation of Finland, 2003.

Haddad, P. The SSRI Discontinuatiion Syndrome. *Journal of Psychopharmacology*, 12, 305–313, 1998.

Haensel, S. M., Klem, T. M., Hop, W. C. and Slob, A. K. Fluoxetine and Premature Ejaculation: a Double-blind, Crossover, Placebo-controlled Study. *Journal of Clinical Psychopharmacology*, 18, 72–77, 1998.

Hammond, W. *Sexual Impotence in the Male*. New York: Bermingham & Co, 1883.

Hartmann, U., Schedlowski, M. and Krüger, T. H. C. Cognitive and Partner-Related Factors in Rapid Ejaculation: Differences Between Dysfunctional and Functional Men. *World Journal of Urology*, 23, 93–101, 2005.

Hastings, D. W. *Impotence and Frigidity*. New York: Little, Brown and Co, 1963.

Hatzimouratidis, K., Amar, E., Eardley, I., Giuliano, F., Hatzichristou, D., Montorsi, F., Vardi, Y., Wespes, E. Guidelines on Male Sexual Dysfunction: Erectile Dysfunction and Premature Ejaculation. *European Urology*, 57, 804–14, 2010.

Hawton, K. Erectile Dysfunction and Premature Ejaculation. *British Journal of Hospital Medicine*, 40, 430–34, 1988.

Hawton, K. and Catalan, J. Prognostic Factors in Sex Therapy. *Behaviour Research and Therapy*, 24, 377–385, 1986.

Healey, D. and Whitaker, C. Antidepressants and Suicide: Risk-Benefit Conundrums. *Journal of Psychiatry & Neuroscience*, 28, 331–335, 2003.

Hellstrom, W. J. G. Emerging Treatments for Premature Ejaculation: Focus on Dapoxetine. *Neuropsychiatric Disease and Treatment*, 5, 37–46, 2009.

Hiemke C, Hartter S. Pharmacokinetics of Selective Serotonin Reuptake Inhibitors. *Pharmacology and Therapeutics*, 85, 11–28, 2000.

Hite, S. *The Hite Report on Male Sexuality*. New York: Dell, 1981.

Holbrook, J. and Cohen, P. Aromatase Inhibition for the Treatment of Idiopathic Hypogonadism in Men with Premature Ejaculation. *Southern Medical Journal*, 45, 544–547, 2003.

Hong, L. K. Survival of the Fastest: On the Origin of Premature Ejaculation. *The Journal of Sexual Research*, 20, 109–122, 1984.

Hudson, W. W. *The Clinical Measurement Package: A Field Manual*. Homewood, Ill.: Dorsey Press, 1982.

Hunt, M. *Sexual Behavior in the 70s*. Chicago: Playboy Press, 1974.

Ince, L. Behavior Modification and Sexual Disorders. *American Journal of Psychotherapy*, 11, 446–451, 1973.

Isidori, A. M., Pozza, C., Esposito, K., Giugliano, D., Morano, S., Vignozzi, L., Corona, G., Lenzi, A., Jannini, E. A. Development and Validation of a 6-Item Version of the Female Sexual Function UIndex (FSFI) as a Diagnostic Tool for Female Sexual Dysfunction. *The Journal of Sexual Medicine*, 7, 1139–1146, 2010.

Jannini, E. A., Lombardo, F. and Lenzi, A. Correlation Between Ejaculatory and Erectile Dysfunction. *International Journal of Andrology*, 28 (2 suppl), 40–45, 2005.

Jannini, E. A., Maggi, M. and Lenzi, A. Evaluation of Premature Ejaculation. *The Journal of Sexual Medicine*, 8 (suppl 4), 328–334, 2011.

Jannini, E. A., McMahon, C., Chen, J., Aversa, J. A. and Perelman, M. The Controversial Role of Phosphodiesterase Type 5 Inhibitors in the Treatment of Premature Ejaculation. *The Journal of Sexual Medicine*, 8, 2135–2143, 2011.

Jehu, D. *Sexual Dysfunction*. New York: John Wiley & Sons, 1979.

Jern, P., Santtila, P., Johansson, A., Varjonen, M., Witting, K., von der Pahlen, B. and Sandnabba, N. K. Evidence for a Genetic Etiology to Ejaculatory Dysfunction. *International Journal of Impotence Research*, 2, 62– 67, 2009.

Jern, P. Twin Studies and Quantitative Genetics in Premature Ejaculation In E. A. Jannini, C. G. McMahon and M. D. Waldinger (Eds). *Premature Ejaculation: From Etiology to Diagnosis and Treatment*. Milan: Springer-Verlag Italia, Chapter 10, 2013.

Jern, P., Eriksson, E. and Westberg, L. A Reassessment of the Possible Effects of the Serotonin Transporter Gene Linked Polymorphism 5-HTTLPR on Premature Ejaculation. *Archives of Sexual Behavior*, 42, 45–9, 2013.

Kaplan, H. S. *The New Sex Therapy*. New York, Brunner/Mazel, 1974

Kaplan, H. S. *The Evaluation of Sexual Disorders: Psychological and Medical Aspects*. New York: Brunner/Mazel, 1983.

Kaplan, H. S. *P E: How to Overcome Premature Ejaculation*. New York: Brunner/Mazel, 1989.

Kaplan, H. S., Kohl, R. N., Pomeroy, W. B., Offit, A. K. and Hogan, B. Group treatment of Premature Ejaculation. *Archives of Sexual Behavior*, 5, 443–452, 1974.

Kara, H., Aydin, S., Yucel, M., Agargun, M. Y., Odabas, O. and Yilmaz, Y. The Efficacy of Fluoxetine in the Treatment of Premature Ejaculation: a Double-blind Placebo Controlled Study. *Journal of Urology*, 156, 1631–1632, 1996.

Kempeneers, P., Andrianne, R., Bauwens, S., Georis, I., Pairoux, J. and Fand Blairy, S. Clinical Outcomes of a New Self-Help Booklet for Premature Ejaculation. *The Journal of Sexual Medicine*, 9, 2417–2428, 2012.

Killmann, P. R. and Auerbach, R. Treatments of Premature Ejaculation and Psychogenic Impotence: A Critical Review of the Literature. *Archives of sexual Behavior*, 8, 81–100, 1979.

Kim, S. and Keun, K. Efficacy and Safety of Fluoxetine, Sertraline and Clomipramine in Patients with Premature Ejaculation. *Journal of Urology*, 159, 425–427, 1998.

Kinsey, A. C., Pomeroy, W. B. and Martin, C. E. *Sexual Behavior in the Human Male*. Philadelphia: W. B. Saunders, 1948.

Kinsey, A. C., Pomeroy, W. B. Martin, C. E. and Gebhard, P. H. *Sexual Behavior in the Human Female*. Philadelphia: W. B. Saunders, 1953.

Kockott, G., Feil, W., Ferstl, R., Alsenhoff, J. and Besinger, U. Psycho-physiological Aspects of Male Sexual Inadequacy: Results of an Experimental Study. *Archives of Sexual Behavior*, 9, 477–493, 1980a.

Kockott, G., Feil, W., Revenstorf, S., Alsenhoff, J. and Besinger, U. Symptomatology and Psychological Aspects of Male Sexual Inadequacy: Results of an Experimental Study. *Archives of Sexual Behavior*, 9, 477–493, 1980b.

Koos Slob, A., van Berkel, A. and van der Werff ten Bosh, J. J. Premature Ejaculation Treated by Local Penile Anaesthesia in an Uncontrolled Clinical Replication Study. *Journal of Sex Research*, 37, 244–247, 2000.

Kraft, T. and Al-Issa, I. The Use of Methohexitone Sodium in the Systematic Desensitization of Premature Ejaculation. *British Journal of Psychiatry*, 14, 351–352, 1968.

Kuhr, C., Heiman, J., Cardenas, D., Bradley, W. and Berger, R. Premature Emission after Spinal Cord Injury. *Journal of Urology*, 153, 429–431, 1995.

Lane, R and Baldwin, D. Selective Serotonin Reuptake Inhibitor-induced Serotonin Syndrome: Review. *Journal of Clinical Psychopharmacology*, 17, 208–21, 1997.

La Pera, G. and Nicastro, A. A New Treatment for Premature Ejaculation: The Rehabilitation of the Pelvic Floor. *Journal of Sex & Marital Therapy*, 22, 1, 22–27, 1996.

Laumann, E. O., Gagnon, J. H., Michael, R. T. and Michaels, S. *The Social Organization of Sexuality. Sexual Practices in the United States*. Chicago: University of Chicago Press, 1994.

Laumann, E. O., Paik, A. and Rosen, R. C. Sexual Dysfunction in the United States: Prevalence and Predictors. *JAMA*, 281, 537–544, 1999.

Laumann, E. O., Nicolosi, A., Paik, A., Gingell, G. and Moriera, E. Sexual Problems among Men and Women Aged 40–80: Prevalence and Correlates Identified in the Global Study of Sexual Attitudes and Behavior. *International Journal of Impotence Research*, 17, 39–57, 2005.

Lazarus, A. A. *Behavior Therapy and Beyond*. New York: McGraw-Hill, 1971.

Leiblum, S. R., Rosen, R. C. and Pierce, D. Group Treatment Format: Mixed Sexual Dysfunctions. *Archives of Sexual Behavior*, 5, 313–322, 1976.

Levine, S. B. Premature Ejaculation: Some Thoughts about its Pathogenesis. *Journal of Sex and Marital Therapy*, 1, 326–334, 1975.

Levine, S. B. Helping Men to Control Ejaculation. *In Sexual Life: A Clinician's Guide*. New York: Plenum, pp. 90–106, 1992.

Liang, C., Zhang, X., Shi, H. and Wang, K. Prevalence of Sexual Dysfunction In Chinese Men with Chronic Prostatitis. *British Journal of Urology International*, 93, 569–570, 2004.

London, L. S. *Mental Therapy: Studies in Fifty Cases*. New York: Couici-Friede, 1957.

LoPiccolo, J. Direct Treatment of Sexual Dysfunction in the Couple. In J. Money and H. Mesaph (Eds). *Handbook of sexology, Volume 5: Selected Syndromes and Therapy*. New York: Elsevier, pp. 1227–1244, 1978.

Lowe, J. C. and Mikulas, W. L. Use of Written Material in Learning Self-Control of Premature Ejaculation. *Psychological Reports*, 37, 295–298, 1975.

Lowen, A. *Bioenergetics*. New York: Coward, McCann & Geoghegan, 1975.

Lowen, A. *Love and Orgasm*. New York: The Macmillan Company, 1965.

Ludovico, G., Corvasce, A., Pagliarulo, C., Cirillo-Marucco, E., Marino, A. and Pagliarulo, E. Paroxetine in the Treatment of Premature Ejaculation. *British Journal of Urology*, 77, 881–882, 1996.

Lue, T. F., Giuliano, F., Montorsi, F., Rosen, R. C., Andersson, K. E., Althof, S., Christ, G., Hatzichristou, D., Hirsch, M., Kimoto,Y., Lewis, R., McKenna, K., MacMahon, C., Morales, A., Mulcahy, J., Padma-Nathan, H., Pryor, J., de Tejada, I. S., Shabsigh, R. and Wagner, G. Summary of the Recommendations on Sexual Dysfunctions in Men. *The Journal of Sexual Medicine*, 1, 6–23, 2004.

Lunde, I., Larsen, G. K., Fog, E. and Garde, K. Sexual Desire, Orgasm, and Sexual Fantaisies: A Study of 625 Danish Women Born in 1910, 1936, and 1958. *Journal of Sex Education & Therapy*, 17, 111–115, 1991.

Manasia, P., Pomerol, J., Ribe, N., Gutierrez del Pozo, R. and Alcocer Garcia, J. Comparison of the Efficacy and Safety of 90 mg Versus 20 mg Fluoxetine in the Treatment of Premature Ejaculation. *Journal of Urology*, 170, 164–165, 2003

Marmor, J. Impotence and Ejaculatory Disturbances. In B. J. Sadock, H. I. Kaplan and A. M. Freedman (Eds). *The Sexual Experience*. Baltimore: Williams & Wilkins, 1976.

Marten, J. *Gonofologium Novum: or, a New System of all the Secret Infirmities and Diseases, Natural, Accidental, and Venereal in Men and Women*. London: N. Crouch, 1709.

Masters, W. H. and Johnson, V. E. *Human Sexual Response*. Boston: Little, Brown, 1966.

Masters, W.H. and Johnson, V.E. *Human Sexual Inadequacy*. Boston: Little, Brown, 1970.

McCabe, M. P. Intimacy and Quality of Life among Sexually Dysfunctional men and women. *Journal of Sex and Marital Therapy*, 23, 276–290, 1997.

McCabe, M. P. Evaluation of a Cognitive Behavior Therapy Program for People with Sexual Dysfunction. *Journal of Sex and Marital Therapy*, 27, 259–271, 2001.

McCarthy, B. W. *Male Sexual Awareness: Increasing Sexual Satisfaction*. New York: Carroll & Graf, 1988.

McCarthy, B. W. Cognitive-Behavioural Strategy and Techniques in the Treatment of Early Ejaculation. In S. R. Leiblum and R. C. Rosen (Eds). *Principles and Practices of Sex Therapy: Up-date for the 1990s*. New York: Guilford, pp. 141–147, 1989.

McCarthy, B. W. Relapse Prevention Strategies and Techniques in Sex Therapy. *Journal of Sex and Marital Therapy*, 19, 142–146, 1993.

McCarthy, B. W. Etiology and Treatment of Early Ejaculation. *Journal of Sex Education and Therapy*, 20, 5–6, 1994.

McMahon, C. G., Althof, S. E., Waldinger, M. D., Porst, H., Dean, J., Sharlip, I. D., Adaikan, P. G., Becher, E., Broderick, G. A., Buvat, J., Dabees, K., Giraldi, A., Giuliano, F., Hellstrom, W. J., Incrocci, L., Laan, E., Meuleman, E., Perelman, M. A., Rosen, R. C., Rowland, D. L. and Segraves, R. An Evidence-based Definition of Lifelong Premature Ejaculation: Report of the International Society for Sexual Medicine (ISSM) Ad Hoc Committee for the Definition of Premature Ejaculation. *The Journal of Sexual Medicine*, 5, 1590–1606, 2008.

McMahon, C. G., McMahon, C. N., Leow, L. J. and Winestock, C. G. Efficacy of Type-5 Phosphodiesterase Inhibitors in the Drug Treatment of Premature Ejaculation: A Systematic Review. *British Journal of Urology International*, 98, 259–72, 2006.

McMahon, C. G. and Touma, K. Treatment of Premature Ejaculation with Paroxetine Hydrochloride as Needed: 2 Single-blind Placebo Controlled Crossover Studies. *Journal of Urology*, 161, 1826–1830, 1999a.

McMahon, C. G. and Touma, K. Treatment of Premature Ejaculation with Paroxetine Hydrochloride. *International Journal of Impotence Research*, 11, 241–245, 1999b.

McMahon, C. G., Abdo, C., Incrocci, L., Perelman, M., Rowland, D., Waldinger, M. and Xin, Z. C. Disorders of Orgasm and Ejaculation in Men. *The Journal of Sexual Medicine*, 1, 58–65, 2004.

McMahon, C. G., Stuckley, B., Andersen, M., Purvis, K., Koppiker, N. and Haughie, S. Efficacy of Sildenafil Citrate (Viagra) in Men with Premature Ejaculation. *The Journal of Sexual Medicine*, 2, 368–375, 2005.

Melnik, T., Althof, S., Atallah, Á. N., Puga, M. E. D. S., Glina, S. and Riera, R. Psychosocial Interventions for Premature Ejaculation (Review). The Cochrane Collaboration. *The Cochrane Library*, Issue 8, 2011.

Mendels, J., Camera, A. and Sikes, C. Sertraline Treatment for Premature Ejaculation. *Journal of Clinical Psychopharmacology*, 15, 341–346, 1995.

Metz, M. E. and McCarthy, B. W. *Coping with Premature Ejaculation*. Oakland: New Harbinger, 2003.

Metz, M. E., Pryor, J. L., Premature Ejaculation: A Psychophysiological Approach for Assessment and Management. *Journal of Sex and Marital Therapy*, 26, 293–320, 2000.

Metz, M. E., Pryor, J. L., Nesvacil, L. J., Abuzzahah Sr., F. and Koznar, J. Premature Ejaculation: A Psychological Review. *Journal of Sex & Marital Therapy*, 23, 3–23, 1997.

Meyer, J. K., Schmidt, C. W. and Wise, T. N. *Clinical Management of Sexual Disorders*. Baltimore: Williams & Wilkins, 1983.

Michetti, P. M., Rossi, R., Bonanno, D., De Dominicis, C., Iori, F. and Simonelli, C. Dysregulation of Emotions and Premature Ejaculation (PE): Alexithymia in 100 Outpatients. *The Journal of Sexual Medicine*, 4, 1462–1467, 2007.

Miller, S. A. and Byers, E. S. Actual and Desired Duration of Foreplay and Intercourse: Discordance and Misperceptions Within Heterosexual Couples. *The Journal of Sex Research,* 41, 301–309, 2004.

Mimoun, S. and Hania, C. 1000 éjaculateurs prématurés: les célibataires et les autres. *Contraception-fertilité-sexualité*, 16, 511–516, 1988.

Montague, D. K., Jarow, J., Broderick, G. A., Dmochowski, R. R., Heaton, J. P., Lue, T. F., Nehra, A. and Sharlip, I. D. AUA Guideline on the Pharmacologic Management of Premature Ejaculation. *Journal of Urology*, 172, 290–4, 2004.

Montejo-Gonzalez, A. L., Llorca, G., Izquierdo, J. A., Ledesma, A., Bousono, M., Calcedo, A., Carrasco, J. L., Ciudad, J., Daniel, E., de la Gandara, J., Derecho, J., Franco, M., Gomez, M. J., Macias, J. A., Martin, T., Perez, V. and Sanchez, J. M., Vicens, E. SSRI-Induced Sexual Dysfunction: Fluoxetine, Paroxetine, Sertraline, and Fluvoxamine in a Prospective, Multicenter, and Descriptive Study of 344 Patients. *Journal of Sex & Marital Therapy*, 23, 176–194, 1997.

Morales, A. Developmental Status of Topical Therapies for Erectile and Ejaculatory Dysfunction. *International Journal of Impotence Research*, 12, 4, 80–85, 2000.

Mrdjenovich, A. J., Bischof, G. H and Menichello, J. L. A Biopsychosocial Approlach to Premature Ejaculation. *The Canadian Journal of Human Sexuality*, 13, 45–55, 2004.

Mulhall, J. P., Goldstein, I., Bushmakin, A. G., Cappelleri, J. C., and Hvidsten, K. Validation of the Erection Hardness Score. *The Journal of Sexual Medicine*, 4, 1626–1634, 2007.

Munjack, D. J. and Crocker, B. Alprazolam Induced Ejaculatory Inhibition. *Journal of Clinical Psychopharmacology*, 6, 57–58, 1986.

Munjack, D. J., Kanno, P. H., Staples, F. R. and Leonard, M. D. Some Psychometric Data on Ejaculatory Disorders: A Further Note. *Psychological Reports*, 46, 1047–1050, 1980.

Nathan, S. G. The Epidemiology of the DSM-III Psychosexual Dysfunctions. *Journal of Sex & Marital Therapy*, 12, 267–281, 1986.

Nichols McCoy, N. and D'Agostino, P. A. Factor Analysis of Sexual Interaction Inventory. *Archives of Sexual Behavior*, 6, 25–35, 1977.

Obler, M. Systematic Desensitization in Sexual Disorders. *Journal of Behavior Therapy and Experimental Psychiatry*, 4, 93–101, 1973.

Olivier, B., van Ooschot, R. and Waldinger, M. D. Serotonin, Serotonergic Receptors, Selective Serotonin Reuptake Inhibitors and Sexual Behaviour. *International Clinical Pharmacolology*, 13 (Suppl 6), S9–S14, 1998.

Organisation mondiale de la santé/World Health Organization. *The ICD-10 Classification of Mental and Behavioural Disorders: Diagnostic Criteria for Research.* Geneva: World Health Organization, 1993.

Ozbek, E., Tacsi, A. I., Tugcu,V., Ilbey, Y. O., Simsek, A., Ozcan, L., Polat, E. C. and Koksal, V. Possible Association of the 5-HTTLPR Serotonin Transporter Promoter Gene Polymorphism with Premature Ejaculation in a Turkish Population. *Asian Journal of Andrology*, 11, 351–355, 2009.

Paick, J. S., Jeong, H. and Park, M. S. Penile Sensitivity in Men with Premature Ejaculation. *International Journal of Impotence Research*,10, 247–50, 1998.

Patrick, D. L., Althof, S. E., Pryor, J. L., Rosen, R., Rowland, D. L., Ho, K. F., McNulty, P., Rothman, M. and Jamieson, C. Premature Ejaculation: An Observational Study of Men and Their Partners. *The Journal of Sexual Medicine*, 2, 358–367, 2005.

Patrick, D. L., Giuliano, F., Ho, K. F., Gagnon, D. D., McNulty, P. and Rothman, M. The Premature Ejaculation Profile: Validation of Self-reported Outcome Measures for Research and Practice. *British Journal of Urology International*, 103, 358–364, 2009.

Pattij, T., Olivier, B. and Waldinger, M. D. Animal Models of Ejaculatory Behavior. *Current Pharmaceutical Design*, 11, 4069–4077, 2005.

Perelman, M. A. Treatment of Premature Ejaculation. In S. R. Leiblum and L. A. Pervin (Eds). *Principles and Practice of Sex Therapy*. New York: The Guilford Press, 1980.

Pirke, K. M., Kockott, G., Aldenhoff, J., Besinger, U. and Feil, W. Pituitary Gonadal System Function in Patients with Erectile Impotence and Premature Ejaculation. *Archives of Sexual Behavior*, 8, 41–48, 1979.

Plomin, R., DeFries, J. O. C., McClearn, G. E. and McGuffin, P. *Behavioral Genetics, (Fourth Edition)*. New York: Worth Publishers, 2001.

Polonsky, D. Premature Ejaculation. In S. Leiblum and R. Rosen (Eds). *Principles and Practice of Sex Therapy*. New York: Guilford, pp 305–342, 2000.

Porst, H. An Overview of Pharmacotherapy in Premature Ejaculation. *The Journal of Sexual Medecine*, 8 (suppl 4), 335–341, 2011.

Porst, H., Montorsi, F., Rosen, R. C., Gaynor, L., Grupe, S. and Alexander, J. The Premature Ejaculation Prevalence and Attitudes (PEPA) Survey: Prevalence, Comorbidities, and Professional Help-seeking. *European Urology*, 51, 816–823, 2007.

Porto, R. Essai en double aveugle de la clomipramine dans l'éjaculation prématurée. *Médecine et Hygiène*, 39, 1249–1253, 1981.

Poudat, F. X. and Jarousse, N. *Traitement comportemental et cognitif des difficultés sexuelles*. Paris: Masson, 1992.

Pryor, J. L., Althof, S. E., Steidle, C., Miloslavsky, M. and Kell, S. Efficacy and Tolerability of Dapoxetine in the Treatment of Premature Ejaculation. *Journal of Urology*, 173, 201, 2005.

Pryor, J. L., Althof, S. E., Steidle, C., Rosen, R. C., Hellstrom, W. J., Shabsigh, R., Miloslavsky, M. and Kell, S. for the Dapoxetine Study Group. Efficacy and Tolerability of Dapoxetine in Treatment of Premature Ejaculation: an Integrated Analysis of two Double-blind, Randomised Controlled Trials. *Lancet*, 368, 929–937, 2006.

Redmond, D. E., Kosten, T. R. and Reiser, M. F. Spontaneous Ejaculations Associated with Anxiety: Psychophysiological Considerations. *American Journal of Psychiatry*, 140, 1163–1166, 1983.

Reich, W. *Character Analysis*. New York: Farrar, Straus & Giroux, 1972.

Reich, W. *The Function of the Orgasm*. New York: Farrar, Straus & Giroux, 1942.

Reinish, J. M. and Beasley, R. *The Kinsey Institute New Report on Sex: What You Must Know to Be Sexually Literate*. New York: St. Martin's Press, 1990.

Revicki, D., Howard, K., Hanlon, J., Mannix, S., Greene, A. and Rothman, M. Characterizing the Burden of Premature Ejaculation from a Patient and Partner Perspective: A Multi-country Qualitative Analysis. *Health and Quality of Life Outcomes*, 6, 33, 2008.

Richters, J., Grunich, A., de Visser, R., Smith, A. and Rissel, C. Sex in Australia: Sexual Difficulties in a Representative sample of Adudlts. *Australian and New Zealand Journal of Public Health*, 27, 164–170, 2003

Riley, A. and Segraves, R. T. Treatment of Premature Ejaculation. *International Journal of Clininical Practice*, 60, 694–697, 2006.

Rivera, P., Gonzalez, R., Gonzalez, F. and Storme, O. Uso de paroxetina a demanda en eyaculacion precoz. *Actas Urológicas Españolas*, 29, 387–391, 2005.

Rosen, R. C. The Premature Ejaculation Prevalence and Attitudes (PEPA) Survey: a Multi-national Survey. *The Journal of Sexual Medicine*, 1 (supp 1), 57–58, 2004.

Rosen, R. C., Lane, R. M. and Menza, M. Effects of SSRIs on Sexual Function: a Critical Review. *Journal Clinical Psychopharmacology*, 19, 67–85, 1999.

Rosen, R. C., McMahon, C. G., Niederberger, C., Broderick, G. A., Jamieson, C., Gagnon, D. D. Correlates to the Clinical Diagnosis of Premature Ejaculation: Results from a Large Observational Study of Men and their Partners. *Journal of Urology*, 177, 1059–1064, 2007.

Rosen, R. C., Riley, A., Wagner, G., Osterloh, I. H., Kirkpatrick, J. and Mishra, A. The International Index of Erectile Function (IIEF): A Multidimensional Scale for Assessment of Erectile Dysfunction. *Urology*, 49, 822–830, 1997.

Rowland, D. L. Psychophysiology of Ejaculatory Function and Dysfunction. *World Journal of Urology*, 23, 82–88, 2005.

Rowland, D. L. and Cooper, S. E. *Risk Factors for Premature Ejaculation: The Intrapsychic Risk Factor* In E. A. Jannini, C. G. McMahon and M. D. Waldinger (Eds). *Premature Ejaculation from Etiology to Diagnosis and Treatment*. Milan: Springer-Verlag Italia, Chapter 8, 2013.

Rowland, D. L., Cooper, S. E. and Schneider, M. Defining Premature Ejaculation for Experimental and Clinical Investigations. *Archives of Sexual Behavior*, 30, 235–253, 2001a.

Rowland, D. L., Cooper, S. E. and Slob, A. K. Genital and Psychoaffective Response to Erotic Stimulation in Sexually Functional and Dysfunctional Men. *Journal of Abnormal Psychology*, 105, 194–203, 1996.

Rowland, D. L., De Gouveia Brazao, C.A. and Slob, A. K. Effective Daily Treatment with Clomipramine in Men with Premature Ejaculation when 25mg (as required) is Ineffective. *British Journal of Urology*, 87, 357–360, 2001b.

Rowland, D. L., De Gouveia Brazao, C. A., Strassberg, D. A. and Slob, A. K. Ejaculatory Latency and Control in Men with Premature Ejaculation: a Detailed Analysis across Sexual Activities Using Multiple Sources of Information. *Journal of Psychosomatic Research*, 48, 69–77, 2000.

Rowland, S. L., Greenleaf, W., Mas, M., Myers, L. and Davidson, J. M. Penile and Finger Sensory Thresholds of Young, Aging, and Diabetic Males. *Achives of Sexual Behavior*, 18, 1–12, 1989.

Rowland, S. L., Haensel, S. M., Blom, J. H. M. and Slob, A. K. Penile Sensitivity in Men with Premature Ejaculation and Erectile Dysfunction. *Journal of Sex & Marital Therapy*, 19, 189–197, 1993.

Rowland, D. L., Patrick, D. L., Rothman, M., and Gagnon, D. D. The Psychological Burden of Premature Ejaculation. *The Journal of Urology*, 177, 1065–1070, 2007.

Rowland, D. L., Perelman, M., Althof, S., Barada, J., McCullough, A., Bull, S., Jamieson, C., Ho, K. F. Self-reported Premature Ejaculation and Aspects of Sexual Functioning and Satisfaction. *The Journal of Sexual Medicine*, 1, 225–232, 2004.

Ryan, M. *Lectures on Impotence and Sterility*. Baltimore: W. R. Lucas, 1835.

Safarinejad, M. R. Polymorphisms of the Serotonin Transporter Gene and their Relation to Premature Ejaculation in Individuals from Iran. *Journal of Urology*, 181, 2656–2661, 2009.

Salem, E. A., Wilson, S. K., Bissada, N. K., Delk, J. R., Hellstrom, W. J. and Cleves, M. A. Tramadol HCL Has Promise in On-demand Use to Treat Premature Ejaculation. *The Journal of Sexual Medicine*, 5, 188–93, 2008.

Salonia, A., Maga, T., Colombo, R., Scattoni, V., Briganti, A., Cestari, A., Guazzoni, G., Rigatti, P. and Montorsi, F. A Prospective Study Comparing Paroxetine Alone Versus Paroxetine Plus Sildenafil in Patients with Premature Ejaculation. *Journal of Urology*, 168, 2486–2489, 2002.

Salzman, L. Psychotherapy with Patients with Sexual Disorders. In M. Hammer (Ed.). *The Theory and Practice of Psychotherapy with Specific Disorders*. Springfield, Ill.: Charles C. Thomas, pp. 108–143, 1972.

Santtila, P., Jern, P., Westberg, L., Walum, H, Pedersen, C. T., Eriksson, E. and Sandnabba, N. K. The Dopamine Transporter Gene (DAT1) Polymorphism is Associated with Premature Ejaculation. *The Journal of Sexual Medicine*, 7, 1538–1546, 2010.

Schnarch, D. *Passionate marriage*. New York: Henry Holt, 1997.

Schover, L.R., Friedman, J.M., Weiler, S.J., Heiman, J.R. and LoPiccolo, J. Multiaxial Problem-Oriented System for Sexual Dysfunctions. *Archives of General Psychiatry*, 39, 614–619, 1982.

Screponi, E., Carosa, E., DiStasi, S., Pepe, M., Carrusa, G. and Janniri, E. A. Prevalence of Chronic Prostatitis in Men with Premature Ejaculation. *Urology*, 58, 198–202, 2001.

Segraves, R. T. Treatment of Premature Ejaculation with Lorazepam. American *Journal of Psychiatry*, 144, 1240, 1987.

Segraves, R. T. Effects of Psychotropic Drugs on Human Erection and Ejaculation. *Archives of General Psychiatry*, 46, 275–284, 1989.

Segraves, R. T. Rapid Ejaculation: A Review of Nosology, Prevalence and Treatment. *International Journal of Impotence Research*, 18, S24–S32, 2006.

Segraves, R.T., Saran, A., Segraves, K. and Maguire, E. Clomipramine versus Placebo in the Treatment of Premature Ejaculation: A Pilot Study. *Journal of Sex & Marital Therapy*, 19, 198–200, 1993.

Semans, J. Premature Ejaculation: A New Approach. *Southern Medical Journal*, 49, 353–358, 1956.

Shamoul, R. and Nashaar, A. Chronic Prostatitis in Premature Ejaculation: A Cohort Study in 153 Men. *The Journal of Sexual Medicine*, 3, 150–154, 2005.

Shapiro, B. Premature Ejaculation: Review of 1130 Cases. *Journal of Urology*, 50, 374–379, 1943.

Shapiro, B. Potency Disorders in the Male: A Review of 1960 Cases of Premature Ejaculation. *Harefuah*, 45, 40–41, 1953.

Sharlip, I. D. Guidelines for the Diagnosis and Management of Premature Ejaculation. *The Journal of Sexual Medicine*, 3, 309–317, 2006.

Shilon, M., Paz, G.F. and Homonnai, Z.T. The Use of Phenoxybenzamine Treatment in Premature Ejaculation. *Fertility and Sterility*, 42, 659–661, 1984.

Simpson, G., McCann, B. and Lowy, M. Treatment of Premature Ejaculation after Traumatic Brain Injury. *Brain Injury*, 17, 723–729, 2003.

Singer, C. and Weiner, W. J. Male Sexual Response Cycle. In C. S. Singer and W. J. Weiner, Editors, *Sexual Dysfunction, a Neuro-Medical Approach*. Armonk: Futura, 1994.

Siroky, M.B., Sax, S. D. and Krane, R. J. Sacral Signal Tracing: The Electrophysiology of the Bulbocavernous Reflex. *Journal of Urology*, 122, 661–664, 1979.

Solano, C. *La sexualité au masculin*. Paris: Marabout, 2000.

Spanier, G. B. Measuring Dyadic Adjustment: New Scales for Assessing the Quality of Marriage and Similar Dyads. *Journal of Marriage and the Family*, 38, 15–28, 1976.

Spiess, W. F. J., Geer, J. H. and O'Donohue, W.T. Premature Ejaculation: Investigation of Factors in Ejaculatory Latency. *Journal of Abnormal Psychology*, 93, 242–245, 1984.

Steggall, M. J., Fowlerc, C. G. and Pryce, A. Combination Therapy for Premature Ejaculation: Results of a Small-scale Study. *Sexual and Relationship Therapy*, 23, 365–376, 2008.

Stekel, W. *Impotence in the Male: The Psychic Disorders of Sexual Function in the Male*. New York: Boni and Liveright, 1927.

Strassberg, D., Gouveia, C., Rowland, D. and Slob, K. Clomipramine in the Treatment of Rapid (Premature) Ejaculation. *Journal of Sex and Marital Therapy*, 25, 89–101, 1999.

Strassberg, D. S., Kelly, M. P., Carroll, C. and Kircher, J. C. The Psychophysiological Nature of Premature Ejaculation. *Archives of Sexual Behavior*, 16, 327–36, 1987.

Strassberg, D., Mahoney, J., Schaugaard, M. et Hale, V. The Role of Anxiety in Premature Ejaculation; A Psycho-physiological Model. *Archives of Sexual Behavior*, 19, 251–257, 1990.

Symonds, T., Perelman, M. A., Althof, S., Giuliano, F., Martin, M., May, K., Abraham, L., Crossland, A. and Morris, M. Development and Validation of a Premature Ejaculation Diagnostic Tool. *European Urology*, 52, 565–573, 2007.

Symonds, T., Roblin, D., Hart, K. and Althof, S. How Does Premature Ejaculation Impact a Man's Life? *Journal of Sex and Marital Therapy*, 29, 361–370, 2003.

Tamam, L. and Ozpoyraz, N. Selective Serotonin Reuptake Inhibitor Discontinuous Syndrome: A Review. *Advances in Therapy*, 19, 17–26, 2002.

Tanner, B. A. Two Case Report on the Modification of the Ejaculatory Response with the Squeeze technique. *Psychotherapy: Theory, Research and Practice*, 10, 297–300, 1973.

Terman, L. M. Correlates of Orgasm Adequacy in a Group of 556 Wives. *Journal of Psychology*, 32, 115–172, 1951.

Tollison, C. D. and Adams, H. E. *Sexual Disorders: Treatment, Theory, Research*. New York: Gardner Press, 1979.

Tordjman, G. L'éjaculation prématurée. *Soins*, 401, 27–31, 1983.

Tordjman, G. Un nouveau traitement de l'éjaculation précoce. *Cahiers de sexologie clinique*, 15, 17–22, 1989.

Trudel, G. *Les Dysfonctions Sexuelles: évaluation et traitement par des méthodes psychologique, interpersonnelle et biologique*. Sillery: Les Presses de l'Université du Québec, 2000.

Trudel, G. and Proulx, S. Treatment of Premature Ejaculation by Bibliotherapy: an Experimental Study. *Sexual and Relationship Therapy*, 2, 163–167, 1987.

Vanden Broucke, H., Everaert, K., Peersman, W., Claes H., Vanderschueren, D. and Van Kampen, M. Ejaculation Latency Times and Their Relationship to Penile Sensitivity in Men With Normal Sexual Function. *Journal of Urology*, 177, 237–240, 2007.

Vander, A. J., Sherman, J. H. and Luciano, D. S. *Human Physiology: The Mechanisms of Body Function*. New York: McGraw-Hill, 1975.

Vignoli, G. C. Premature Ejaculation: New Electrophysiologic Approach. *Urology*, 1, 81–82, 1978.

Wainberg, J. Essai d'interprétation ontogénique de l'éjaculation prématurée. In J. Buvat and P. Jouannet (Eds). *L'éjaculation et ses perturbations*. Lyon-Villeurbanne: Simep., pp. 112–116, 1984.

Waldinger, M. D. The Neurobiological Approach to Premature Ejaculation. *Journal of Urology*, 168, 2,359–2,267, 2002.

Waldinger, M. D. Lifelong Premature Ejaculation: From Authority Based to Evidence Based Medicine. *British Journal of Urology International*, 93, 201–207, 2004.

Waldinger, M. Risk Factors in Premature Ejaculation: The Genetic Risk Factor. In E. A. Jannini, C. G. McMahon and M. D. Waldinger (Eds). *Premature Ejaculation: From Etiology to Diagnosis and Treatment*. Milan: Springer-Verlag Italia, Chapter 9, 2013.

Waldinger, M. D., Berendsen, H. H., Blok, B. F., Olivier, B. and Holstege, G. Premature Ejaculation and Serotonergic Antidepressants-induced Delayed Ejaculation: the Involvement of the Serotonergic System. *Behavioural Brain-Research*, 92, 111–118, 1998a.

Waldinger, M. D., Hengeveld, M. W. and Zwinderman, A. H. Paroxetine Treatment of Premature Ejaculation: a Double-bind, Randomized, Placebo-controlled Study. *American Journal of Psychiatry*, 151, 1377–1379, 1994.

Waldinger, M. D., Hengeveld, M. W., Zwinderman, A. H., Olivier, B. An Empirical Operationalization Study of DSM-IV Diagnostic Criteria for Premature Ejaculation. *International Journal of Psychiatry in Clinical Practice*, 4, 287–293, 1998b.

Waldinger, M. D., Hengeveld, M. W., Zwinderman, A. H., Olivier, B. Effect of SSRI Antidepressants on Ejaculation: a Double-bind, Randomized, Placebo-controlled Study with Fluoxetine, Fluvoxamine, Paroxetine and Sertraline. *Journal of Clinical Psychopharmacology*, 18, 274–281, 1998c.

Waldinger, M. D., Janssen, P. K. C. and Schweitzer, D. H. Hardy Weinberg Equilibrium in Genetic PE Research Remains Critical to Avoid Misinterpretation. *Asian Journal of Andrology*, 11, 524, 2009a.

Waldinger, M. D., Janssen, P. K. C. and Schweitzer, D. H. Re: Polymorphisms of the Serotonin Transporter Gene and their Relation to Premature Ejaculation in Individuals from Iran: M.R. Safarinejad. *Journal of Urology*,181, 2656–2661, 2009a; *Journal of Urology*, 182, 2983–2984, 2009b.

Waldinger, M. D. and Olivier, B. Selective Serotonin Reuptake Inhibitor-induced Sexual Dysfunction. Clinical and Research Considerations. *International Clinical Psychopharmacology*, 13 (Suppl. 6), S27–S33, 1998.

Waldinger, M. D. and Olivier, B. Utility of Selective Serotonine Re-Uptake Inhibitors in Premature Ejaculation. *Current Opinion in Investigational Drugs*, 5, 743–747, 2004c.

Waldinger, M. D., Quinn, P. Dilleen, M., Mundayat, R., Schweitzer, D. H. and Boolell, M. A Multinational Population Survey of Intravaginal Ejaculation Latency Time. *The Journal of Sexual Medicine*, 2, 492–497, 2005a.

Waldinger, M. D., Rietschel, M., Nothen, M. M., Hengeveld, M. W. and Olivier, B. Familial Occurrence of Primary Premature Ejaculation. *Psychiatric Genetics*, 8, 37–40, 1998d.

Waldinger, M. and Schweitzer, D. H. The Use of Old and Recent DSM Definitions of Premature Ejaculation in Observational Studies: A Contribution to the Present Debate for a New Classification of PE in the DSM-V. *The Journal of Sexual Medicine*, 5, 1079–87, 2008.

Waldinger, M. D., Schweitzer, D. H. and Olivier, B. Dapoxetine Treatment of Premature Ejaculation. *Lancet*, 368, 1869–1870, 2006.

Waldinger, M. D., Zwinderman, A. H. and Olivier, B. Antidepressants and Ejaculation: A Double-Blind, Randomised, Fixed-Dose Study with Mirtazapine and Paroxetine. *Journal of Clinical Psychopharmacology*, 23, 467–470, 2003.

Waldinger, M. D., Zwinderman, A. H. and Olivier, B. On-Demand Treatment or Premature Ejaculation with Clomipramine and Paroxetine: A Randomized, Double-Blind, Fixed-Dose Study with Stopwatch Assessment. *European Urology*, 46, 510–516, 2004a.

Waldinger, M. D., Zwinderman, A. H., Schweitzer, D. H. and Olivier, B. Relevance of Methodological Design for the Interpretation of Efficacy of Drug Treatment of Premature Ejaculation: a Systematic Review and Meta-analysis. *International Journal of Impotence Research*. 16, 369–381, 2004b.

Waldinger, M. D., Zwinderman, A. H., Olivier, B. and Schweitzer, D. H. Proposal for a Definition of Lifelong Premature Ejaculation Based on Epidemiological Stopwatch Data. *The Journal of Sexual Medicine*, 2, 498–507, 2005b.

Waldinger, M. D., Zwinderman, A. H., Olivier, B. and Schweitzer, D. H. Thyroid-Stimulating Hormone Assessments in a Dutch Cohort of 620 Men with Lifelong Premature Ejaculation without Erectile Dysfunction. *The Journal of Sexual Medicine*, 2, 865–870, 2005c.

Wallin, P. A Study of Orgasm as a Condition of Women's Enjoyment of Intercourse. *Journal of Social Psychology*, 51, 191–198, 1960.

Weakland, J., Fish, R., Watzlawick, P. and Bodin, A. Brief Therapy: Focused Problem Resolution. *Family Process*, 13, 141–167, 1974.

Weiss P., and Brody S. Women's Partnered Orgasm Consistency is Associated with Greater Duration of Penile-vaginal Intercourse but not of Foreplay. *The Journal of Sexual Medicine*, 6,135–141, 2009.

Williams, V. S., Baldwin, D. S., Hogue, S.L., Fehnel, S. E., Hollis, K. A. and Edin, H. M. Estimating the Prevalence and Impact of Antidepressant-induced Sexual Dysfunction in 2 European Countries: a Cross-sectional Patient Survey. *The Journal of Clinical Psychiatry*, 67, 204–210, 2006.

Wise, T.N. Sertraline as a Treatment for Premature Ejaculation. *Journal of Clinical Psychiatry*, 55, 417, 1994

Wolpe, J. *Psychotherapy by Reciprocal Inhibition*. Stanford, Calif: Stanford University Press, 1958.

Wolpe, J. *The Practice of Behavior Therapy (Second Edition)*. New York: Pergamon Press, 1973.

World Health Organization. *The ICD-10 Classification of Mental and Behavioral Disorders: Clinical Description and Diagnostic Guidelines*. Geneva: World Health Organization, 1993.

Xin, Z., Choi Lee, S. and Choi, H. Efficacy of a Topical Agent SS-Cream in the Treatment of Early Ejaculation: Preliminary Clinical Studies. *Yonsei Medical Journal*, 38, 91–100, 1997.

Yilmaz, U., Tatlisen, A., Turan H., Arman, F. and Ekmekcioglu, O. The Effects of Fluoxetine on Several Neuro-Physiological Variables in Patients with Premature Ejaculation. *Journal of Urology*, 161, 107–111, 1999.

Yuan, Y. M., Xin, Z. C., Jiang, H., Guo, Y. J., Liu, W. J., Tian, L. and Zhu, J. C. Sexual Function of Premature Ejaculation Patients Assayed with Chinese Index of Premature Ejaculation. *Asian Journal of Andrology*, 6, 121–6, 2004.

Zeiss, R. A. Self-Directed Treatment for Premature Ejaculation. *Journal of Consulting and Clinical Psychology*, 6, 1234–1241, 1978.

Zeiss, R. A., Christensen, A. and Levine, A. G. Treatment for Premature Ejaculation Through Male-Only Groups. *Journal of Sex & Marital Therapy*, 4, 139–143, 1978.

Zeiss, R. A. and Zeiss, A. M., *Prolong Your Pleasure*. New York: Pocket Books, 1978.

Zeiss, R. A. and Zeiss, A. M., *Prolonger votre plaisir*. Montréal: Québécor, 1985.

Zhang, G. X., Yu, L. P., Bai, W. J. and Wang, X. F. Selective Resection of Dorsal Nerves of Penis for Premature Ejaculation. *International Journal of Andrology*, 35, 873–879, 2012.

Zilbergeld, B. Group Treatment of Sexual Dysfunction in Men Without Partners. *Journal of Sex and Marital Therapy*, 1, 204–214, 1975.

Zilbergeld, B. *The New Male Sexuality*. Toronto: Bantam, 1992.

Zorgniotti, A. W. Elevated Penile Blood Pressures in Patients with Premature Ejaculation. *Urology*, 13, 161–162, 1979.